FROMMERS

LONDON

DARWIN PORTER

□

1989–1990

Published by Prentice Hall Trade Division
A Division of Simon & Schuster, Inc.
Gulf + Western Building
One Gulf + Western Plaza
New York, NY 10023

ISBN 0-13-047911-X
ISSN 0899-2886

Manufactured in the United States of America

Text Designed: Levavi & Levavi Inc.

*Although every effort was made to ensure the accuracy
of price information appearing in this book,
it should be kept in mind that prices
can and do fluctuate in the course of time.*

CONTENTS

Frommer's Dollarwise Travel Club—How to Save Money on All Your Travels . . .

MAPS

THE DOLLAR AND THE POUND

The currency conversions from pounds to dollars appearing in parentheses throughout these pages were prepared on the basis of £1 = $1.75. That rate may not be accurate by the time you travel, as it varies from day to day, depending on the relative values of both currencies on world markets. Use our currency conversions, therefore, only as a gauge of what you'll be spending, and check with a banker before you leave for England to determine what the actual rate of exchange is at that time.

INFLATION ALERT: We don't have to tell you that inflation has hit London as it has everywhere else. In researching this book we have made every effort to obtain up-to-the minute prices, but even the most conscientious researcher cannot keep up with the current pace of inflation. As we go to press, we believe we have obtained the most reliable data possible. Nonetheless, in the lifetime of this edition—particularly its second year (1990)—the wise traveler will add 15% to 20% to the prices quoted throughout these pages.

CHAPTER I

CITY WITH A PAST

□ □ □

London is a city that has never quite made up its mind about its own size. For the "City of London" proper is merely one square mile of (very expensive) real estate around the Bank of England, inhabited by a few hundred nightwatchmen and caretakers, several score police officers, and innumerable cats.

All the gargantuan rest is made up of separate cities, boroughs, and corporations called Westminster, Chelsea, Hampstead, Kensington, Camden Town, etc., each with its own mayor and administration and ready to fight for its independent status at the drop of an ordinance.

Together, however, they add up to a mammoth metropolis, once the largest on the globe. However, the 1988 *World Almanac* now places London in the 13th position.

The millions of people loosely governed by the Greater London Council live spread out over 609 square miles. Luckily, only a minute fraction of this territory need concern us: the rest is simply suburbs, stretching endlessly into the horizon, red-roofed and bristling with TV antennas.

But the heart, the brick and mortar core of this giant, is perhaps the most fascinating area on earth. For about a century, one-quarter of the world was ruled from there. And with every step you take, you'll come across some sign of the tremendous influence this city has exerted over our past thoughts and actions . . . and still wields today.

London is a very old city, even by European standards. The Roman conquerors of Britain founded Londinium in A.D. 43 by settling and fortifying two small hills on the north bank of the River Thames and linking them via a military road network with the rest of the island.

More than a thousand years later, another conqueror turned the city into his capital. This was William of Normandy, who defeated the last Saxon ruler of England, Harold Godwin, in 1066. There isn't much left of the Roman period, but William the Conqueror left his imprint on London for all time to come.

For a start, he completed and had himself crowned in Westminster Abbey. Every British monarch has been crowned there since, right up to the present Queen. He also built the White Tower, which today forms part of the Tower of London.

William did more than transform London (or rather Westminster) into a royal capital. He and his nobles superimposed their Norman French on the country's original Anglo-Saxon language and thus concocted English as we speak it today. Both the richness and the maddening illogicality of our tongue are direct results of that transplant.

The Normans weren't exactly gentle rulers, but the nation they created did pretty well. No one, for instance, has ever successfully invaded Britain since William's time . . . unless you count North American visitors.

CROWN VERSUS PARLIAMENT: London, as mentioned before, is a mass of contradictions, some of them dating way back in her history. On the one hand, she's a decidedly royal city, studded with palaces, court gardens, coats-of-arms, and other regal paraphernalia. Yet she is also the home of mankind's second-oldest parliamentary assembly. And when handsome and rash King Charles I tried to defy its representatives, he found himself swept off his throne and onto a scaffold long before the French got around to dealing likewise with their anointed monarch.

The huge, gray building that houses the "Mother of Parliaments," with its famous clock, Big Ben, is more truly symbolic of London than Buckingham Palace. For it was there that Prime Minister William Pitt intoned, "You cannot make peace with dictators—you have to defeat them!" at a time when England, alone, stood against the might of Napoleon. And it was there that Winston Churchill repeated these sentiments in even better phrases when England—again alone—held out against Hitler.

Nevertheless, London was largely shaped by the monarchs who ruled her: imposingly by the tough Tudors, beautifully by the wicked Georges, clumsily by the worthy Victoria. To get an idea of the taste abyss between the straitlaced queen and her rakish predecessors, look at the classical elegance of Regent Street and then, say, at the Albert Memorial, perhaps the most exquisitely awful piece of statuary extant.

THE FIRE AND THE BLITZ: Much of London is also the result of disasters, both accidental and premeditated.

The first was the Great Fire of 1666, which swept away most of the old wooden Tudor-style houses and resulted in a new city, built of brick.

The cause of the fire—like that of the great Chicago conflagration—remains unknown. Considering the fire hazards of those tightly packed timber dwellings, the remarkable thing is that the town didn't burn down annually.

As it was, the blaze gutted three-quarters of London: about 13,300 homes, churches, and public buildings. But it also gave England's greatest architect, Christopher Wren, the chance to design St. Paul's Cathedral as it is today, as well as 51 other superb churches, and the Royal Hospitals at Chelsea and Greenwich.

The Blitz Hitler unleashed on the city during 1940–1941 also had one beneficial result. Along with beautiful structures, the rain of incendiary bombs demolished vast patches of the pestilential slum areas around Whitechapel in the East End. This region—made equally famous by Charles Dickens and Jack the Ripper—had been London's festering sore, boasting possibly the worst housing conditions in the Western world. With slum clearance courtesy of the Luftwaffe, the L.C.C. rebuilt most of the area into rather drab, but infinitely superior, apartment blocks.

There was something else the Blitz gave London: a world image as the embattled fortress of freedom, caught unforgettably by the wartime news photo showing the white dome of St. Paul's silhouetted against the black smoke of a dozen simultaneous fires.

The postwar building boom may have made London a little less "quaint," but it also made her a healthier, happier place to live in. And it provided the overture of her present phase of . . .

LIVELY LONDON: Contemporary London really does jump: it has more rock groups than New York, more discos than Paris, more nude shows than Tokyo. Her youngsters dress more zanily than American youths, and her theater is the most experimental.

London is currently the only major capital city that permits gambling clubs to flourish. And if you study the little handwritten ads you'll see in some shop windows in Soho, you'll get an idea of just how permissive a society can get.

The burst of joie de vivre beginning in the late '60s was not a uniquely modern novelty for London. London was merely reverting to type. Throughout most of her long, long history, London was a distinctly wild and wicked town. Shakespeare, Marlowe, and their roistering, hot-blooded tavern cronies personified London life during the reign of "Good Queen Bess." Seventeenth-century London shocked visiting Frenchmen. A hundred years later, it even managed to shock the visiting Casanova. One look at some of Hogarth's paintings in a museum will tell you just what a boozing, wenching, gambling place it was.

For only a very short period—from around 1830 to 1950—did Britain's capital don Mrs. Grundy's tight corsets, which she had worn briefly during Cromwell's short-lived Puritan Commonwealth. There were various reasons for this: the industrial revolution and the surge of the bourgeoisie, the task of empire-building and defending, the personal stuffiness of Queen Victoria. But 120 years is merely a punctuation pause in the chronicle.

After winning two World Wars and losing an empire in the process, her people have rediscovered the zest for life that characterized their ancestors' "Merry England." For a little while it had been almost smothered by the cult of the "British Raj," the "stiff upper lip," the pervasive idea of "setting an example," and the activities of the most ludicrously hidebound censorship to be found outside of Russia.

Now London is almost her old self again.

LONDON FOR AMERICANS: Despite the historic fact that they fought two wars against each other, no two countries have stronger links than America and Britain. Throughout this book we'll be coming upon the mementos of a common heritage that cuts right across political and economic conflicts.

In London they virtually crowd in on you. Stand in front of the **National Gallery** and you'll find George Washington gazing at you. His bronze statue looks out over Trafalgar Square.

Visit **Westminster Abbey** and you'll see a memorial tablet to President Roosevelt, a bust of Longfellow in the Poet's Corner, and the graves of Edward Hyde (Hyde Park, N.Y., was named after him) and James Oglethorpe, who founded the state of Georgia.

Grosvenor Square, in the heart of the West End, is known as "Little America." Overlooked by a statue of FDR, it contains the sumptuously modern U.S. Embassy and the home of John Adams when he was minister to Britain.

Norfolk House, St. James Square, was General Eisenhower's Allied Headquarters during World War II, the spot from which he directed the Normandy landing in 1944.

At **36 Craven Street,** just off the Strand, stands Benjamin Franklin's London residence. And in **St. Sepulchre,** at Holborn Viaduct, lies the grave of Capt. John Smith of Pocahontas fame, who had been prevented from sailing in the *Mayflower* because the other passengers considered him an "undesirable character."

The most moving reminder of national links is the **American Memorial Chapel** at St. Paul's Cathedral. It commemorates the 28,000 U.S. servicemen who lost their lives while based in Britain during World War II. The Roll of Honor containing their names was handed over by General Eisenhower on the Fourth of July 1951, and the chapel—with the Roll encased in glass—has become an unofficial pilgrimage place for visiting Americans.

UNDERSTANDING THE ENGLISH: For an American it can

be a disheartening experience to discover that the English in fact speak *English*. *We* speak *American*. There are just enough differences between the two lingos to result in totally crossed wires, and occasional communication breakdowns. For although the British use words and phrases you think you understand, they often have quite different connotations from their U.S. equivalents.

When they call someone "mean" they mean stingy. "Calling" denotes a personal visit, not a phone call. To "queue up" means to form a line. A "subway" is an underground pedestrian passage. The actual subway system is "the Underground." The term "theater" only refers to the live stage; a movie theater is a "cinema," and what's playing in them "the pictures."

In a grocery you don't buy canned goods but "tins" of this and that. Rutabagas are "swedes," chops are "cutlets," and both cookies and crackers are "biscuits" which can be either "dry" or "sweet." That is, except for graham crackers which—unaccountably—are "digestives."

The going gets rougher when you're dealing with motor vehicles. Gas, for a start, is "petrol," and a service station is a "petrol station." And when talking about the actual vehicle, very little means the same except the word "car." The hood is the "bonnet." The windshield is the "windscreen," bumpers are "fenders," and the dashboard is the "fascia." The trunk is the "boot" and what you do on the horn is "hoot."

Luckily most of us know that an English apartment is a "flat" and that an elevator is a "lift." But are you aware that what you wash your hands in is a "bowl"? The term basin, to the English, is a utensil you mix salads in.

Please note that none of the above terms are slang. For in that particular realm madness lies, particularly if you are foolhardy enough to try to unravel Cockney. Cockneys are indigenous Londoners, although strictly speaking the label refers only to people born within the sound radius of the bells of St. Mary-le-Bow in Cheapside.

The exact derivation of the word Cockney is lost in the mist of antiquity, but it's supposed to have meant an "odd fellow." And the oddest feature about this fellow is undoubtedly the rhyming slang he concocted over the centuries, based on the rhyme—or the rhyme of a rhyme—that goes with a particular word or phrase.

You'll get some idea of its dazzling intricacy when you learn that a buddy is a "China" (from china plate—mate), a hat a "titfer" (from tit-for-tat), children are "Godforbids," a wife is "trouble and strife," feet are "pieces o' meat," and stairs are "apples" (from apples and pears.) And these are merely a few primitive basics. So take my advice and don't try to delve further, unless you happen to be Professor Higgins—pardon me—'iggins.

. . . AND MEETING THE LONDONER: The first thing you notice about Londoners is their perpetual air of preoccupation. Don't be put off by this. It's merely a mask, a kind of detachable face they wear in public.

Approach them about anything and you'll find them possibly the most courteous and helpful people you're ever likely to meet. They'll go blocks out of their way to show you directions, explain where, when, and for how much you can buy whatever you need, and draw little diagrams to clarify some transportation problem. No matter how ignorant you appear of local currency, rarely will taxi drivers, barmaids, or shopkeepers shortchange you. And they will patiently expound for your benefit all the immensely complicated rules that govern English drinking hours, club admissions, and telephone communications.

But . . . you have to approach them first! Londoners are not given to opening casual conversations, even when they share tables or bus seats or breast a bar alongside you. And this is not through lack of sociability but from a deeply rooted respect for privacy. All people who live on densely populated islands develop that trait, and with Londoners it's almost an unwritten law.

Their reserve vanishes the moment *you* start talking. Then follows a ritualistic exchange about the weather. After that, the ice is considered broken and actual conversation begins.

All of which may strike you as rather quaint and formal. But look around you and note how with a minimum of friction the wheels of this giant city turn. How that touch of dignified politeness saves nervous tension. How few people you ever see snarling at each other. And then you'll realize that London's formality fulfills the same purpose as the air in a motor tire: it makes for a smoother ride.

CHAPTER II

THE ABC'S OF LONDON

□ □ □

The aim of this "grab bag" section—dealing with the minutiae of your stay—is to make your adjustment to the British way of life easier. It's maddening to have your trip marred by an accident that could have been avoided if you had been tipped off earlier. To prevent this from happening, I'll try to anticipate the addresses, data, and information that might come in handy on all manner of occasions.

AMERICAN EXPRESS: The main office is 6 Haymarket, S.W.1 (tel. 01/930-4411, Tube: Piccadilly Circus). There are some ten other London locations.

BABYSITTERS: These are hard to find, and the only safe way is to get your hotel to recommend someone, possibly a staff member. Expect to pay the cost of travel to and from your hotel by taxi. There are a number of organizations advertised in the Yellow Pages of the telephone directory that provide sitters using registered nurses and carefully checked mothers, as well as trained nannies.

One such company is **Childminders,** 67A Marylebone High St., W. 1 (tel. 935-9763). This is London's leading babysitting service, covering all of London, the suburbs, even some country areas. You pay £18 ($31.50), plus VAT, for a membership, then £2.40 ($4.20) per hour in the daytime, £1.75 ($3) to £2.10 ($3.75) per hour at night, depending on the day of the week. The membership fee is paid to the agency, while pay for the job goes to the employee, together with reasonable transportation costs. Tube: Regent's Park.

Universal Aunts, 250 King's Rd., S.W.3 (tel. 351-5767),

provides personal services such as all child care, mother's help, proxy parents, and nannies. Tube: Sloane Square.

BANKS: They are generally open from 9:30 a.m. to 3:30 p.m. Monday to Friday. There are also Bureaux de Change which charge for cashing traveler's checks or personal checks (U.K. ones only), or for changing foreign currency into sterling. These bureaus are often open seven days a week, 12 hours a day. You're best advised to use the bureaus at travel agencies such as Thomas Cook or American Express, as some shops charge very high fees. Ask first, and use one of the major banks if possible. There are branches of the main banks at London airports (always use banks for your best rates).

CIGARETTES: Most U.S. brands are available in London. Expect to pay £1.50 ($2.65) to £1.60 ($2.80) or more for a pack of 20. Smoking is banned in the Underground, although it is allowed in certain train cars and on top of buses.

CRIME: Theft is not as bad, perhaps, as it is in the U.S. In the main, mugging is limited to the poor areas. As for murder and assault, reports say that most of these occur within families and related groups. The best advice is to use discretion and a little common sense and keep to well-lit areas.

CUSTOMS: Overseas visitors may import 400 cigarettes and one quart of liquor. If you have obtained your allowance on a ship or plane, then you may import only 200 cigarettes and one liter of liquor. (See intro to Chapter VII for information on U.S. Customs upon your return.) There is no limit on money, film, or other items that are for your own use except that *all drugs* other than medical supplies are illegal. Do not try to import live birds or animals. You may be subjected to heavy fines, and the pet will be destroyed.

DENTIST: To find the nearest dentist in an emergency, phone 677-6363 or 584-1008. You will be directed to whichever dental surgery in or near your area can attend to your needs.

DOCTORS: Hotels have their own list of local practitioners, for whom you'll have to pay. (Look under "Hospitals" for 24-hour emergency service.)

DOCUMENTS FOR ENTRY: U.S. citizens, Canadians, Australians, New Zealanders, and South Africans all fall under the same category for entry into the United Kingdom. A passport is definitely required, but no visa is necessary. Immigration officers prefer to see a passport with two months' remaining validity. Much depends on the criteria and observations of Immigration officers. The one checking you through will want to be satisfied that you have the means to return to your original destination (usually a round-trip ticket) and visible means of support while you're in Britain. If you are planning to fly from, say, the U.S. to the U.K. and then on to a country which requires a visa (India, for example), it's wise to secure the India visa before your arrival in Britain. Even the amount of time spent in the British Isles depends for holiday-makers on the Immigration officer.

DRUGSTORES: In Britain they're called "chemist shops." Every police station in the country has a list of emergency chemists. Dial "0" (zero) and ask the operator for the local police. The only 24-hour druggist in London is **Bliss the Chemist,** 50–56 Willesden Lane, Kilburn, N.W.6 (tel. 624-8000), and 5 Marble Arch, W.1 (tel. 723-6116).

ELECTRICAL APPLIANCES: The current is 240 volts, AC (50 cycles). Buy a transformer and an adapter before leaving home as they may not be readily available in Britain. A good adapter will convert your plug to almost any other sort of plug.

EMBASSY AND HIGH COMMISSION: The **U.S. Embassy** is at 24 Grosvenor Square, W.1 (tel. 499-9000; Tube: Bond Street). The **Canadian High Commission** is at Canada House, Trafalgar Square, S.W.1 (tel. 629-9492; Tube: Tralfagar Square).

EMERGENCY: In London, for police, fire, or an ambulance, dial 999.

GLASSES: Lost or broken? Try **Imperial Optical of Selfridges,** a branch of the well-known Canadian optical company, at Selfridges Department Store, 400 Oxford St., W.1 (tel. 629-1234, ext. 3889). An eye exam costs £20 ($35), and the least expensive pair of eyeglasses with an uncomplicated prescription costs an additional £50 ($87.50). Multifocal lenses sometimes take two to three working days to complete, but simple prescriptions may be filled in two to three hours. You will pay more for designer frames. It's always wise to take a copy of your glasses prescription with you when you travel. Tube: Bond Street.

HOLIDAYS AND FESTIVALS: Christmas Day, Boxing Day

(December 26), New Year's Day, Good Friday, and Easter Monday, May Day, and spring and summer bank holidays.

HOSPITALS: The following offer emergency care in London 24 hours a day, and the first treatment is free under the National Health Service. These include **Royal Free Hospital,** Pond Street, N.W.3 (tel. 794-0500; Tube: Belsize Park), and the **University College Hospital,** Gower Street, W.C.1 (tel. 387-9300; Tube: Euston Square). Many other London hospitals also have Accident and Emergency Departments, including among others, St. Mary's Hospital, Paddington; London Hospital, Whitechapel; King's College Hospital, Denmark Hill; Charing Cross Hospital; and St. Bartholomew's Hospital. Only emergency treatment is free.

LIQUOR LAWS: No alcohol is served to anyone under the age of 18. Children under 16 aren't allowed in pubs, except in special rooms. Pub hours vary, but as a general guide they are open from 11:30 a.m. to 2:30 p.m. and 6 to 10:30 p.m. Monday to Saturday (Sunday hours are noon to 2:30 p.m. and 7 to 10 p.m.). These laws are under review and may change during the lifetime of this edition. Don't drink and drive. Penalties are high and inconvenient, even if you are an overseas visitor.

LOST PROPERTY: To find property lost in London on the tube or in a taxi—or elsewhere—report the loss to the police first, and they will advise you where to apply for its return. Taxi drivers are required to hand property left in their vehicles to the nearest police station. London Transport's Lost Property Office will try to assist personal callers only at their office at the Baker Underground station. For items lost on British Rail, go to the Euston Lost Property Office (tel. 01/922-6477). For lost passports, credit cards, or money, report the loss and circumstances immediately to the nearest police station. For lost passports, you should then go directly to your embassy. The address will be in the telephone book, or see "Embassy and High Commission," above. For lost credit cards, report to the appropriate organization; the same holds true for lost traveler's checks.

LUGGAGE SHIPPED: London Baggage Company Ltd., 262 Vauxhall Bridge Rd., S.W.1 (tel. 828-2400), offers worldwide service shipping unaccompanied baggage, at rates usually below the normal excess-baggage charges of airlines.

MEDICAL SERVICES: Medical Express, Chapel Place, W.1

(tel. 499-1991), is just off Oxford Street, almost equidistant from the Oxford Circus and Bond Street Underground stations. It's a medical center where you can have a consultation and full medical/clinical examinations, such as a blood-pressure test, an ECG, and X-rays. The cost is £37 ($64.75), plus £15 ($26.25) if you get a prescription. For £5 ($8.75) you can get the British equivalent of your U.S. prescription here, if they decide that it is bona fide. The center is open Monday to Friday from 8 a.m. to 8 p.m., on Saturday from 9 a.m. to 6 p.m. Full specialist services available by appointment include E.G., gynecology, ENT, dermatology, and cardiology, among others, at consultation fees of £47 ($82.25).

NEWSPAPERS: *The Times* is tops, then the *Telegraph,* the *Daily Mail,* and the *Guardian,* all London papers carrying the latest news. The *International Herald Tribune,* published in Paris, and an international edition of *USA Today,* beamed via satellite, are available daily.

OFFICE HOURS: Business hours are 9 a.m. to 5 p.m. Monday to Friday. The lunch break lasts an hour, but most places stay open all day.

POSTAL SERVICE: Letters and parcels to be called for may, as a rule, be addressed to you at any post office except a town suboffice. The words "To Be Called For" or "Poste Restante" must appear in the address. When claiming your mail, always carry some sort of identification. Letters generally take seven to ten days to arrive from the U.S. Post Restante service is provided solely for the convenience of travelers, and it may not be used in the same town for more than three months. It can be redirected, upon request, for a one-month period, unless you specify a longer time, not to exceed three months, on the application form you will be asked to fill out. Post offices and sub-post offices are centrally located and open from 9 a.m. to 5:30 p.m. Monday to Friday, 9:30 a.m. to noon on Saturday. The Chief Post Office in London is on King Edward Street, E.C.1, near St. Paul's Cathedral (Tube: St. Paul's). The Trafalgar Square Post Office (Tube: Trafalgar Square) is open from 8 a.m. to 8 p.m. Monday to Saturday. All post offices are closed on Sunday.

RELIGIOUS SERVICES: Times of services are posted outside the various places of worship. Almost every creed is catered to in London. The **Interdenominational American Church** is on Tottenham Court Road, W.1 (tel. 580-2791). Tube: Goodge Street.

REST ROOMS: These are usually found at signs saying "Public Toilets." Expect to pay from 2p (5¢) to 5p (10¢) for women; men are usually free.

SENIOR DISCOUNTS: Be warned: these are only available to holders of a British pension book.

SHOP HOURS: In general, they are from 9 a.m. to 5:30 p.m. Monday to Saturday.

TAXES: There is no local sales tax, but 15% **VAT** (value added tax) is added to all hotel and restaurant bills. VAT is also included in the cost of many of the items you purchase to take home with you. When purchasing, inquire as to the tax-free export scheme which may save you that 15% tax.

TELEGRAMS: For messages sent within the United Kingdom, the current cost is £4.50 ($8) for the first 50 words, £2.50 ($4.50) for each additional 50 words. The concierge of a hotel or the switchboard of a hotel can telex or phone in your message. If you're dialing from a private house in London, dial 193. Special-occasion cards, giving impersonal and mass-produced acknowledgments of birthdays, births, anniversaries, whatever, cost 80p ($1.40) each. These prices do not include VAT. The international version of a telemessage is called a mailgram. The message is telexed by British TeleCom to the North American postal service, then delivered through the regular mails, usually the next working day. These cost £7.25 ($12.75) for the first 50 words, £3.60 ($6.25) for each additional 50 words. Naturally, the address is included in the 50 words. On many occasions it would be easier and cheaper to phone instead.

TELEPHONES: British TeleCom is carrying out a massive improvement program of its public pay-phone service. During the transitional period, you could encounter four types of pay phones. The old style (gray) pay phone is being phased out, but there are a lot still in use. You will need 10p (18¢) coins to operate such phones, but you should not use this type for overseas calls. Its replacement is a blue-and-silver push button model that accepts coins of any denomination. The other two types of phone require cards instead of coins to operate. The Cardphone takes distinctive green cards especially designed for it. They are available in five values—£1 ($1.75), £2 ($3.50), £4 ($7), £10 ($17.50), and £20 ($35)—and they are reusable until the total value has expired.

Cards can be purchased from news agencies and post offices. Finally, the Credit-call pay phone operates on credit cards—Access, VISA, American Express, and Diners—and is most common at airports and large railway stations.

Phone numbers in Britain outside of the major cities consist of an exchange name plus telephone number. In order to dial the number, you will need the code of the exchange being called. Information sheets on call-box walls give the codes in most instances. If your code is not there, however, call the operator by dialing 100. In major cities, phone numbers consist of the exchange code and number (seven digits in all). These seven digits are all you need to dial if you are calling from within the same city. If you are calling from elsewhere, you will need to prefix them with the dialing code for the city. Again, you will find these codes on the call-box information sheets. If you do not have the telephone number of the person you want to call, dial 192 for any town within the U.K. except London. Give the operator the name of the town and then the person's name and address. Dial 142 for this information if the number you want is within the London postal-code area.

A guide to telephone costs: A call at noon from London to Reading, 40 miles away, lasting three minutes, costs 80p ($1.40). This charge is more than halved between 6 p.m. and 8 a.m. and on weekends. A local call costs 20p (35¢) for three minutes at all times. The charges quoted are for pay phones. You will have to pay far more if you use a hotel operator at any time.

The **Westminster Communications Center,** 1A Broadway, S.W.1, (Tube: St. James Park) is open daily except Sunday from 9 a.m. to 7 p.m. Here you can call all countries not available from a call box. Receptionists are available to help you in case of difficulty and to take your payment once your call is finished. You can pay in cash, by check, credit card, or traveler's checks in pounds sterling. A range of other services is also available, including telex, telegrams, telemessages, word processing, photocopying, radio paging, voice bank, cellular radio rental, and facsimile. Call 222-4444.

The area code for London is 01.

TELEX: These are mostly restricted to business premises and hotels. If your hotel has a telex, they will send a message for you and you may have to arrange in advance for the receipt of a message back.

TIME: England is based on Greenwich Mean Time (five hours ahead of Eastern Standard Time), with British Summer Time lasting (roughly) from the end of March to the end of October.

TIPPING: Many establishments add a service charge. If service has been good, it's customary to add an additional 5% to that. If no service is added to the bill, give 10% for poor service, otherwise 15%. If service is bad, tell them and don't tip. Taxis expect about 20%, but never less than 20p (35¢) for a 75p ($1.30) ride.

CHAPTER III

GETTING TO KNOW LONDON

□ □ □

There is—fortunately—an immense difference between the sprawling vastness of Greater London and the pocket-size chunk that might be called Tourist Territory.

For a start, all of the latter is *north* of the River Thames. Except for a couple of quick excursions, we'll never have to penetrate the southern regions at all.

Our London begins at Chelsea, on the north bank of the river, and stretches for roughly five miles up to Hampstead. Horizontally, its western boundary runs through Kensington while the eastern lies five miles away at Tower Bridge.

Within this five- by five-mile square, you'll find all the hotels and restaurants and nearly all the sights that are usually of interest to visitors.

Make no mistake: this is still a hefty portion of land to cover and a really thorough exploration of it would take a couple of years. But it has the advantage of being flat and eminently walkable, besides boasting one of the best public transport systems ever devised.

The logical (although not geographical) center of this area is **Trafalgar Square,** which we'll therefore take as our orientation point.

The huge, thronged, fountain-splashed, pigeon-infested square was named after the battle in which Nelson destroyed the combined Franco-Spanish fleets and lost his own life. His statue tops the towering pillar in the center, and the natives maintain that the reason he's been up there all these years is that nobody has told him the lions at the base are made of stone.

If you stand facing the steps of the imposing National Gallery, you're looking northwest. That is the direction of **Piccadilly Circus**—the real core of tourist London—and the maze of notorious streets that make up Soho. Farther north runs Oxford Street, London's gift to moderately priced shopping, and still farther northwest lies Regent's Park with the Zoo.

At your back—that is, south—runs **Whitehall,** which houses or skirts nearly every British government building, from the Ministry of Defence to the official residence of the prime minister in Downing Street. In the same direction, a bit farther south, stand the Houses of Parliament and Westminster Abbey.

Flowing southwest from Trafalgar Square is the table-smooth Mall, flanked by magnificent parks and mansions and leading to Buckingham Palace, residence of the Queen. Farther in the same direction lie **Belgravia** and **Knightsbridge,** the city's plushest residential areas, and south of them **Chelsea,** with its chic flavor, plus Kings Road, the freaky shopping drag.

Due west from where you're standing stretches the superb and distinctly high-priced shopping area bordered by Regent Street and Piccadilly (the street, *not* the Circus). Farther west lie the equally elegant shops and even more elegant homes of **Mayfair.** Then comes Park Lane and on the other side Hyde Park, the biggest park in London and one of the largest in the world.

Running north from Trafalgar Square is Charing Cross Road, past Leicester Square and intersecting with Shaftesbury Avenue. This is London's theaterland, boasting an astonishing number of live shows as well as first-run movie houses. A bit farther along, Charing Cross Road turns into a browser's paradise, lined with new and secondhand bookshops.

Finally it funnels into St. Giles Circus. This is where you enter **Bloomsbury,** site of the University of London, the awesome British Museum, some of our best budget hotels, and erstwhile stamping ground of the famed "Bloomsbury Group," led by Virginia Woolf.

Northeast of your position lies **Covent Garden,** known for its Royal Opera House.

Follow the Strand eastward from Trafalgar Square and you'll come into Fleet Street, the most concentrated newspaper section on earth, the place every reporter in the English provinces dreams about reaching one day.

At the end of Fleet Street lies Ludgate Circus . . . and only there do you enter the actual **City of London.** This was the original

walled settlement and is today what the locals mean when they re-
fer to "The City." Its focal point and shrine is the Bank of England
on Threadneedle Street, with the Stock Exchange next door and
the Royal Exchange across the road.

"The City" is unique insofar as it retains its own separate police force (distinguished by a crest on their helmets) and Lord
Mayor. Its 677 acres are an antheap of jammed cars and rushing
clerks during the week and totally deserted on Sunday, because
hardly a soul lives there. Its streets are winding, narrow, and fairly
devoid of charm. But it has more bankers and stockbrokers per
square inch than any other place on the globe. And in the midst of
all the hustle rises St. Paul's Cathedral, a monument to beauty and
tranquility.

At the far eastern fringe of the City looms the Tower of London, shrouded in legend, blood, and history, and permanently be-
sieged by battalions of visitors.

And this, as far as we will be concerned, concludes the London circle.

A TANGLE OF STREETS: Now I'd like to be able to tell you
that London's thoroughfares follow a recognizable pattern in
which, with a little intelligence, even a stranger can find his or her
way around. Unfortunately they don't and you can't.

London's streets follow no pattern whatsoever, and both
their naming and numbering seems to have been perpetrated by a
group of xenophobes with an equal grudge against postmen and
foreigners.

So be warned that the use of logic and common sense will get
you nowhere. Don't think, for instance, that Southampton Row is
anywhere near Southampton Street and that either of these places
has any connection with Southampton Road.

And this is only a mild sample. London is checkered with innumerable squares, mews, closes, and terraces, which jut into or
cross or overlap or interrupt whatever street you're trying to follow, usually without the slightest warning. You may be walking
along ruler-straight Albany Street and suddenly find yourself
flanked by Colosseum Terrace (with a different numbering system). Just keep on walking and after a couple of blocks you're
right back on Albany Street (and the original house numbers)
without having encountered the faintest reason for the sudden
change in labels.

House numbers run in odds, evens, clockwise, or counter-
clockwise as the wind blows. That is, when they exist at all, and
frequently they don't. And every so often you'll come upon a

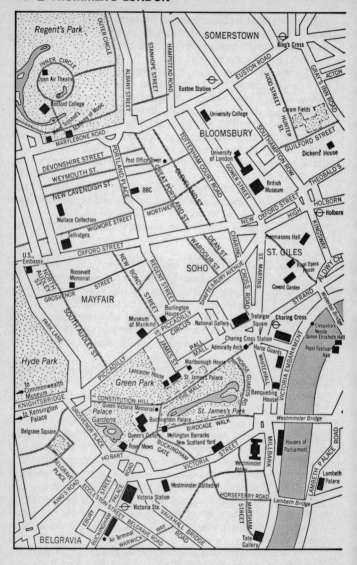

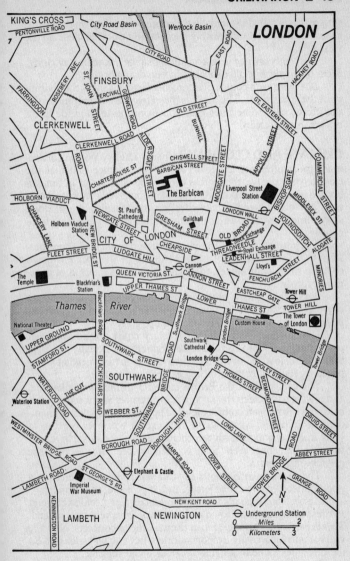

LONDON

KING'S CROSS
PENTONVILLE ROAD
City Road Basin
Wenlock Basin

CITY ROAD
EAST ROAD
HACKNEY ROAD

FARRINGDON
ROSEBERY AVE.
ST. JOHN STREET
PERCIVAL
GOSWELL ROAD
FINSBURY
OLD STREET
BUNHILL
GT. EASTERN STREET
APOLLO STREET
COMMERCIAL STREET

CLERKENWELL
CLERKENWELL ROAD
ALDERSGATE STREET
CHISWELL STREET
BARBICAN STREET
The Barbican
MOORGATE STREET
Liverpool Street Station
BISHOPSGATE
MIDDLESEX ST.
HOUNDSDITCH

HOLBORN VIADUCT
CHANCERY LANE
CHARTERHOUSE ST.
NEWGATE STREET
St. Paul's Cathedral
Holborn Viaduct Station
CITY OF LONDON
GRESHAM STREET
Guildhall
LONDON WALL
OLD BROAD
ALDGATE

NEW BRIDGE ST.
FLEET STREET
LUDGATE HILL
CHEAPSIDE
THREADNEEDLE
Stock Exchange
Royal Exchange
LEADENHALL STREET
Lloyd's
FENCHURCH STREET
MINORIES

The Temple
Blackfriar's Station
QUEEN VICTORIA ST.
Cannon
CANNON STREET
EASTCHEAP GATE
Tower Hill
TOWER HILL

UPPER THAMES ST.
LOWER
THAMES ST.
Custom House
The Tower of London

Thames River
Blackfriars Bridge
Southwark Bridge
London Bridge
Tower Bridge

National Theater
UPPER GROUND
STAMFORD ST.
SOUTHWARK STREET
Southwark Cathedral
London Bridge
TOOLEY STREET

WATERLOO ROAD
THE CUT
Waterloo Station
BLACKFRIARS ROAD
SOUTHWARK
BRIDGE
ROAD
SOUTHWARK
ST. THOMAS STREET
BERMONDSEY STREET
DRUID STREET

WEBBER ST.
BOROUGH HIGH
LONG LANE
ABBEY STREET

WESTMINSTER BRIDGE ROAD
BOROUGH ROAD
SOUTHWARK
HARPER ROAD
GT. DOVER STREET
TOWER BRIDGE ROAD
GRANGE ROAD

LAMBETH ROAD
KENNINGTON ROAD
ST. GEORGE'S RD.
Elephant & Castle
Imperial War Museum
NEW KENT ROAD
N

LAMBETH
NEWINGTON
Underground Station
Miles 2
Kilometers 3

square that is called a square on the south side, a road on the north, a park on the east, and possibly a something-or-other close on the west side.

Your only chance is to consult a map or ask your way along. Most of the time you'll probably end up doing both.

But there are a couple of consoling factors. One is the legibility of the street signs. The other is the extraordinary helpfulness of the locals, who sometimes pass you from guide to guide like a bucket in a fire chain.

CLIMATE AND CLOTHING: Charles Dudley Warner (in a remark most often attributed to Mark Twain) once said that the trouble with the weather is that everybody talks about it, but nobody does anything about it. Well, Londoners talk more weather than any other breed of city dwellers, but they have also done something. It's called air-pollution control and it's enforced ferociously.

The result has been the virtual disappearance of those pea-soup fogs that regularly blanketed the city in Sherlock Holmes's day. Up till now, however, they haven't found a method of generating sunshine.

A typical London area weather forecast any given summer day predicts "scattered clouds with sunny periods and showers, possibly heavy at times." This sums it up nicely.

London may be moist, but it's very rarely humid. Summer temperatures seldom rise above 78° Fahrenheit. Equally rarely do they drop below 35° in winter, which makes for a somewhat damp but fairly stable climate, avoiding extremes at both ends.

The catch is that the British consider chilliness wholesome, and always try to keep their room temperatures about ten degrees below the American comfort level. They're also hopelessly enamored of fireplaces, which warm little except whatever portion of your anatomy you turn toward them. Hotels, of course, have central heating, but even that is usually kept just above the goosebump margin.

The most essential items of your wardrobe are, therefore, a good raincoat, a sweater or jersey, and, if possible, an umbrella.

Apart from this, it's wise to remember that Londoners tend to dress up rather than down and that they dress very well indeed. This is particularly noticeable in theaters and at concerts. Nobody will bar you for arriving in sports clothes, but you will stick out. So include at least one smart suit or dress in your luggage.

Better-class restaurants usually demand that male diners wear ties and that women don't wear shorts, but those are the only clothing rules enforced. As a final thought, *do* bring along a pair of reasonably sturdy walking shoes. The most interesting areas of the city can be properly enjoyed only on foot.

MONEY: Britain's monetary system is based on the **pound (£)**, a medium-size greenish bill called a "quid" by the Cockneys. One pound, as of this writing, is worth approximately $1.75 in U.S. terms. It's made up of 100 new **pence**, written **"p."**

Since the rate of exchange fluctuates from day to day, the conversions that appear in this book may not be accurate by the time you reach London. I advise you to check with your banker before leaving home.

Here are some approximate conversions, based on the value of the pound when this edition was written:

Pence	U.S.$	Pounds	U.S.$
1	.02	1	1.75
2	.04	2	3.50
3	.05	3	5.25
4	.07	4	7.00
5	.09	5	8.75
10	.18	7.50*	13.13
25	.44	10	17.50
50	.88	15	26.25
75	1.31	20	35.00

*Note: You read £7.50 as 7 pounds, 50 pence.

GETTING AROUND LONDON: The area known as Greater London possesses one of the (if not *the*) finest transportation systems in the world.

London Transport—the outfit that operates the area's public transportation—has a large Underground and bus network, covering 630 square miles of urban territory with more than 4,000 Underground cars and 5,000 buses, carrying nearly 190 million passengers per year.

The service it provides is not only fast, frequent, clean, and comfortable, but also (by U.S. standards) amazingly cheap. However, London Transport suffers from one grave drawback: it keeps lamentably early hours. Nearly all buses and trains stop running around midnight (11:30 p.m. on Sunday), forcing you to take taxis after a night out.

Transportation in Greater London

London Regional Transport Travel Information Centres are located at Victoria (Underground and British Rail), King's Cross, Euston, Oxford Circus, Piccadilly Circus, St. James's Park, Heathrow Central and Terminals 1, 2, 3, and 4, and West Croydon Bus Station.

Travelcards, for use on Underground and bus services and available in any combination of adjacent zones, and **Capitalcards,** good on British Rail, Underground, and bus services in Greater London and in any combination of adjacent zones, are available at Travel Information Centres and Underground stations.

For a short stay in London or for special excursions, a great bargain is the **One-Day Travelcard.** This ticket can be used on most bus and Underground services throughout Greater London after 9:30 a.m. Monday to Friday and at any time during weekends and on public holidays. The ticket is available at Underground stations, bus garages, certain post offices, and many news kiosks. Four- and five-zone versions are offered. For £1.70 ($3), you can travel anywhere by Underground and the Docklands Light Railway in zones 1, 2, 3a, and 3b or in zones 2, 3a, 3b, and 3c. For £2 ($3.50), you get the freedom of all zones. A Child One-Day Travelcard allows travel throughout all five zones for 70p ($1.25).

A one-day Capitalcard, giving you the advantages of a Travelcard plus use of British Rail also, is offered for a journey taken during the same hours as are good on the One-Day Travelcard. The Capitalcard costs £2.50 ($4.50) for adults, £1.25 ($2.25) for children for all zones; £2 ($3.50) for adults, £1 ($1.75) for children for zones 1, 2, 3a, and 3b. These cards can be purchased at Underground and British Rail stations.

The cost of a Travelcard good for seven days, with no restriction as to hours of use, is £5 ($8.75) for adults (not available at lower price for children) in the central zone; £6 ($10.50) for adults and £1.70 ($3) for children for zones 1 and 2; £8.80 ($15.50) for adults and £2.50 ($4.50) for children for zones 1, 2, and 3; £11.50 ($20.25) for adults and £3.40 ($6) for children in zones 1, 2, 3a, and 3b; and £14.30 ($25) for adults and £3.40 ($6) for children in zones 1, 2, 3a, 3b, and 3c.

Capitalcards for seven days of travel cost £7 ($12.25) for adults, £3.50 ($6.25) for children, for two zones; £10.20 ($17.75) for adults, £5.10 ($9) for children, for three zones;

£13.20 ($23) for adults, £6.60 ($11.50) for children, for four zones; and £16.30 ($28.50) for adults, £8.15 ($14.25) for children, for five zones.

To purchase either a Travelcard or a Capitalcard, you must present a **Photocard.** For persons 16 years old or older, the Photocard is easy to get. Just take a passport-style picture of yourself when you buy your first Travelcard, and the Photocard will be issued free. Child-rate Photocards are issued at post offices in the London area, at bus garages, or at British Rail stations, as well as at the Travel Information Centres listed above. In addition to a passport-style photograph, proof of age is required (like a passport or a birth certificate). Travelcards are not issued at child rates unless supported by a Photocard. Older children (14 or 15) are charged adult fares on *all* services unless in possession of one of the cards. A child-rate Photocard is not, however, required for child-rate London Explorer tickets or for tours.

These fares, although valid at the time of writing, will very likely change during the lifetime of this edition and are therefore presented only for general background information so that you will know the range of travel options open to you.

The London Transport Information Centres provide information on a wide range of facilities and places of interest in addition to that on bus and Underground services. They sell special visitors' tickets, take reservations for London Transport's guided tours (see below "Official London Sightseeing Tour," and "Organized Tours" in Chapter VI), and have free Underground and bus maps and other information leaflets. A 24-hour telephone information service is available (tel. 222-1234).

Airports

London has two main airports, **Heathrow** and **Gatwick.** It takes 35 to 45 minutes by Underground train from Heathrow Central to central London, costing £1.50 ($2.65) for adults and 40p (70¢) for children. From Heathrow, you can also take an airbus, which gets you into central London in about an hour. The cost is £3 ($5.25) for adults, £1.50 ($2.65) for children.

Gatwick Airport, where many charter and some scheduled flights come in, lies 30 miles south of London. Trains leave from there every 15 minutes until midnight, and every hour after midnight. Also, there is an express bus from Gatwick to Victoria Station every half hour from 6:30 a.m. to 8 p.m. and every hour from 8 to 11 p.m. Flightline bus 777, it costs £4 ($7) per person.

The Underground, airbus, and train are, of course, far cheaper means of transport than a private taxi. For example, a taxi from Heathrow into central London is likely to cost more than £20 ($35).

A bus service connects the two airports, leaving every hour for the 70-minute trip. In addition, there is also an expensive helicopter service that takes only 15 minutes between airports.

For flight information, telephone Heathrow at 01/759-4321 or Gatwick at 0293/31299.

Heathrow Airport has four passenger terminals. The most recent one, Terminal Four is located on the south side of the airport some distance away from the other terminals. There are land side and air side transfer buses, but it takes about 15 minutes to make it around the perimeter, so it's best to aim for the correct terminal at the start. Terminal Four is used by British Airways intercontinental, Amsterdam, and Paris services, as well as by Air Malta.

The Underground

Known locally as the "tube," this is the fastest and easiest (although not the most interesting) way to get from place to place. The tube has a special spot in the hearts of Londoners . . . during the Blitz thousands of people used its underground platforms as air-raid shelters, camping down there all night in reasonable safety from the bombs.

All Underground stations are clearly marked with a red circle and blue crossbar. You descend either by stairways or escalators or huge elevators, depending on the depth. Some subway stations have complete shopping arcades underground and several boast gadgets such as pushbutton information machines.

Compared to, for instance, its New York counterpart, the tube is a luxury cruiser. The stations are clean, ventilated, orderly, and fairly quiet. Above all, they're superbly signposted, and in such a well-calculated fashion that it takes a certain amount of talent to catch the wrong train.

You pick the station for which you're heading on the large diagram displayed on the wall, which has an alphabetical index to make it easy. You note the color of the line it happens to be on (Bakerloo is brown, Central is red, etc.). Then, by merely following the colored band, you can see at a glance whether and where you'll have to change and how many stops there are to your destination.

That's all there is to it. It's so simple and logical that I can't imagine why all other subway systems in the world haven't copied it.

If you have the right change, you can get your ticket at one of

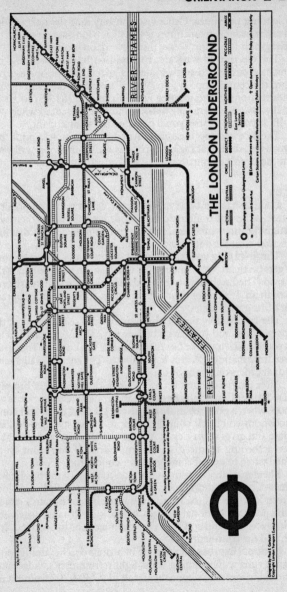

the vending machines. Otherwise you buy it at the ticket office. You can transfer as many times as you like so long as you stay in the Underground and don't leave the network on ground level.

The electric subways are, to begin with, comfortable—the trains have cushioned seats, no less. The flat fare for one journey within the central zone is 50p (90¢). Trips from the central zone to destinations in the suburbs range from 60p ($1.05) to £2.40 ($4.20). *Be sure to keep your ticket;* it must be presented when you get off. If you owe extra, you'll be billed by the attendant.

The line serving Heathrow Airport to central London has trains with additional luggage space as well as moving walkways from the airport terminals to the Underground station.

Buses

London has just two types of buses, which you can't possibly confuse—the red double-decked monsters that bully their way through the inner-city areas, and the green single-deckers that link the center with the outlying towns and villages.

The first thing you learn about London buses is that nobody just gets on them: you "queue up," that is, form a single file, at the bus stop. The English do it instinctively, even when there are only two of them. It's one of their eccentricities, and you get to appreciate it during rush hours.

The comparably priced bus system is almost as good as the Underground, and you have a better view. To find out about current routes, pick up a free bus map at one of the London Transport Travel Information Centres listed above. The map is available to personal callers only, not by mail.

After you've queued up for the red, double-decker bus and selected a seat downstairs or on the upper deck (the best seats are on top, where you'll see more of the city), a conductor will come by to whom you'll tell your destination. He or she then collects the fare and gives you a ticket. As with the Underground, the fare varies according to the distance you travel. If you want to be warned when to get off, simply ask the conductor.

The departure point from London to most of the bus lines is **Victoria Coach Station,** Buckingham Palace Road, S.W.1, a block up from Victoria Railroad Station. It is the hub of Britain's largest coach operators, National Express, whose long-distance coach network covers England and Wales with connections to Scotland, Ireland, and the continent.

National Express Rapides are luxurious coaches doing long-distance runs with reclining seats, light refreshments, video, and no-smoking areas. To phone them, call 01/730-0202 from 8 a.m.

to 10 p.m. daily. The National Express ticket office for England and Wales is open daily from 6 a.m. to midnight. The ticket bureau for Scotland, Ireland, and the continent is open daily from 7:30 a.m. to 10:30 p.m. You can also arrange coach excursions here, as well as sightseeing tours, and purchase rail and ferry travel tickets, even get hotel accommodations.

For information on bus sightseeing tours of London, see "Organized Tours" in Chapter VI.

Taxis

London cabs are specially designed for their function, have a glass partition to prevent driver and passengers from bothering each other, and have the maneuverability of fighter planes. At first glance they seem oddly staid and upright, but you quickly learn to appreciate the headroom they provide and the uncanny U-turns they can execute. They are, in fact, the best-designed taxis anywhere.

However, they share the drawback of their ilk the world over. Meaning that they encircle you in massed columns when you don't want them and become invisible the moment you do. And their drivers have precisely the same tendency as their Stateside brethren of going off duty when it starts to rain.

Otherwise, the drivers are immeasurably more polite, know their streets better, and thank you for tips.

You can pick up a cab in London either by heading for a cab rank or by hailing one in the street (the taxi is free if the light on the hood is on). Or else you can phone 253-5000, 272-0272, or 272-3030 for a radio cab. The minimum fare is 80p ($1.40) for the first 924 yards or three minutes and 18 seconds, with increments of 20p (35¢) thereafter, based on distance or time. Each additional passenger is charged 20p ($35¢). From 8 p.m. to midnight Monday to Friday and from 6 a.m. to 8 p.m. on Saturday, after the 80p ($1.40) minimum, increments are 40p (70¢). From midnight to 6 a.m. Monday to Friday and between 8 p.m. on the day before until 6 a.m. on the day after Sunday and public holidays, the meter clicks over at 60p ($1.05). From 8 p.m. on December 24 to 6 a.m. on December 27 and from 8 p.m. on December 31 to 6 a.m. on January 1, the flag still drops at 80p ($1.40), but increments are £2 ($3.50). Passengers are charged 10p (20¢) for each piece of luggage in the driver's compartment and any other item more than two feet long. All these tariffs include VAT. It's recommended that you tip about 20% of the fare, and never less than 15%.

If you have a complaint about the taxi service you get, or if you leave something in a cab, phone the Public Carriage Office, 15 Penton St., N.1 (tel. 278-1744). If it's about a complaint, you must have the cab number, which is displayed in the passenger compartment.

Be warned. If you phone for a cab, the meter starts running when the taxi receives instructions from the dispatcher. So you could find 80p ($1.40) or more on the meter when you get inside the taxi.

Cab sharing is now permitted in London, as British law allows cabbies to offer shared rides for two to five persons. The taxis accepting riders sharing display a notice of yellow plastic, with the words "Shared Taxi." These shared rides are mainly available at Heathrow Airport, main train stations, and the some 200 taxi stands in London. The savings per person is as follows: Each of two riders sharing are charged 65% of the fare a lone passenger would be charged. Three persons pay 55%, four are charged 45%, and five (the seating capacity of all new London cabs) pay 40% of the single-passenger fare.

The journey between Heathrow and central London costs about £20 ($35). If you are traveling between central London and Gatwick Airport, you must negotiate a fare with the driver before you get in the cab, as the meter does not apply. (This is necessary because Gatwick is outside the Metropolitan Police District.)

Rented Cars

Driving around London is a tricky business even for the native motorist. While London isn't quite as permanently stalled as Rome, and traffic is much better disciplined than in Paris, it is still a warren of one-way streets, and parking sports are at a premium.

In England, as you probably know, you drive on the left and overtake on the right. Roadsigns are clear and internationally unmistakable.

Petrol prices (gas to you) are pretty steep, due to a truly savage 25% tax on motor fuels. Incidentally, an Imperial gallon is one-fifth bigger than the U.S. measure.

Car rentals are reasonable and London offers a large array of companies to choose from. Most of them will accept your U.S. driving license, providing you're over 21 and have held it for more than a year. Don't forget, however, that the car you get will have the steering wheel on the "wrong" side.

Herewith a survey of some rental firms and rates:

Budget Rent-a-Car, (Central reservations, tel. 01/441-5882) is, in my experience, one of the best and least expensive and maintains offices at both Gatwick and Heathrow Airports, as well as at eight inner London locations, including Earl's Court,

Knightsbridge, Mayfair, Piccadilly, and the Tower of London, as well as Victoria Station.

The cheapest Budget car available is a peppy and maneuverable but pint-size Austin Mini, with two doors and manual transmission, for £79 ($138.25) per week. If this is too small for your taste, there is the Ford Fiesta, three doors and manual transmission, for £89 ($155.75) per week with unlimited mileage. You pay for your own fuel (called "petrol" here), of course. Larger cars, and those with automatic transmission, are more expensive.

The above prices are meant only as a guideline and do not include additional charges of around 15% as tax.

For Budget information call their toll-free number in the U.S. or Canada—800/527-0700—anytime between 7 a.m. and midnight (Central Standard Time) seven days a week. Ask for the international department.

Hertz, 35 Edgware Rd., Marble Arch, W.2 (tel. 01/402-4242), or at Heathrow Airport (tel. 01/679-1799), has 14 other major offices in London including one at Gatwick Airport. Their most economical and smallest car is the Ford Fiesta, seating four passengers. If you book seven days in advance, they'll charge you £119 ($208.25) for a seven-day rental. Government tax is 15% extra.

Avis also maintains offices at Heathrow Airport (tel. 01/897-9321), at Gatwick, and all other major airports in the United Kingdom. The charge for a Ford Fiesta with manual transmission was £112 ($196) at press time. Special rates offered for 21 days-plus start at only £19 ($33.25) per day, including collision damage waiver and tax.

Warning: Pedestrian crossings are marked by striped lines (zebra striping) on the road. Also, flashing lights near the curb indicate that drivers must yield the right of way if a pedestrian has stepped out into the zebra zone to cross the street.

The wearing of seatbelts is mandatory in the British Isles.

Bicycles

This is the cheapest transportation apart from what you walk on. You can rent bikes by the day or by the week from a number of outfits.

One popular place to rent a bicycle is **Savile's Stores,** 97 Battersea Rise, Battersea, S.W.11 (tel. 228-4279), which has been renting out bikes for more than 73 years. Stan Savile's father started the company back in 1912! The price is £22 ($38.50) per week, which is about half the charge of most of its competitors. This firm is not only the cheapest but also the most reliable bike-rental company I have found. A deposit of £10 ($17.50) is required with a passport, £20 ($35) without. Padlocks are provided free, and insurance costs £2 ($3.50) for any one rental period. It's open Monday to Saturday from 9 a.m. to 5:30 p.m.

London: Average Monthly Temperatures			
January	41.1	July	64.1
February	41.3	August	63.8
March	44.7	September	59.5
April	49.1	October	52.5
May	55.9	November	45.4
June	60.9	December	41.8

TRAIN TRAVEL OUTSIDE LONDON: There's something magical about traveling on a train in Britain. You sit in comfortable compartments, on upholstered seats, next to the reserved and well-dressed British. A rail journey outside London is a relaxing interlude.

BritRail Pass

If you plan to venture by train into the environs of London, perhaps visiting Oxford or Stratford-upon-Avon, you should be warned that your *Eurailpass is not valid on trains in Great Britain.* But the cost of rail travel in England, Scotland, Northern Ireland, and Wales can be quite low, particularly if you take advantage of certain cost-saving travel plans, including the **BritRail Pass.**

This pass gives unlimited rail travel in England, Scotland, and Wales, and is valid on all British Rail routes. It is not valid on ships between Great Britain and the continent, the Channel Islands, or Ireland.

Gold (first-class) and **silver** (economy-class) **passes** are sold for travel periods of varying lengths. An 8-day gold pass costs $230, and a silver ticket goes for $166. For 15 days, a gold pass costs $350; silver, $249. For 22 days, gold is $440; silver, $319. And for one month, gold is $520; silver, $369. Children up to 5 years of age travel free, and those from 5 to 15 go for half the adult price. Travelers from 16 to 25 may ride at reduced rates in economy class, but they must pay the full adult fare if they choose to go first class.

Youth passes, all silver, are $139 for 8 days, $209 for 15 days, $269 for 22 days, and $309 for a month. BritRail also offers a **Senior Citizen gold pass** to those age 60 and over, costing less than the regular gold pass. Prices are $195 for 8 days, $295 for 15 days, $375 for 22 days, and $445 for a month. All prices for BritRail passes are higher for Canadian travelers.

BritRail Passes cannot be obtained in Britain, but should be secured before leaving North America either through travel agents or by writing or visiting BritRail Travel International, 630 Third Ave., New York, NY 10017; Suite 603, 800 S. Hope St., Los Angeles, CA 90017; 333 N. Michigan Ave., Chicago, IL 60601; or Cedar Maple Plaza, 2305 Cedar Springs, Dallas, TX 75201. Canadians can write to 94 Cumberland St., Toronto M5R 1A3, or 409 Granville St., Vancouver, BC V6C1T2.

BritRail Passes do not have to be predated. Validate your pass at any British Rail station when you start your first rail journey.

London Travel Pak

The London Travel Pak is a package market by **BritRail Travel International, Inc.,** which includes a four-day BritRail Pass valid for unlimited rail travel in England, Scotland, and Wales for four consecutive days, a three-day London Visitors Travelcard (see "Transportation in Greater London," above), giving access to London Transport's red buses and Underground as well as transfers to and from Gatwick Airport by BritRail train or from and to Heathrow Airport by Underground.

The Travel Pak costs $149 for adults and $75 for children in first class, $119 for adults and $60 for children in economy class. Senior citizens can purchase a Travel Pak first class for $134.

The Britexpress Card

This offers one-third off all adult journey tickets purchased on Britain's Express Coach Network, valid for a 30-day period throughout the year. Travel where and when you wish with a choice of 1,500 destinations. All it costs is £10 ($17.50) for a discount card to travel around the network. Other bonuses are Flightline (Heathrow and Gatwick Airport services to London) and Jetlink (Heathrow to Gatwick Airport services) which offer similar discounts. The Britexpress Card can be purchased from your U.S. travel agent or on your arrival in London at the Victoria Coach Station. Examples of some approximate one-way fares and travel times are: London–Edinburgh, £12.50 ($22), 9 hours; London–Stratford-upon-Avon, £8 ($14), 3 hours, 10 minutes; London–York (Rapide Service), £13.50 ($23.75), 4½ hours; London–Cambridge, £6 ($10.50), 1 hour, 50 minutes. For information, phone 01/925-0188 in London.

Railroad Information

Personal callers can receive assistance at the British Rail / Sealink office, 4-12 Lower Regent St., S.W.1, and at the British Rail Travel Centres in the main London railway stations—Waterloo, King's Cross, Euston, Victoria, and Paddington—where each deals mainly with its own region. For general information, call the appropriate station. All numbers are listed in the telephone directory. Travel agents displaying a British Rail license can also help you.

BARGAIN TIPS FOR SIGHTSEEING: English Heritage, an

organization similar to the National Trust, is a foundation set up by the government (but independent of it) to care for more than 400 sites open to the public throughout the country. On their books in London are such important attractions as the Tower of London, Kensington Palace, and Hampton Court. Membership in the society gives you an annual season ticket for free entrance to all their sites, together with a map and regular up-to-the-minute information on activities and innovations. Even if you don't plan to tour the country, membership will provide information and free entrance to a number of attractions in and around the London area. Membership is £10 ($17.50) for adults. You can also purchase a family ticket covering both parents and all children under 16 for £20 ($35) per year. Join when you are in England at any English Heritage property or write to English Heritage, Membership Department, P.O. Box 43, Ruislip, Middlesex HA4 OXW, England (tel. 01/734-6010).

The **National Trust,** as mentioned, specializes in historic and stately homes. They offer a year-long membership in the Royal Oak Foundation for £16 ($28). This can be purchased at the National Trust, 36 Queen Anne's Gate, London, S.W.1 (tel. 01/222-9251). Tube: St. James's Park. Hours are weekdays from 9:30 a.m. to 5:30 p.m.

The U.S. headquarters for Royal Oak is at 41 E. 72nd St., New York, NY 10021 (tel. 212/861-0529). Membership can be purchased here, and it's considered a tax-deductible charitable contribution. The purpose of the Royal Oak Foundation is for the maintenance and continued exposure of British monuments and stately homes to the public. With membership, you're entitled to visit properties in Great Britain administered by the National Trust.

If you're planning to tour the country, you might also be interested in an **Open to View** ticket, which includes free admission to more than 500 properties in Great Britain. These include

Edinburgh Castle, Churchill's Chartwell, Woburn Abbey, Hampton Court Palace, and Windsor Castle. A 15-day ticket sells for $24 (U.S.), a one-month ticket for $36. In the United States, inquire at BritRail Travel International at addresses listed above, under BritRail Pass.

LONDON INFORMATION: Tourist information is available from the London Tourist Board's facilities. The **Tourist Information Centre,** Victoria Station Forecourt, S.W.1 (Tube: Victoria Station), can and will help you with almost anything of interest to a tourist in the U.K. capital. Staffed by courteous, tactful, sympathetic, patient, and understanding men and women, the center deals chiefly with accommodations in all size and price categories, from single travelers, family groups, and students to large-scale conventions. They also arrange for tour ticket sales and theater reservations and operate a bookshop. Hours are 9 a.m. to 8:30 p.m. daily from early April to the end of October; 9 a.m. to 7 p.m. Monday to Saturday, to 5 p.m. on Sunday, November to April. The bookshop is open from 9 a.m. to 7 p.m. Monday to Saturday and 9 a.m. to 4 p.m. on Sunday; hours are extended in July and August. For most types of service, you must apply in person.

The **Tourist Board** also has offices at:

Harrods, Knightsbridge, S.W.3, on the fourth floor. Open during store hours. Tube: Knightsbridge.

Selfridges, Oxford Street, W.1, basement services area, Duke Street entrance. Open during store hours. Tube: Bond Street.

The Tower of London, West Gate, E.C.3. Open early April to the end of October from 10 a.m. to 6 p.m. daily. Tube: Tower Hill Station.

Heathrow Airport Terminals 1, 2, and 3, Underground Concourse, open from 9 a.m. to 6 p.m.; and Terminal 2, Arrivals Concourse, open from 9 a.m. to 7 p.m. daily.

Telephone inquiries may be made to the bureau by calling 730-3488 Monday to Friday from 9 a.m. to 6 p.m. Written inquiries should be addressed to the London Tourist Board, Central Information Unit, 26 Grosvenor Gardens, London SW1W ODU.

For riverboat information, phone 730-4812.

The British Tourist Authority has a **British Travel Centre** at Rex House, 4-12 Lower Regent St., London S.W.1. This center offers a full information service on all parts of Britain, a British Rail ticket office, a travel agency, a theater ticket agency, hotel booking service, a bookshop, and a souvenir shop, all under one roof. Tube: Piccadilly Circus.

CHAPTER IV

WHERE TO STAY

□ □ □

London boasts some of the most famous hotels in the world. These include such hallowed temples of luxury as Claridge's, Grosvenor House, where top film stars like to stop off, the Ritz (which originated the slang term "ritzy" for smart), the Connaught, the Savoy, and their recent-vintage rivals, the Inn on the Park and the Park Lane Hilton.

All these establishments are superlative, but nobody would call them budget hotels. It is in that bracket that you get the most fantastic contrasts, both in terms of architecture and comfort. Most of London's hotels were built around the turn of the century, which gives the majority a rather curlicued appearance. But whereas some have gone to no ends of pain to modernize their interiors, others have remained at Boer War level, complete with built-in drafts and daisy-strewn wallpaper.

In between, however, you come across up-to-the-minute structures that seem to have been shifted bodily from Los Angeles. These aren't necessarily superior, for what the others lack in streamlining they frequently make up in personal service and spaciousness.

My task is to pick the raisins out of the pudding, so to speak. To select those hotels that combine maximum comfort with good value, in all price categories.

In most, but not all, of the places listed, there's a service charge ranging from 10% to 15% added to the bill. Again in most, although not all, the rates include breakfast, either a full English one or a continental one.

In the spring of 1973, however, the British government introduced a special Value Added Tax (VAT). At present 15% is added to your bill.

All hotels, motels, inns, and guesthouses in Britain with four bedrooms or more (including self-catering accommodations) are required to display notices showing minimum and maximum overnight charges. The notice must be displayed in a prominent position in the reception area or at the entrance. The prices shown must include any service charge and may include VAT, and it must be made clear whether or not these items are included. If VAT is not included, then it must be shown separately. If meals are provided with the accommodation, this must be made clear too. If prices are not standard for all rooms, then only the lowest and highest prices need be given.

And now, a brief summary of local hotel peculiarities.

Very few English hotels provide free matches for their patrons, hardly any supply a washcloth (bring your own), and most keep their soap tightly rationed; a private reserve bar is a good idea.

What is termed "continental breakfast" consists of coffee or tea and some sort of roll or pastry. An "English breakfast" is a fairly lavish spread of tea or coffee, cereal, eggs, bacon, ham or sausages, toast, and jam. Don't expect fruit juice, however. That's strictly a luxury item.

If you want to remain undisturbed, don't forget to hang the "Do Not Disturb" sign on your doorknob. English hotel maids—most of whom aren't English—have a disconcerting habit of bursting in simultaneously with their knock.

Elevators are called "lifts" and some of them predate Teddy Roosevelt's Rough Riders and act it. They are, however, regularly inspected and completely safe.

And, as mentioned earlier, hotel rooms are somewhat cooler than you're accustomed to. It's supposed to be healthier that way.

For those who demand really superior accommodations, I'll lead off with a selection among deluxe and first-class hotels.

DELUXE TRADITIONAL HOTELS

The Dorchester, Park Lane, W.1 (tel. 01/629-8888). A series of socially prominent buildings had stood on the site for as long as anyone could remember, but in 1929, with an increased demand for hotel space in the expensive Park Lane district, a famous mansion—whose inhabitants had been known for everything from great debauchery to great aesthetic skills—was torn down. In its place was erected the finest hotel London had seen in many years. Breaking from the neoclassical tradition which contemporary critics felt had hidebound the city into one homogenized unit, the most ambitious architects of the era designed a building of reinforced concrete clothed with terrazzo slabs. The superstructure was erected in little more than three months, a speed unheard of. One way designers muffled noise from the street (indeed, the rooms today are almost soundless) was with the compression of layers of seaweed between slabs of concrete.

The dozens of maids' rooms, included at the time, have since been converted into regular rooms with their own private baths. The hotel was constructed in such a way that as many rooms as needed could be occupied without anyone going into an outside corridor, thanks to interconnecting doors.

The façade facing Hyde Park rises into a graceful concave art deco sweep. An array of uniformed doormen greet newcomers with courtesy, and visitors register at an imposingly beautiful reception desk. The smiling concierge, one of the first woman concierges of any grand hotel in Britain, is Jackie Harris, who receives mail addressed directly to her from grateful clients, for which she has done everything from arrange a marriage license to get an impossible ticket to a hit West End production.

Throughout the hotel, you find a 1930s interpretation of Regency motifs. The arrangements of flowers and elegance of the main hall seem appropriate for a diplomatic reception, yet it contains a kind of sophisticated comfort in which guests from all over the world feel comfortable. All this production is presided over and skillfully managed by one of London's most deservedly famous hoteliers, Ricci Obertelli.

Owned by the publicity-shy Sultan of Brunei, the hotel is a member of one of Europe's most dynamic reservation agencies, Steigenberger Reservations System. The Dorchester contains 280 opulently furnished and spacious bedrooms. Linen sheets are a standard feature, as well as all the electronic gadgetry you'd expect from a world-class hotel. Singles range from £123 ($215.25) to £145 ($253.75), and doubles or twins go for £165 ($288.75) to £180 ($315), plus VAT. Suites, some designed by Oliver Messel, have sheltered everyone from Elizabeth Taylor to Stephanie Powers, from Jack Nicholson to assorted magnates of the world's social, political, and financial hierarchy. Tube: Hyde Park Corner.

The Savoy, The Strand, W.C.2 (tel. 01/836-4343), is a London landmark, with eight stories behind a façade of light terracotta-glazed tiles, rising majestically between the Strand and the Thames. The hotel, opened in 1889, was built by Richard D'Oyly Carte, impresario, for the use of people going to his theater to see the Gilbert and Sullivan operas he staged. Through the Savoy's portals have passed famous personages of yesterday and today, everybody from royalty to stars of stage, screen, TV, and rock.

Under the direction of Willy Bauer, its German-born managing director and general manager, the hotel has regained the impeccable hospitality, service, and splendor of its early years, which had faded somewhat for a couple of decades.

The hotel has 200 bedrooms, many with their own sitting rooms. Each has a different décor, with color-coordinated accessories, and all have private baths, comfortable chairs, solid furniture, and large closets. The units contain a blend of antiques, an eclectic combination of such pieces as gilt mirrors, Queen Anne chairs, and Victorian sofas. Guests find fresh flowers and fruit in their rooms on arrival, and at night beds are turned down and a chocolate placed on the pillows. Singles cost £145 ($253.75). Doubles and twins go for £175 ($306.25) to £235 ($411.25).

The world-famous Savoy Grill has long been popular with a theatrical clientele. Sarah Bernhardt was among its most celebrated customers in her time. The room has wood paneling and new carpeting, and a harpist plays in the evening. The even more elegant Savoy Restaurant is in a prime position, with tables looking toward the Thames. A four-person band plays in the evening for dancing on the intimate dance floor surrounded by tables. Tube: Temple, Embankment, or Covent Garden.

Claridge's, Brook Street, W.1 (tel. 01/629-8860), in Mayfair, dates from the mid-Victorian age under the present name, although an earlier "lodging house" complex occupied much of the hotel's area as far back as the reign of George IV. It has cocooned royal visitors in an ambience of discreet elegance since the time of the Battle of Waterloo. Queen Victoria visited the Empress Eugénie of France here, and afterward, Claridge's lent respectability to the idea of ladies dining out in public. The hotel took on its present modest exterior appearance in 1898. Inside, art deco was added in the 1930s, and much of it still exists agreeably along with antiques and TV.

The 209 bedrooms (55 are suites) are spacious, many having generous-size bathrooms complete with dressing rooms and numerous amenities. Suites can be connected by private foyers away from the main corridors, providing self-contained, large units suitable for a sultan and his entourage. Tariffs, including VAT and service, are £120 ($210) to £165 ($288.75) in a single, from £185 ($323.75) to £210 ($367.50) in a twin-bedded double, and from £350 ($612.50) in a suite. It's necessary to reserve a room at Claridge's far in advance.

Excellent food is stylishly served in the intimacy of the Causerie, renowned for its lunchtime smörgåsbord and pre-theater suppers, and in the more formal restaurant with English and French specialties. From the restaurant, the strains of the Hungarian

Quartet, a Claridge's institution since 1902, can be heard from the adjacent foyer during luncheon and dinner. Both the Causerie and the restaurant are open from noon to 3 p.m. The Causerie serves evening meals from 5:30 to 11 p.m., and dinner is offered in the restaurant from 7:30 to 11 p.m. Tube: Bond Street.

The Ritz, Piccadilly, W.1 (tel. 01/493-8181), has undergone an extensive four-year renovation program, costing millions of dollars, keeping it in the ranks of London's most luxurious hotels. The original color scheme of apricot, cream, and dusty rose enhances gold-leafed molding, marble columns, and potted palms. The oval-shaped Palm Court, dominated by a gold-leafed statue, *La Source,* adorning the fountain, is still the most fashionable place in London to meet for afternoon tea, enjoying a selection of finger sandwiches including cucumber and smoked salmon and specially made French pastries, scones, and cake.

The bedrooms and suites, each with its own character, are spacious and comfortable, all with modern private bathrooms, color television, Ceefax, radio, in-house films, and 24-hour room service. Prices are £150 ($262.50) for a single room, from £185 ($323.75) to £230 ($402.50) for twins and doubles. VAT and service are included.

The Louis XVI Restaurant, one of the loveliest dining rooms in London, has also been faithfully restored to its original splendor. Service is efficient yet unobtrusive, and the tables are spaced to allow the most private of conversations, perhaps the reason Edward and Mrs. Simpson dined so frequently at the Ritz. Tube: Green Park.

The Connaught, Carlos Place, W.1 (tel. 01/499-7070), captures an elegant old English atmosphere perhaps more than any other hotel in London. It ranks at the top with Claridge's for prestige and character. Its position is supreme, in the center of Mayfair, two short blocks from both Berkeley and Grosvenor Squares. The Connaught is a 19th-century architectural treasure house of a way of life fast disappearing. It's a brick structure, with a formal entrance, and its tall French windows overlook two curved, tree-lined streets.

As you enter, the staircase reminds you of an estate in the English countryside. Throughout the hotel are excellent antiques, such as in the drawing room with its formal fireplace, soft lustrous draperies at high windows, and bowls of fresh flowers. The cost of staying here is the same year round: a single with bath is £120 ($210), and a double or twin with bath runs £143 ($250.25) to £165 ($288.75), inclusive of VAT. All meals are extra, and the service charge is 15%. The bedrooms vary in size, but all are furnished with well-selected antiques and tasteful reproductions. All the rooms have well-equipped bathrooms and niceties galore. It is imperative to reserve well in advance.

The paneled bar-lounge is old-school-tie conservative; the fashionable (everybody from movie stars to bestselling novelists) dining room is also wood paneled, but it glitters with mirrors and crystal. The chef has perfected the English cuisine and a selection of French dishes. The bowing, attentive waiters and the fresh flowers set the proper mood. Luncheon or dinner from the à la carte menu will cost £35 ($61.25) to £70 ($122.50) per person. The food lives up to its reputation as superb. Reservations are essential for nonresidents of the hotel.

Grosvenor House, Park Lane, W.1 (tel. 01/499-6363), is an art deco marvel, a bastion of luxury, tradition, and elegance, the flagship of Trusthouse Forte. It was named after the famous residence of the Duke and Duchess of Westminster which around the turn of the century occupied this gilt-edged frontage along Hyde Park. To build the hotels, the efforts of the architects were spearheaded by Sir Edwin Lutyens, whose domestic architecture redefined the concept of how a fine house should be erected. The Grosvenor House came into being from 1927 to 1929, and today it is practically a miniature city unto itself, with 160 apartments (which lie within a separate tower) and 468 bedrooms and suites. Along tastefully furnished hallways lie some of the most engaging and spacious accommodations on Park Lane, each different from its neighbor, each filled with English chintz, inlaid headboards, and traditional furnishings. Accommodations contain large tile or marble baths, color TV, radio, trouser press, mini-bar, and phone. Singles rent for £160 ($280) to £185 ($323.75); doubles or twins, £165 ($288.75) to £195 ($341.25).

Since the days of Edward VIII the hotel has been noted for its banqueting rooms, which are said to be the largest in Europe. The biggest of them is almost as wide as the Suez Canal. The eight art deco chandeliers of the main ballroom have witnessed use as an officers' mess in World War II, as well as the traditional site of London's annual Caledonian Ball, where 1,500 dancers do the Scottish reel.

You enter a plushly upholstered, turquoise-colored lobby. On the premises is one of London's most superlative restaurants (more about that in the next chapter), called Ninety Park Lane. The hotel also has an array of other dining and drinking facilities for any occasion, plus one of the most sought-after health clubs in London in its basement. In addition to its stylish modern design, the club has a 65-foot swimming pool, along with a sauna, steambath, and exercise and aerobics room. Tube: Marble Arch.

First built in 1908, **Le Meridien Piccadilly,** Piccadilly, W.1

(tel. 01/734-8000), is now happily enjoying its reincarnation. At the time of its original opening, the Ionic arcade capping the limestone of its arched neoclassical façade was considered the height of Edwardian extravagance. It was instantly pronounced the grandest hotel in London, but its huge expense bankrupted its creator. One design factor that contributed to his financial demise was the hotel's 40-foot-deep foundations, deep enough to permit the installation of three underground floors. New owners continued to make the hotel one of the most stylish in the world, receiving such luminaries as Mary Pickford accompanied by Douglas Fairbanks, and much earlier, Edward VII. After World War II the hotel sank into a kind of musty obscurity until the revitalization of the Piccadilly theater district and the lavish refurbishment of the hotel, both of which coincided.

Today, after the expenditure of some $30 million, the hotel is considered the European flagship of the French-owned Meridien chain. It has enough elaborately detailed plasterwork, stained glass, and burnished oak paneling to make any Francophile feel at home, yet offers enough old-world service and style to satisfy even the most discerning British. Except for the intricate beauty of the skylit reception area, the centerpiece of the hotel is the soaring grandeur of its oak-paneled tea room, where gilded sculptures and chandeliers of shimmering Venetian glass re-create Edwardian styles.

The hotel offers a formal and very elegant restaurant and a less formal, sun-flooded eyrie under the greenhouse walls of the façade's massive Ionic portico (the Terrace Restaurant). There is, as well, a very British bar sheathed in hardwoods and permeated with music from a live pianist. The hotel is also proud of Champney's, one of the most exotic health clubs in London. Graced with a pool almost 50 feet long, whose tilework looks like something from the grand art deco days of Budapest, it features saunas, steambaths, aerobic workshops, squash courts, billiard tables, and a private membership clientele. Each of the nearly 300 handsome bedrooms contains ample amounts of space, private bath, TV, radio, phone, and a mini-bar, plus a chosen array of fine and conservatively tasteful furniture. Singles rent for £140 ($245) to £165 ($288.75); doubles or twins, £165 ($288.75) to £190 ($332.50). Tube: Piccadilly Circus.

DELUXE MODERN HOTELS

Inn on the Park, Hamilton Place, Park Lane, W.1 (tel. 01/499-0888). It's a commercial fact of life that among the dozens of luxury hotels of London, only a handful will attain the stratospheric heights which are derived from a combination of superb service, beauty, and famous connections. Inn on the Park has captured the imagination of the glamour-mongers of the world ever since it was inaugurated by Princess Alexandra in 1970.

Bordered with a smallish triangular garden and ringed by one of the most expensive neighborhoods in the world, it sits behind a tastefully modern façade. Its clientele includes heads of state, superstars, and business executives, among others. Howard Hughes, who could afford anything, chose it as a retreat, but his sprawling eighth-floor suite has since been subdivided into more easily rentable rooms.

Visitors enter a modern reception area ringed with burnished paneling. The acres of superbly crafted paneling and opulently conservative décor create the impression that the hotel is far older than it is. Piano music accompanies afternoon tea, served among excellent copies of Chippendale and Queen Anne furniture. A gently inclined stairway leads in the grandest manner to a symmetrical grouping of Chinese and European antiques flanked by cascades of fresh flowers.

One of my favorite bars in London, the Empire Bar, serves drinks in a room where Wellington might have felt at home, all to the tune of a pianist. A pair of restaurants creates a most alluring rendezvous, including the highly starred Four Seasons, which is both elegant and stylish, with superb views opening onto Park Lane. The finest wines and continental specialties dazzle guests either at lunch or dinner, which is served until 11 p.m. The alternative dining choice is the less expensive Lanes Restaurant, and many members of London's business community come here to partake of the hors d'oeuvres table.

The 228 rooms are large and beautifully outfitted with well-chosen chintz patterns, reproduction antiques, and plush upholstery, along with dozens of well-concealed electronic extras. The hotel has one of the highest occupancy rates in London. Singles cost £155 ($271.25) to £165 ($288.75), and doubles, £185 ($323.75), plus VAT. The hotel is a member of the Four Seasons group. Tube: Hyde Park Corner.

London Hilton on Park Lane, Park Lane, W.1 (tel. 01/493-8000), is better than ever. It's been a legend ever since it was built in 1963, and in 1984 the 500-room deluxe hostelry was completely renovated and upgraded in a tasteful, conscientious program.

A skyscraper, it offers bedrooms facing Hyde Park. When it was built, one of the most persistent stories alleged that from some of the high-altitude windows (28 floors) you could look down into Elizabeth's boudoir. Not so! It would take a powerful spyglass to see the Queen putting on her diamond tiara.

The Hilton rooms have such amenities as extra-long beds, TV, radio and baby-listening systems, air conditioning, message signal lights, showers in the baths, and circulating ice water. Year-round rates, with VAT included, range from £125 ($218.75) to £157 ($274.75) in a single and £144 ($252) to £181 ($316.75) in a twin-bedded chamber.

As part of a major renovation, floors 24 to 27 now have nine luxury suites, two executive suites, and six junior suites, along with 38 bedrooms and a private lounge. Separate check-in and check-out facilities are offered on these floors.

The Hilton's major restaurant is called "The British Harvest," which serves only the best and freshest of local produce in season. Pickled pine, a high coffered ceiling, and arched windows combine with pink marble, cherry-colored upholstery, and plant-filled troughs to achieve an airy, cheerful effect. Breakfast here includes poached haddock, calves' liver, kedgeree, kippers, and deviled kidneys, along with eggs, bacon, sausage, and steak. Lunch and dinner feature seasonal "harvest" menus.

The front lobby of the Hilton is a modern interpretation of 18th-century Georgian traditions. Finishes are predominantly of mahogany and marble, with accessories in crystal and brass. The adjacent Lobby Lounge has become a favorite London rendezvous. Earth colors—brown, beige, peach, ochre, rust, and tan—predominate, and the furnishings reflect a Hepplewhite and Chippendale influence. A dramatic marble-and-brass spiral staircase sweeps up to the first-floor level and the British Harvest Restaurant.

Other hotel facilities include a library of video films, a host of concessionaires in the arcade (where you can arrange car rentals, book theater tickets, etc.), a sauna, massage showers, and massage service. There has also been a major upgrading of the fire-detection, air-conditioning, and safety systems. Tube: Hyde Park Corner.

Hyatt Carlton Tower, 2 Cadogan Place, S.W.1 (tel. 01/235-5411). Its location and its height made this luxurious hotel a landmark even before Hyatt transformed it into its European flagship. After an army of decorators, painters, and antique dealers left, it became one of the most plushly decorated and best-maintained hotels in London.

It overlooks one of the most civilized gardens in London, whose Regency-era town houses were originally built as part of an 18th-century planning initiative. Its marble-floored lobby, with a resident harpist, looks a lot like the private salon of an 18th-century merchant, complete with the lacquered and enameled treasures he might have brought back from the Far East. Even the pink-and-blue dragons and flowers which cover the thick woolen carpets were made especially for the Hyatt in Hong Kong.

A massive bouquet of flowers almost, but not quite, dominates the clusters of Chippendale-style chairs and sideboards, creating a haven for breakfast, light lunches, afternoon teas, and nightcaps, which are served with rhythmical efficiency by a bevy of attractive employees. In fact, after the publicity it received once as "Britain's Tea Place of the Year," the hotel has been considered one of the capital's most fashionable corners in which to enjoy a midafternoon pick-me-up. Of course, scones, Devonshire clotted cream, arrays of pastries and delicate sandwiches, and music are all part of the experience.

The hotel contains a pair of restaurants and a few hideaway bars as well. The Rib Room is for relatively informal meals in a warmly atmospheric setting. The Chelsea Room, considered one of the great restaurants of London, is covered separately in the dining chapter.

Bedrooms are opulently outfitted, the beneficiary of the more than $15 million that the Hyatt spent on the décor. Each contains all the modern comforts you'd expect, as well as marble-lined bathrooms, imaginative artwork, air conditioning, and in-house movies. In the past few years Hyatt has spent $30 million on improvements, and its 223 bedrooms are opulently outfitted. Singles rent for £132 ($231) to £158 ($276.50), and doubles or twins, £160 ($280) to £188 ($329). Suites are more expensive, of course. A family plan allows children under 18 sharing a room with their parents to stay free.

Of particular note is a chic and desirable health club, whose two stories of shimmering glass encompass a sweeping panorama of the old trees of Cadogan Place. Filled with the most up-to-date exercise machines and staffed by a bevy of health and beauty experts, the club provides a genuine release from the pressures of a stressful day in London. On its upper floor, a neo-Grecian bar serves health-conscious light meals, and it's also preferred as an early rendezvous place for its breakfast buffet. Tube: Sloane Square.

Berkeley Hotel, Wilton Place, S.W.1 (tel. 01/235-6000). The original hotel so beloved by Noël Coward was moved, along with the loyalty of its well-heeled clients, to a travertine-faced building near Hyde Park in 1972. The restrained detailing of its French-inspired façade conceals a world of impeccable service, flickering fireplaces, richly textured oak paneling, and the accumulated traditions of the best hotel standards in both England and France.

The property abounds with such niceties as a news-service

telex machine between the Ionic marble columns of the lobby, formally dressed receptionists, a penthouse swimming pool designed like a modernized Roman bath, and lots of hideaway corners for drinks and conversations in elegant surroundings. The Restaurant, as it is called, serves a superb French cuisine in a décor of bleached paneling, masses of flowers, gracious proportions, and well-chosen English chintz.

Each of the accommodations is extremely comfortable, but the hotel is perhaps best known for its opulent suites, many of which contain exquisite paneling and gargantuan bathrooms. With VAT included, singles cost £126 ($220.50) to £175 ($306.25), while doubles go for £175 ($306.25) to £210 ($367.50). Tube: Knightsbridge.

FIRST-CLASS HOTELS

The **Stafford Hotel,** 16–18 St. James's Pl., S.W.1 (tel. 01/493-0111), dates from Edwardian days as a hostelry, romantically lying in a cul-de-sac off St. James's Street and Green Park. It can be entered via St. James's Place or else through the more colorful Blue Ball Yard (but only when the hotel's cocktail bar is open).

Built in the 19th century as a private home, the Stafford has retained a home-like, country-house atmosphere which has made it a favorite London address for visitors looking for something elegant and comfortable, with modern amenities yet without the cold anonymity of big, chain hotels, although it is owned by the Cunard group. David Ward, general manager, and his dedicated and capable staff make staying here an experience to remember.

Comfort is the keynote in the tastefully decorated public rooms. The elegant dining room, lighted by a handsome chandelier and wall sconces plus candles on the tables, gleams with silver and white napery. Here you can lunch or dine on classic dishes concocted by the chef's staff, using fresh, select ingredients and practiced know-how. A set lunch or dinner costs from £20 ($35). The bar of the hotel is a cozy attraction.

The 62 bedrooms are individually decorated and of varying shapes, in keeping with the private-home background of the structure. Rates are £125 ($218.75) in a single, £145 ($253.75) to £165 ($288.75) in a double, including VAT and service. The Stafford is often used by those who need a place of tranquility in the heart of London, to be near court and the embassy and political life of the city. There's easy access to good shopping and to "theaterland." Tube: Green Park.

London Marriott, Grosvenor Square, W.1 (tel. 01/493-1232). Its breakfast room is a decorator's dream, filled with a carefully researched cluster of Chippendale antiques and the kind of chintz which goes perfectly with the dramatic masses of seasonal flowers. The property was built in a grander era as the very conservative Hotel Europa. After Marriott poured millions of dollars into its refurbishment, only the very best elements, and of course much of the tradition, remained.

This triumph of the decorator's art sits proudly behind a red-brick and stone Georgian façade on one of the most distinguished parks in London, Grosvenor Square. Its polite battalions of porters, doormen, and receptionists wait near the entrance along a side street. The American Embassy is just a few doors away, adding even more distinction.

Throughout the hotel's carefully crafted interior, the same colors are consistently used in alluring combinations of pink, peach, ivory, and green. One of my favorite retreats is the Diplomat Bar, where leather wing chairs, well-rubbed paneling, and oil portraits of Edwardian statesmen imbue the place with the air of a very exclusive club. In the adjacent Diplomat Grill, elegant meals are impeccably served with the assistance of such culinary niceties as rolling silver trolleys with cabriole legs and claw-and-ball feet.

The 229 accommodations are plushly upholstered in Georgian design, containing all the electronic extras you'd expect. Singles cost £165 ($288.75) to £190 ($332.50); doubles, £190 ($332.50) to £215 ($376.25). Tube: Green Park.

Dukes Hotel, 35 St. James's Pl., S.W.1 (tel. 01/491-4840), provides elegance without ostentation. A hotel since 1908, it stands in a quiet courtyard off St. James's Street with its romantic, turn-of-the-century gas lamps. From the hotel it's possible to walk to Buckingham Palace, St. James's Palace, and the Houses of Parliament. Shoppers will be near Bond Street and Piccadilly. At St. James's Place, Oscar Wilde lived and wrote for a period. Each of the well-furnished bedrooms, 40 in all, plus 14 suites, is decorated in the style of a particular period.

There is central heating throughout, and every bedroom has its own private bath and direct-dial phone. A total renovation has made rooms brighter and more spacious than ever. A single rents for £128 ($224) to £138 ($241.50), and a double or twin goes for £170 ($297.50) to £195 ($341.25), including service charge and VAT. Room service is available 24 hours a day. Main meals are served in Dukes Restaurant from 12:30 to 2:30 p.m. and 6 to 10:30 p.m. Tube: Piccadilly Circus.

Hilton International Kensington, 179 Holland Park Ave., W.11 (tel. 01/603-3355), is a superb example of skillful space distribution. Although with 606 bedrooms it actually houses more guests than its Park Lane relative, it manages to look smaller. That's because the beautiful beige structure lies horizontally rather than towering vertically, thus blending nicely with the Kensington skyline. Yet the interior is spacious, with a lobby that never seems crowded and rooms offering all the elbow space you may crave.

The Kensington is one of the most finely designed and equipped Hiltons anywhere. Happily it is also considerably cheaper than its Park Lane counterpart. The reason for the price difference has nothing to do with comfort: simply, it boasts fewer restaurants, bars, lounges, and other peripherals.

One hotel restaurant, the Hiroko of Kensington, features authentic Japanese cuisine and handsome décor. The Market Restaurant dispenses English meals and international potations, and on Sunday the hotel offers the best-value brunch in town. You will find a magnificent buffet laid out with a full selection of breakfast and luncheon dishes.

The hotel's bedrooms strike a balance between eye-pleasing decor and practical gadgetry. The color schemes—pale pinks and greens—are blended for soothing restfulness. The lighting is both discreet and effective, the carpeting rich, the beds wide, soft, and slumbersome. Apart from bath and shower, hairdryer, dial telephone, color TV, radio, and fingertip-control air conditioning, the rooms also come with one of the handiest hotel installations ever invented. This is a self-service combination of bar and refrigerator plus breakfast dispenser. On insertion of the appropriate key, this contraption disgorges 12 different alcoholic drinks as well as soft beverages, coffee, tea, *and* a continental breakfast! You just pick your fancy, press a button and *voilà*! Instant room service. All rooms have satellite TV channels. The "Uniqey" electronic door-lock system has replaced the conventional key-lock system, affording guests greater security. Single rooms start at £86 ($151.50), and twins cost from £110 ($192.50), VAT included. The Crescent Lounge, just off the lobby, serves beverages and light snacks 24 hours a day. Tube: Holland Park.

The Park Lane Hotel, Piccadilly, W.1 (tel. 01/499-6321), is one of the long established "Park Lane sisters," having its own loyal clients and winning new converts all the time. It was begun in 1913 by an entrepreneurial former member of the Life Guards, using advanced engineering techniques to construct the foundations and an intricately detailed iron skeleton. When its creator was tragically killed in World War I, local gossips mockingly referred to the echoing and empty shell as "the bird cage." In 1924 one of London's leading hoteliers, Bracewell Smith, completed the construction, and a short time later the Park Lane became one of the leading hotels of Europe.

Today you'll enter an intensely English hotel which sits behind a discreet stone-block façade. One of its gateways, the Silver Entrance, is considered such an art deco marvel that its soaring columns have been used in many films, including *Brideshead Revisited, The Winds of War,* and *Shanghai Surprise* with Madonna. The hotel's restaurant, Bracewell's, is recommended separately.

This is the last of the Park Lane deluxe hotels to be privately owned by an English family. Designed in a "U" shape, with a view overlooking Green Park, it has more than 350 luxurious and comfortable accommodations, which are among the least expensive of any of the other major Park Lane competitors. Each contains a private bath, color TV, radio, mini-bar, phone, and double glazing for interior peace and quiet. Many of the suites offer marble fireplaces and the original marble-sheathed bathrooms. Depending on the season and the accommodation, singles cost £120 ($210) to £135 ($236.25); doubles or twins, £142 ($248.50) to £160 ($280). For afternoon tea, you can enter the beautifully decorated yellow-and-white lobby, capped by a glass ceiling and filled with palms evoking the Edwardian era. Tube: Hyde Park Corner.

Halcyon Hotel, 81 Holland Park, W.11 (tel. 01/727-7288, called "by far the grandest of London's small hotels," was formed from a pair of Victorian mansions originally built in 1860 by upper-class Londoners wanting to live on former meadowland owned by Lady Holland. Today their successful union contains a hotel of charm, class, fashion, urban sophistication, and much comfort. Since it opened in 1985, its clientele has included a bevy of international film and recording stars who like the privacy and anonymity provided by this place, where maids, dressed in black with starched white pinafores, glide silently through the corridors. Until British entrepreneur Peter James took over, the buildings had descended into seedy hotels for budget-minded students. After the expenditure of millions of pounds, the hotel is today directed by Gibraltar-born James Caetano, managing a staff of more than 60 people, several of whom earned their experience in some of the most important hotels of London.

More than half the 44 accommodations are classified as suites, and each unit is lavishly outfitted with the kinds of furnishings and textiles you might find in an Edwardian country house. Several accommodations are filled with such whimsical touches as tented ceilings, and each contains all the modern luxuries you'd expect in a hotel of this caliber. Rates in a single range from £95 ($166.25) to £175 ($306.25); in a double or twin, £150 ($262.50) to £250 ($437.50); and in a suite, £250 ($437.50) to £375 ($656.25).

The public rooms are inviting oases, with trompe-l'oeil paintings against backgrounds of turquoise. The designer of the hotel

was an American, Barbara Thornhill, who had worked at the
Georgetown Inn in Washington and for royal palaces in Saudi Arabia. She traveled the world on a massive shopping expedition to
provide the right objects for the hotel. As you arrive at the hotel,
you may think at first you're at the wrong address, as only a small
brass plaque distinguishes the aptly named Halycon from other
buildings on the street. A complimentary limousine service takes
clients to and from the West End, and there's a host of extras, including 24-hour room service, one-hour pressing of clothes, and a
message-paging system that extends 20 miles from the hotel. The
hotel's superb restaurant, Kingfisher, is recommended in the next
chapter. Tube: Holland Park.

Drury Lane Moat House, 10 Drury Lane, High Holborn,
W.C.2 (tel. 01/836-6666), is set in Covent Garden, with its
memories of Nell Gwynne, Sarah Siddons, and David Garrick. A
steel-and-glass structure originally built in 1978 and intended as
an office building, with terraced gardens and its own plaza, the hotel is elegantly decorated in greens and beiges, its extensive planting evoking a garden effect. The bedrooms are well furnished, each
containing a tile bath, color TV, and individually controlled central heating. Singles cost £90 ($157.50) to £110 ($192.50), and
doubles, £115 ($201.25) to £130 ($227.50). Tariffs include VAT
and service. Maudie's Bar makes a good pre-theater rendezvous,
and Maudie's Restaurant is open for lunch and dinner seven days a
week. Who was the original Maudie? She's Sir Osbert Lancaster's
famous arbiter-of-chic cartoon character Maudie Littlehampton.
Tube: High Holborn.

Brown's Hotel, Dover Street and Albemarle Street, W.1 (tel.
01/493-6020), is highly recommended for those who want a fine
hotel among the top traditional choices. This upper-crust, prestigious establishment was created by James Brown, a former manservant of Lord Byron. He and his wife, Sarah, who had been Lady
Byron's personal maid, wanted to go into business for themselves.
Brown knew the tastes of gentlemen of breeding and wanted to
open a dignified, club-like place for them, his dream culminating
in the opening of the hotel in a town house at 23 Dover St. in
1837, the year Queen Victoria ascended the throne of England.

Today, Brown's Hotel occupies some 14 historic houses on
two streets, in an appropriate location—in Mayfair, just off Berkeley Square. To this day, old-fashioned comfort is dispensed with
courtesy. A liveried doorman ushers you to an antique reception
desk where you check in. The lounges on the street floor are inviting, including the Roosevelt Room, the Rudyard Kipling Room
(the famous author was a frequent visitor here), and the paneled
St. George's Bar for the drinking of "spirits." A good, old-

fashioned English tea is served in the Albemarle Room. Men are required to wear jackets and ties for teas and for dining in the dining room, which has a quiet dignity and unmatched service. À la carte meals are served, plus a set luncheon menu at £24 ($42) and a set dinner at £25 ($43.75), including service and VAT.

The bedrooms vary considerably and are a tangible record of the past history of England. Even the wash basins are semi-antiques. The rooms show restrained taste in decoration and appointments, with good soft beds and phones. The rates for a single room are £111 ($194.25) to £140 ($245), £155 ($271.25) to £165 ($288.75) for a twin-bedded unit. The hotel also has bed-sitting rooms for two, renting for £190 ($332.50), and studio suites, also for two, going for £180 ($315). All rates include VAT and service. Tube: Green Park.

Rising like a concrete cylinder, the **Sheraton Park Tower,** 101 Knightsbridge, S.W.1 (tel. 01/235-8050), is not only one of the most convenient hotels in London, virtually at the doorstep of Harrods, but one of the best. It rises with its unusual circular architecture contrasting with the well-heeled 19th-century neighborhood around it. From its windows guests have a magnificently landscaped view of Hyde Park. The front door isn't where you'd think it would be—that is, at the front. Instead it's discreetly placed in the rear of the building where taxis can deposit guests more conveniently.

Opened in the summer of 1973 by Skyline of Toronto, the hotel was originally built as an office structure. Seven floors of the original design were removed to satisfy local demand. After a roller-coaster ride, the management of Sheraton stepped in in 1977, and the hotel has never been better run. They wanted two things: a flagship for their European enterprises and, in the words of one spokesperson, "a modern version of the Connaught."

Designers redecorated the wedge-shaped rooms into a tastefully international kind of plushness. Each of the accommodations, 295 in all, contains air conditioning, central heating, soundproof windows, in-house movies, radio, and phone. Room service and babysitting are also available. Commercial travelers, along with visiting diplomats and military delegations, often book the rooms which are, incidentally, opposite the French Embassy. Singles range from £135 ($236.25) to £145 ($253.75), and doubles or twins go for £150 ($262.50) to £160 ($280), plus VAT.

Its busy travertine-covered lobby bustles with scores of international clients who congregate on one of the well-upholstered sofas or amid the Edwardian comfort of the hideaway bar. In the rotunda, near the ground-floor kiosks, you can be served afternoon tea. The champagne bar offers you a choice of either a glass or a silver tankard filled with bubbly, along with oysters, dollops of caviar, and iced vodka. The food is exceptionally good at "The Restaurant," open from 7 a.m. to midnight, ideal for an after-theater supper. You can dine on such dishes as English crab, potted salmon, medallions of venison, and Scottish lamb. The restaurant has its own entrance on Knightsbridge. Tube: Knightsbridge.

Blakes, 33 Roland Gardens, S.W.7 (tel. 01/370-6701), is one of the best small hotels in London, certainly the most sophisticated. The neighborhood may be staunchly middle class, but Blakes is strictly an upper-class bastion of privilege. It's so glamorous, in fact, that guests might see Princess Margaret dining in its basement-level restaurant. The hotel is the creation of a talented actress, Anouska Hempel. You enter a richly appointed lobby furnished with Victorian-era campaign furniture, probably brought back by some empire-builder from a sojourn in India. Near an ornate wire birdcage (a miniature version of a mogul's palace), a well-spoken receptionist quotes rates for singles from £100 ($175) and doubles or twins from £150 ($262.50). Rooms tend to be smallish, yet impeccably outfitted with unusual accessories and furniture, some of it antique.

London's parade of the young and stylish, including "rag trade" types, photographers, and actors, dine downstairs in what is one of the best-reputed restaurants in town. Reservations are strictly observed by a youthful maître d'hôtel. After going down a flight of steps, you enter a black-lacquered room festooned with Japanese screens, silk-tufted cushions, and coffee-table books. The dramatically lit dining room is outfitted with pin spotlights shining onto a collection of Japanese helmets. Menu items are in tune with the times. Your salad of foie gras with Landais truffles might be served by an alluring Française from the region that produced the ingredients. Equally tempting might be an appetizer of quail eggs on a purée of mushrooms. Main courses include deliciously flavored varieties of teriyaki, poached salmon in a champagne sauce, and roast partridge with juniper berries. None of this, of course, comes cheaply. The price of a meal, with wine and service, might come to £50 ($87.50). Tube: South Kensington (but a taxi's better).

The **Royal Garden Hotel,** Kensington High Street, W.8 (tel. 01/937-8000), is another of Kensington's deluxe hostelries, well known for its stylish accommodations and supper club, the Royal Roof (see the nightlife chapter). A large modern building, the Royal Garden towers on the fringe of Kensington Gardens next to Kensington Palace where the Prince and Princess of Wales live, and fronts one of London's most fashionable shopping streets.

The hotel has 390 large bedrooms and suites, two restaurants, three bars, and seven conference and exhibition rooms. The Garden Café offers all-day dining of an international flavor and is adjacent to the Garden Bar, a sunken area with settees especially designed for lounging and sipping. In the Royal Roof, the cuisine is French and is served with a selection of well-chosen wines in elegant traditional English surroundings.

The bedrooms are modern, with décor in warm colors and facilities that include radio, color TV, in-house films, direct-dial phones, air conditioning, electronic message system, refrigerated bars, hairdryers, dual-voltage power points, sitting-room area, dressing room, and private bathroom and shower. Rates start at £101.50 ($177.75) for a single, increasing to £130 ($227.50) to £135 ($236.25) for a twin. These rates include tax. The Reserve Club wing on the tenth floor has spacious and elegant rooms patronized by well-heeled business people and other guests seeking the best in accommodations. These rooms have such amenities as crystal stemware and the personal services of a butler. Tube: High Street Kensington.

The Westbury, Conduit Street, W.1 (tel. 01/629-7755), offers all the ingredients for a prestigious West End address. Run by Trusthouse Forte, it was constructed in 1955 by an American polo enthusiast as a sister to the New York original. In 1987 it received a major refurbishment, giving it a new lease on life. It lies in the vicinity of some of the finest shops, art galleries, and antique auction houses.

The 243 bedrooms are individually designed, including standard and superior singles and doubles, as well as mini-suites and more spacious suites. You get comfort here in quiet elegance, with personal service. All bedrooms have individually controlled air conditioning, color TVs, and mini-bars, and there is 24-hour room service, plus a valet service. Singles range from £125 ($218.75) to £135 ($236.25); twins, £150 ($262.50) to £170 ($297.50). After afternoon tea served from silver and fine china, you may later in the evening want to patronize the Polo Restaurant, known for its French cuisine, later enjoying a nightcap in the Polo Bar. The Westbury has car parking and the convenience of being within walking distance of Bond Street (the nearest tube stop), Oxford Circus, Piccadilly, and Green Park.

The **Cavendish Hotel,** Jermyn Street, S.W.1 (tel. 01/930-2111), has an old name but a new body with a lively spirit. It was built in 1966 on the site of the old Cavendish, the subject of numerous stories about the days of Edward VII, when it was thronged with theatrical and royal personages. The hotel grew to fame under its colorful proprietor, Rosa Lewis, known as "The Duchess of Jermyn Street" in a biography written about her. In the St. James's district (Royal London), just off Piccadilly and a five-minute walk from Pall Mall, this former landmark has been transformed into a contemporary hotel. Its first two floors are devoted to shops, lounges, restaurants, and bars. The 253-bedroom tower is set back, rising above it.

The rooms are bright and airy, decorated in pastels, with wall-to-wall curtains, a sitting area, mini-bar, video, and TV. Double-thickness windows keep out traffic noises. All rooms have private bath. Singles rent for £110 ($192.50), and doubles cost from £145 ($253.75), with VAT and service included in the rates.

A traditional cocktail bar, the Sub Rosa, named for the famous former proprietor, is on the ground floor. On an upper level is the Cavendish Restaurant under the supervision of the head chef, Jack Rivas, who serves an excellent cuisine. Here you can enjoy a full English breakfast, à la carte or table d'hôte luncheon, pretheater dinner, or an à la carte candlelit repast. The Gallery offers a continental buffet breakfast, a buffet luncheon, and a unique menu throughout the day. Tube: Green Park.

The **Belgravia-Sheraton,** 20 Chesham Place, S.W.1 (tel. 01/235-6040), a modern block tower situated close to Harrods, Hyde Park, Knightsbridge, and Buckingham Palace, is ideal for the individual traveler looking for a comfortable home while in London.

All 90 guest rooms and suites are decorated tastefully and have full air conditioning, direct-dial phones, 24-hour room service, color TVs with remote control, free in-house films, and radios. Six-day laundry service and valet service is offered. Rates in a single are £115 ($201.25) to £130 ($227.50), while those in a double or twin range from £122 ($213.50) to £137 ($239.75), plus VAT.

The hotel's restaurant has an English-French menu with many traditional dishes prepared by the English chef, Michael Neal. The Lobby Lounge is an ideal place for morning coffee, snacks at lunchtime, or afternoon tea. Tube: Sloane Square.

The Capital, 22 Basil St., S.W.3 (tel. 01/580-5171), is one of the most personalized hotels in the West End. Small and modern, it's a stone's throw from Harrods. The proud owner, David Levin, has created a warm town-house ambience, the result of an extensive refurbishment program. The elegant *fin de siècle* decoration is matched by the courtesy and professionalism of the staff. From the lobby, an elevator takes guests to each floor, the corridors and staircase all being treated as an art gallery, with original oil paintings. In all, 60 rooms are offered, all with air conditioning, direct-dial phones, full audio and video service, and twin or king-size beds. Singles rent for £110 ($192.50) to £120 ($210), and doubles for £135 ($236.25) to £155 ($271.25).

The Capital Restaurant is among the finest in London, offering such exquisitely prepared main dishes as entrecote grill with béarnaise sauce and carré d'agneau (lamb) persillé with herbs from Provence. Fresh vegetables are used, and the dessert list is tempting. Tube: Knightsbridge.

Hotel Russell, Russell Square, W.C.1 (tel. 01/836-6470), is a late Victorian hotel facing the gardens of this famous square and within easy reach of theaters and shopping. It is run by Trusthouse Forte and offers 318 rooms, all with private baths or showers. Rates for a single are from £80 ($140), from £95 ($166.25) in a twin. The public rooms have been refurbished and include an excellent carvery restaurant and the Oakroom Grill. The Kings Bar serves cocktails in the atmosphere of a London club, and you can enjoy draft beer in the country-pub ambience of the Trade Winds Bar. The hotel has 24-hour room service. Other facilities include a theater-ticket agency, secretarial services, and car rental. Tube: Russell Square.

The **Strand Palace Hotel,** The Strand, W.C.2 (tel. 01/836-8080), is ideally situated for those who want to be in the theater district, near points such as Trafalgar Square, yet within a block of the Thames Embankment. Rooms have wall-to-wall draperies, innerspring mattresses, and other comfortable furnishings. Sun-bright colors contrast vividly with chalk-white walls. Behind the scenes is a staff of more than 400 standing by to provide personalized service. Rates are £65 ($113.75) in a single, £79 ($138.25) in a double or twin, and £85 ($148.75) in a triple. VAT and service are included, and all rooms have private baths or showers.

One of the assets of the Strand Palace is its restaurants, including a carvery where you can gorge yourself every day on England's finest roasts. There's also the coffeeshop that attracts show people. Favored is the intimate Mask Bar. To complete the dining possibilities, there is the Italian Connection, where you can select from an à la carte menu. Tube: Embankment, Charing Cross, or Covent Garden.

The **Royal Westminster Thistle Hotel,** Buckingham Palace Road, S.W.1 (tel. 01/834-1821), has one of the most fashionable addresses in London, within minutes of Buckingham Palace (in fact this hotel is passed during the Changing of the Guard).

The elegantly furnished hotel charges from £125 ($218.75) to £155 ($271.25) in a double or twin, £105 ($183.75) to £125 ($218.75) in a single. Rates are inclusive of service charge and

Privacy Plus

Bailey's Hotel, 140 Gloucester Rd., S.W.7 (tel. 01/373-6000), has been around since 1880, but it isn't on the usual tourist list. This six-story, handsome, red-brick structure, with white stone trim and a mansard roof, was in its day a pacesetter (the first hotel, for example, to install an "ascending room," that is, an iron cage elevator). To this day it harbors those who admire an aura of Victoriana. Social memories recall a great ball attended by 700 members of the nobility, including the Prince of Wales. It has been taken over by the Taj International Group of Hotels of India.

The hotel's 149 bedrooms have private bath/shower, color TV, radio, and direct-dial telephone. An extensive upgrading program has been carried out, resulting in many amenities, such as automatic elevators, a daily in-house movie facility, a good coffeeshop, and a hotel bar with a first-class restaurant, the Bombay Brasserie, specializing in Indian food. There's also a fully computerized reservation and billing system.

Single rooms cost £45 ($78.25) to £65 ($113.75), and twin rooms rent for £50 ($87.50) to £105 ($183.75) per night. All prices are inclusive of VAT and service. Tube: Gloucester Road.

VAT. Each bedroom is spacious, with many fine touches. All have individually controlled air conditioning, double glazing, direct-dial phones with extensions at the bedside, on the writing desk, and in the bathroom, radios, color TVs with teletext and in-house movies, hairdryers, trouser presses, mini-bars, and personal safes. In the bathrooms are bathrobes and toiletries. There is 24-hour room service and complimentary morning and evening newspapers, if you wish them.

The Restaurant St. Germain is the hotel's à la carte restaurant, which features an evocative mural on one wall depicting a gentle fantasy scene that is purely French in inspiration. The cuisine is mainly French and international. The attractive Le Café next to the Brasserie is open all day. There patrons can order any of up to 20 different imported beers from nearly as many countries, cocktails, and an appetizing range of hot and cold dishes. Tube: Victoria Station.

The **Goring Hotel,** Beeston Place, Grosvenor Gardens, S.W.1 (tel. 01/834-8211), was built in 1910 by Mr. O. R. Goring. It was the first hotel in the world to be equipped with a private bathroom in every bedroom. It was also the world's first hotel to be centrally heated. The hotel was erected just behind Buckingham Palace, and it lies within easy reach of the royal parks, Victoria Station, the West London air terminals, Westminster Abbey, and the Houses of Parliament.

Today top-quality service is still provided, this time by the founding father's grandson, George Goring. Rooms here are called apartments. Singles rent for £87.50 ($153.25), doubles or twins for £130 ($227.50); a suite is £165 ($288.75). Color television sets are included in the tariffs, as are service and VAT. You can have a three-course luncheon for £15.50 ($27.25) and dinner from £18 ($31.50). Some of the chef's specialties include a fine duckling pâté, calves' liver (with bacon and onions), venison, and roast boned best end of lamb. The charm of a traditional English country hotel is reflected in the paneled drawing room, where fires burn in the ornate fireplaces on nippy evenings. Nearby is a sunroom with a view of the gardens in the rear and a bar situated by the window. Tube: Victoria Station.

THE BEST OF THE REST

All the following hotels offer rooms with full private bath; but with one or two exceptions, many of them also contain many rooms with hot and cold running water only, which the British themselves are fond of booking. If you find that a medium-priced room with private bath is more than you can afford—and you want something fancier than a "bed-and-breakfast" house—then consider asking for one of the bathless rooms. You'll enjoy the same facilities, the same central location, the same hotel services, but you'll be paying far less.

OFF PICCADILLY: The following hotel is on Half Moon Street, a small, svelte thoroughfare connecting Piccadilly with Curzon Street. It's smack in the heart of the West End, right among the theaters and nightspots, yet fringed with greenery and removed from din. It's in what the British would call a "favored position." And if you don't mind the lack of a private bath, you can stay at the largest hotel in Europe (see below).

Flemings Hotel, 7–12 Half Moon St., W.1 (tel. 01/499-2964), is a traditional-style hotel set in a quiet street off Piccadilly. The reception area and spacious lounge have an air of peaceful charm and elegance with elaborate chandeliers and period furniture. The Langoustine Restaurant and Claridge Bar offer a wide choice from à la carte and table d'hôte menus served in a warm and relaxing atmosphere. There are 135 charmingly decorated rooms, all with private baths, color TVs with in-house movies, radios, direct-dial phones, refrigerators, and hairdryers. Rates are £70 ($122.50) for a single, rising to £95 ($166.25) for a double or twin. Executive twins cost £115 ($201.25). An extra bed can be set up in rooms occupied by two people for £14 ($24.50). Tariffs include service and VAT. Tube: Green Park.

BELGRAVIA: The aristocratic quarter of London, Belgravia, south of Hyde Park, challenges Mayfair for grandness. It reigned in glory with Queen Victoria, but today's aristocrats are more likely to be the top echelon in foreign embassies, along with a rising new monied class of actors and models. Belgravia is near Buckingham Palace Gardens and Brompton Road. Its center is Belgrave Square, one of the more attractive plazas in London. A few town houses once occupied by eminent Edwardians have been discreetly turned into moderately priced hotels (others were built specifically for that purpose). For those who prefer a residential address, Belgravia is choice real estate.

The **Diplomat Hotel,** 2 Chesham St., S.W.1 (tel. 01/235-1544). Part of its multiple allure lies in its status as a small, reasonably priced family-operated hotel in an otherwise prohibitively expensive neighborhood filled with privately owned Victorian homes and high-rise first-class hotels. It was originally built by one of the neighborhood's most famous architects in the 19th century on a wedge-shaped street corner near the site of the Belgravia Sheraton. You register at a desk whose borders are framed by the sweep of a partially gilded circular staircase beneath the benign gaze of cherubs looking down from the borders of a Regency-era chandelier.

Each of the 28 comfortable bedrooms contains a modern bath, color TV, phone, a high ceiling, and well-chosen wallpaper in vibrant Victorian-inspired colors. Each comes with such extra touches as a hairdryer and morning newspapers. The staff is very helpful, and each accommodation is named after one of the famous streets in this posh district. Singles rent for £47 ($82.25), and doubles or twins are £64 ($112), plus VAT. An extra bed can be set up in a room for another £18 ($31.50) per person. A continental breakfast, served in your room, is included in the price. Tube: Sloane Square.

The **Regent Palace Hotel,** Piccadilly Circus, W.1 (tel. 01/734-7000), one of the largest hotels in Europe, has 1,034 bedrooms, all with hot and cold running water, hot-beverage facilities, radios, and color TVs. It stands in the center of London, with theaterland around the corner and Oxford Circus a five-minute walk away. It charges £37 ($64.75) in a single, £49 ($85.75) in a twin- or double-bedded room. Rates include an English breakfast, VAT, and service. The hotel's Carvery is a good place to dine, and the Winter Garden coffeeshop is open for pre-theater meals. Drinks are served in the Half Sovereign bar and the Planters bar. The Palace has a wide range of services you can learn about at the hall porter's desk. Tube: Piccadilly Circus.

AT KNIGHTSBRIDGE: A top residential and shopping district
of London just south of Hyde Park, Knightsbridge is close in character to Belgravia, although much of this section to the west of Sloane Street is older, dating back in architecture and layout to the 18th century.

The **Beaufort,** 33 Beaufort Gardens, S.W.3 (tel. 01/584-5252), is one of London's most charming small hotels, sitting behind two Victorian porticos and an iron fence added when the hotel was constructed in the 1870s. The entrepreneurial management combined a pair of adjacent houses, ripped out the old décor, and created a stylishly updated ambience of merit and charm. You register at a small alcove extending off a bay-windowed parlor, and later you climb the stairway used by the Queen of Sweden during a stay here.

Each of the 29 bedrooms contains at least one well-chosen painting by a London art student, a thoughtfully modern color scheme, plush carpeting, and a kind of grace throughout. Amenities include a private bath, color TV, earphone radio, and phone, as well as flowers and a selection of books to read. With breakfast and VAT included, with fresh bread and just-squeezed orange juice and homemade marmalade, singles cost from £95 ($166.25); doubles or twins, £105 ($183.75) to £143 ($250.25). Suites are more expensive. One added advantage of this place is the mostly female staff and the inspired direction of its owner, Diana Wallis, a television producer. She did everything she could to create the feeling of a private house in the heart of London. Tube: Knightsbridge.

The **Basil Hotel,** Basil Street, S.W.3 (tel. 01/581-3311), has long been a favorite little hotel of discerning British who make an annual pilgrimage to London to shop at Harrods and perhaps attend the **Chelsea Flower Show.**

This Edwardian charmer is totally unmarred by pseudo-modernization, with guests who can appreciate this highly individualistic hotel preferred. The open mahogany staircase seems ideal as a setting for the entrance line of a drawing room play: "You're just in time for tea, Braddie." There are several spacious and comfortable lounges, appropriately furnished with 18th- and 19th-century decorative accessories. Off the many rambling corridors are smaller sitting rooms.

The pleasantly furnished bedrooms are priced according to size and location. Single rooms range from £45 ($78.75) to £85 ($148.75), the latter with private baths. Doubles without bath go for £68 ($119), increasing to £110 ($192.50) with bath.

A three-course table d'hôte luncheon is served in the dining room, and dinner is à la carte. Candlelight and piano music recreate the atmosphere of a bygone era. The Upstairs Restaurant serves lighter meals and snacks, and the Downstairs Wine Bar, wines and inexpensive food. Tube: Knightsbridge.

The **Claverley Hotel**, 13–14 Beaufort Gardens, S.W.3 (tel. 01/589-8541). Set on a quiet street in Knightsbridge, this pleasant and tasteful hotel lies just a few blocks from Harrods. In many ways it's one of the very best hotels in the neighborhood, especially considering its price. It's a small, cozy place with a highly prized location and Georgian-era accessories. The lounge is one of the hotel's most desirable features, containing 19th-century oil portraits, a Regency fireplace, and a collection of elegant antiques and leather-covered sofas much like an ensemble you'd find in a private country house.

Awarded the British Tourist Authority's Certificate of Distinction for Bed-and-Breakfast Hotels in 1986, the Claverley continues to maintain the high standards that won it the award. You take a small elevator to one of the 36 bedrooms, all but six of which have a private bath. Several contain open-air balconies overlooking a wide-angle view of the rear end of Harrods. Most rooms have a frilly Victorian-inspired wallpaper, wall-to-wall carpeting, and comfortably upholstered armchairs. With a full English breakfast included, as well as VAT, singles cost £47 ($82.25) to £53 ($92.75); doubles or twins, £53 ($92.75) to £65 ($113.75). Tube: Knightsbridge.

The **Knightsbridge Hotel**, 10 Beaufort Gardens, S.W.3 (tel.01/598-9271), sandwiched between the restaurants and fashionable boutiques of Beauchamp Place and Harrods, still retains the feeling of a traditional British hotel. On a tranquil, tree-lined square, free from traffic, it has a subdued Victorian charm.

The place is small—only 20 bedrooms—and personally run by the manager, Robert A. Novella. Units have phones, radios, and central heating, and there's a lounge with a color "telly" and a bar on the premises. Most expensive are rooms with private baths, costing £39.50 ($69.25) in a single, from £64.90 ($113.50) in a twin. The best for the budget are the bathless specials, from

£28.60 ($50) in a single and from £40.70 ($71.25) in a twin. There are also rooms with showers. For example, a family room with shower for three guests rents for £60.50 ($106) per night. All tariffs include a continental breakfast, VAT, and service charge. Tube: Knightsbridge.

Knightsbridge Green Hotel, 159 Knightsbridge, S.W.1 (tel. 01/584-6274). This unusual establishment was constructed a block from Harrods in the 1890s. In 1966, when it was converted into a hotel, the developers were careful to retain the wide baseboards, cove molding, high ceilings, and spacious proportions of the dignified old structure.

None of the accommodations contains a kitchen, but the result comes close to apartment-style living. Many of the doubles or twins are suites, each well furnished with access to the second-floor "club room" where coffee and pastries are available throughout the day. Each of the units contains a private bath, phone, and TV set. Singles rent for £50 ($87.50) a night, doubles or twins for £60 ($105), and suites for £75 ($131.25), including VAT. Tube: Knightsbridge.

The **Executive Hotel,** 57 Pont St., S.W.1 (tel. 01/581-2424). It was built in 1870 as a private house behind an ornate neo-Romanesque façade of red brick. After costly restoration by a hard-working and savvy entrepreneur, it was restored and is now one of the most appealing and convenient small hotels in the district. Part of its charm lies in its Adam-style frieze, which ascends and curves around the high ceilings and graceful stairway of the main entrance. From the front you see only a discreet metal plaque announcing the establishment's status as a hotel. But once inside, you find 29 comfortable, modernized, and unfrilly bedrooms. Each of these contains simple built-in furniture, a high ceiling, radio, color TV, phone, private bath, and central heating. With a full English breakfast included, singles cost £45 ($78.75) to £53 ($92.75), and doubles or twins run £64 ($112), plus VAT. An elevator takes guests to one of the five upstairs floors. A cozy modern bar occupies one of the rooms off the lobby, and the location, near the attractions of Knightsbridge (the nearest tube stop), make the Executive very, very central.

NEAR OXFORD STREET: The next hotel is as choicely located: close to London's main shopping drag, but tucked away from the traffic noise.

The Londoner, 57–59 Welbeck St., W.1 (tel. 01/935-4442), has retained its traditional façade but completely modernized its interior. The contrast, the moment you walk in, is delightful. Tucked away in Mayfair, off Wigmore Street (near Cavendish

Square and Wigmore Hall), the hotel is an excellent remake of an older building.

All of its 142 comfortably furnished bedrooms contain private bath, phone, radio, and TV. There's also 24-hour room service. Singles rent for £65 ($113.75), and with doubles or twins cost from £84 ($147), inclusive of VAT. Oliver's Restaurant is comfortably traditional and welcoming, serving British fare at breakfast, lunch, and dinner. The Chesterfield Bar offers a range of "spirits" and beer. Tube: Bond Street.

AROUND VICTORIA STATION: Directly south of Buckingham Palace is a section in Pimlico often referred to as "Victoria," with its namesake, sprawling, bustling Victoria Station as its center. Known as "the Gateway to the Continent," Victoria Station is where you get boat trains to Dover and Folkestone for that trip across the Channel to France.

The section also has many other advantages from the standpoint of location, as the British Airways Terminal, the Green Line Coach Station, and the Victoria Coach Station are all just five minutes from Victoria Station. Your best bet in this area is to walk about Ebury Street, which lies directly to the east of Victoria Station and Buckingham Palace Road. There you will find some of the best moderately priced lodgings in central London. My favorite recommendations along this street are:

Ebury Court, 26 Ebury St., S.W.1 (tel. 01/730-8147), was created out of a group of small town houses. You notice the country-house flavor right away. The place is brightly painted (turquoise and white), with railings to match and flower-filled window boxes. The little reception rooms are informal and decorated with flowery chintz and quite good antiques. Best of all, there is a cordial and informal staff.

The rate in a single ranges from £40 ($70) to £44 ($77), from £62 ($108.50) in a bathless twin-bedded room or a double. Doubles with private bathrooms cost from £72 ($126). All 38 rooms have hot and cold running water, as well as a telephone and radio. An English breakfast and VAT are included in the rates. You can order either a lunch or dinner in the small restaurant.

A special feature of this establishment is the bar, which caters only to guests and to members of the Ebury Court Club, a group of local people who enjoy their drinks in a congenial atmosphere. A night porter is on duty to look after late arrivals. The A1 bus, which goes to Heathrow every 20 minutes, leaves from Grosvenor Gardens, about 1½ minutes from the Ebury Court. Hotel porters will help you with your luggage on a trolley if required. Tube: Victoria Station.

The **Elizabeth Hotel,** 37 Eccleston Square, S.W.1 (tel. 01/828-6812), is an intimate, privately owned establishment overlooking the attractive, quiet gardens of a stately square. It is an excellent place to stay, convenient to Belgravia, Chelsea, and Westminster, and not far from Buckingham Palace. Of its 24 rooms, three have baths or showers, and good facilities are available for the bathless rooms, which have hot and cold water basins. Singles cost from £24 ($42) without bath, and bathless twins or doubles are priced from £37 ($64.75). Doubles with shower cost from £41 ($71.75). A large double or twin room with bath or shower, toilet, color TV, and refrigerator rents from £46 ($80.50) to house three persons, £52 ($91) for four persons. Prices include either an English or a continental breakfast. The friendly reception staff will help guests find good pubs and restaurants in the neighborhood, as well as advising on how to enjoy London. Tube: Victoria Station.

Collin House, 104 Ebury St., S.W.1 (tel. 01/730-8031), provides a good, clean B&B under the watchful eye of its resident proprietors, Mr. and Mrs. D. L. Thomas.

Everything is well maintained here, and all bedrooms, the majority with private showers and toilets, have fitted carpets, hot and cold running water, built-in wardrobes, and comfortable divan beds. Single rooms with private bath/shower and toilet cost £30 ($52.50), with doubles renting for £35 ($61.25) without bath, £40 ($70) with bath. All rates are inclusive of a full English breakfast, VAT, and the use of showers and toilets for those who don't have private facilities. There are a number of family rooms here. The main bus, rail, and Underground terminals are about a five-minute walk from the hotel. Tube: Victoria.

Lewis House, 111 Ebury St., S.W.1 (tel. 01/730-2094). A benign brass face stares back at visitors from the door-knocker of this town house which used to shelter Noël Coward. The building was sold by Coward's father in 1929. Noël remained a tenant for three years, composing many of his songs here and entertaining luminaries of London society. Eventually the parties became too raucous and he was requested to leave the premises, which he promptly did, moving on to greener pastures.

During World War II military bigwigs were housed here, each with a direct phone line to the Admiralty or War Office.

Today the establishment is sometimes fully booked for weeks in advance. If you're lucky enough to get a room, you'll meet the Evans family, who, with John Evans as manager, maintain this Regency house with warm-hearted comfort. The Evanses have completely refurbished the establishment, adding more private showers in rooms and restyling the breakfast room. It has pictures of Noël Coward adorning the walls, old play programs, Coward's old top hat, and other memorabilia of the Coward era. Bathless singles rent for £26 ($45.50). The price of twins and doubles is £35 ($61.25) to £40 ($70), depending on the plumbing. Triples with shower are offered for £55 ($96.25), and suites for four people, with toilet and shower, are £80 ($140). Charges include VAT and a full English breakfast. Tube: Victoria Station.

CHELSEA: This stylish district stretches along the Thames, south of Hyde Park, Brompton, and South Kensington. It begins at the historic and charming Sloane Square. If you lodge here, you'll be close to the shopping districts of Knightsbridge and Sloane Street, with the famous department stores of Harrods and Peter Jones at your doorstep. Nearby is King's Road, with its exciting boutiques, antique shops, and restaurants.

The **Wilbraham Hotel,** Wilbraham Place, off Sloane Street, S.W.1 (tel. 01/730-8296), is as dyed-in-the-wool British as you can get. On a quiet little street, just a few hundred yards from busy Sloane Square, three Victorian town houses have been joined together as one hotel.

It has an intimate sitting room and an attractively old-fashioned bar/lounge where you can have simple meals at both lunch and dinnertime. There are 57 rooms in all, plus 42 baths, and prices range according to plumbing. Singles go for £30 ($52.50) to £41 ($71.75) and twins or doubles for £50 ($87.50) to £64 ($112), the latter for a deluxe chamber. VAT is added. Tube: Sloane Square.

Willett Hotel, 32 Sloane Gardens, S.W.1 (tel. 01/730-0634), opening onto the gardens, is a 19th-century town house with many architectural curiosities, including a Dutch-style roof and bay windows. It is currently undergoing restoration so the level of accommodation will vary. Each of the bedrooms has a radio, TV, direct-dial phone, hairdryer, dressing table, and facilities for making coffee or tea. Best of all is the full English breakfast served in a club-style room with black leather chairs.

Most of the accommodations contain private baths. Singles rent for £30 ($52.50), and doubles or twins for £42 ($73.50). An extra single bed in a family room costs an additional £12 ($21). Tube: Sloane Square.

The **Blair House Hotel,** 34 Draycott Pl., S.W.3 (tel. 01/581-2323), is a good, moderately priced choice for those who'd like to anchor deep in the heart of Chelsea. An old-fashioned building of architectural interest, it has been modified and completely refurnished.

Rooms are usually small but still comfortable and contain

such conveniences as phones, radios, and facilities for making tea or coffee, along with TV sets. Most rooms have a private bath or shower and are more expensive. Singles range in price from £30 ($52.50) without bath to £44 ($77) with. A bathless twin goes for £46 ($80.50), a twin with complete bath costs £56 ($98), including a continental breakfast and VAT. Tube: Sloane Square.

ST. MARYLEBONE: Below Regent's Park, northwest of Piccadilly Circus, is the district of St. Marylebone (pronounced Mar-li-bone), a residential section that faces Mayfair to the south and extends north of Marble Arch.

A small, homey place to stay, the **Dorset Square Hotel,** 39–40 Dorset Square, N.W.1 (tel. 01/723-7874), is made up of two Georgian Regency town houses similar to their neighbors on the small square near Regent's Park. Hotelier Tim Kemp and his wife, Kit, have transformed the former dwellings into a hotel whose interior is so designed that its public rooms, bedrooms, and baths still give the impression of being in an elegant private home. The bedrooms are decorated in chintz or print materials that complement the furniture, a mix of antiques and reproductions. Rates are £55 ($96.25) for singles, £70 ($122.50) to £90 ($157.50) for doubles, with suites going for £105 ($183.75) to £120 ($210), depending on whether or not there's a view.

The handsome restaurant, Country Manners, is graced by a mural showing Dorset Square when it was the home of the Marylebone Cricket Club. The menu, featuring the best of English cuisine, changes daily, offering such dishes as Stilton soup and venison (in season) and poached Scottish salmon with hollandaise sauce. Tube: Baker Street or Marylebone.

Durrants Hotel, George Street, W.1 (tel. 01/935-8131), is a 200-year-old hotel with a sprawling Georgian façade of brown brick. Someone has made an admirable attempt to establish a small garden of ivy and seasonal flowers near the foundation. Since its ownership by the Miller family for the past century, several neighboring houses have been incorporated into the original structure, making a walk through the pine- and mahogany-paneled public rooms a tour through another century.

The in-house restaurant serves full afternoon teas and satisfying meals in one of the most beautiful Georgian décors in the neighborhood. The less formal breakfast room is ringed with 19th-century political cartoons by the noted Victorian artist Spy.

You'll even find such 18th-century niceties as a letter-writing room sheathed with old paneling and a popular neighborhood pub with Windsor chairs, an open fireplace, and a décor which probably hasn't changed very much in 200 years. The establishment's oldest bedrooms face the front and contain slightly higher ceilings than the newer ones. Even the most recent accommodations, however, have elaborate cove moldings, very comfortable furnishings, and a solid feeling of well being. Each has color TV, phone, radio, and private bath. Singles cost £48 ($84) to £65 ($113.75); doubles, £70 ($122.50) to £122 ($213.50). Tube: Bond Street.

The **Hart House Hotel,** 51 Gloucester Pl., Portman Square, W.1 (tel. 01/935-2288), is a well-preserved building, part of a group of Georgian mansions occupied by the French nobility during the French Revolution. The hotel is in the heart of the West End and is convenient for shopping and theaters. It's within easy walking distance of Oxford Street, Selfridges, Marble Arch, Hyde Park, Regent's Park, the Zoo, Madame Tussaud's, and the Planetarium.

Hart House is centrally heated, and all rooms have hot and cold running water, color TVs, radios, and phones. This is a small family hotel with 15 bedrooms, all clean and comfortable. It is run by the proprietors, Mr. and Mrs. Bowden, and their son, Andrew, who offer their guests warm hospitality. Prices, which include an English breakfast and VAT, range from £27 ($47.25) for a single, £40 ($70) for a twin or double, and £56 ($98) to £63 ($110.25) for a family room. Tube: Marble Arch or Baker Street.

Bryanston Court Hotel, 56–60 Great Cumberland Pl., W.1 (tel. 01/262-3141). Each of the three individual houses that were joined together to form this hotel was built about 190 years ago. Today this is one of the most elegant hotels on the street, thanks partly to the decorating efforts of its owners, the Theodore family. There's a gas fire burning in the Chesterfield-style bar, plus a stairway leading up to the 56 bedrooms.

Each of these contains a private bath, color TV, phone, and radio. The opulently red dining room, the Brunswick Restaurant, is furnished in an early 19th-century style with antiques and oil portraits. After you pass through the iron gate in front under the awnings, you'll be quoted a single rate of £50 ($87.50) a night, £64 ($112) in a double or twin. An extra bed can be set up for £15 ($26.25) a night. A continental breakfast is included in the price. Tube: Marble Arch.

The **Hotel Concorde,** 50 Great Cumberland Pl., W.1 (tel. 01/402-6316), is a small hotel with style. The reception desk, nearby chairs, and part of the tiny bar area were at one time part of a London church. A display case in the lobby contains an array of reproduction English silver, each piece of which is for sale. This establishment was built as a private house and later converted into a 30-room hotel.

Each of the accommodations is pleasantly decorated with flowered wallpaper and has a color TV, direct-dial phone, and a private bath. Owned by the Theodore family, the hotel is managed by sons Martin and Michael, daughter Linda, and their father. Breakfast is the only meal served. Guests can patronize the just-recommended Bryanston Court for à la carte lunches and dinners. Singles rent for £45 ($78.75), while doubles or twins cost £55 ($96.25). An extra bed can be set up in any room for another £15 ($26.25) per night. A continental breakfast is included in the rates. Tube: Marble Arch.

The **Edward Lear Hotel,** 30 Seymour St., W.1 (tel. 01/402-5401), is a popular hotel, made all the more desirable by the bouquets of fresh flowers set up around the public rooms. It's one block from Marble Arch in a pair of brick town houses, both of which date from 1780. The western house was the London home of the 19th-century artist and poet Edward Lear, whose illustrated limericks adorn the walls of one of the sitting rooms.

Steep stairs lead up to the 30 bedrooms, 11 of which contain private baths or showers. The cozy units are fairly small but have all the usual facilities, including color TVs, radios, phones, and hot-beverage equipment. Singles cost £30 ($52.50) to £35 ($61.25), and doubles go for £44 ($77) to £50 ($87.50). Tariffs include VAT and a large English breakfast. The owner, Peter Evans, and his capable manager, Duncan McGlashan, are helpful to guests. Tube: Marble Arch.

The **Hallam Hotel,** 12 Hallam St., Portland Place, W.1 (tel. 01/580-1166), is a heavily ornamented stone-and-brick Victorian house, one of the few on the street to escape bombing in World War II. Today it's the property of one of the most charming families in the neighborhood, the Bakers. Earl and his sons, Grant and David, maintain it well. There is a bar for residents.

An elevator leads to the 23 simple but comfortable bedrooms, each with TV, phone, radio, and 24-hour room service. A light English breakfast is included in the price of the rooms, which cost £34 ($59.50) to £41 ($71.75) in a single, £57 ($99.75) to £62 ($108.50) in a double. The bright breakfast room overlooks a pleasant patio. Tube: Oxford Circus.

IN PADDINGTON: The area separated from Hyde Park by pulsating Bayswater Road is pleasantly residential, yet lively enough to be interesting, equally close to sweeping parklands and to some of the best shopping centers.

The **Colonnade Hotel,** 2 Warrington Crescent, W.9 (tel. 01/286-1052), is an imposing town house in a pleasant residential area, just a block from the Warwick Avenue tube station.

Owned and managed for some 40 years by the Richards family, the hotel is run in a personal and friendly manner. Mr. Richards emphasizes: "Every bedroom, bathroom, and corridor is centrally heated 24 hours a day from the first chill wind of autumn until the last breath of retreating winter, even in summer if necessary." He's installed a water-softening plant as well.

The bedrooms are spacious (some with balconies) and are equipped with either private baths/showers or hot and cold water basins. All have TV, video, radio, phone, hairdryer, and trousers press. There are 16 special rooms with four-poster beds. Some are air-conditioned, and some have Jacuzzis. The rates, including a full English breakfast, are £28.50 ($50) for a bathless single, £40 ($70) for a bathless double. With bath, the price range is wide, as the accommodations are widely varied, going from basement units to superior rooms. Singles pay £32 ($56) to £75 ($131.25) and doubles from £46 ($80.50) to £100 ($175). VAT is included.

The hotel has a new restaurant and a cocktail piano bar called Cascades, which has become so popular that you need to have a reservation even to get a martini.

Mornington Lancaster Hotel, 12 Lancaster Gate, W.2 (tel. 01/262-7361), brings a touch of Swedish hospitality to the center of London. Just north of Hyde Park and Kensington Gardens, the hotel has been completely redecorated with a Scandinavian-designed interior. The bedrooms, 70 in all, are not only tastefully conceived and most comfortable, but each unit is complete with private bath and shower, a color TV, plus a phone and radio. Rates are £45 ($78.75) to £56 ($98) in a single, rising to anywhere from £56 ($98) to £74 ($129.50) in a double or twin. If you're traveling with a child, the Swedish-speaking staff will place an extra bed in your room for an additional charge. Tariffs include a Scandinavian buffet breakfast, service, and VAT. Naturally, there's a genuine Finnish sauna, but you'll also find a well-stocked bar where you can order snacks and, if you're back in time, afternoon tea. In the library, visitors wind down, entertaining their friends or making new ones. Considering what you get, especially the comfort and service, the price is most competitive for London. Tube: Lancaster Gate.

SOUTH KENSINGTON:
South of Kensington Gardens and Hyde Park, South Kensington is essentially a residential area, not as elegant as bordering Belgravia and Knightsbridge. However, the section is rich in museums, and it has a number of colleges.

The **Alexander Hotel,** 9 Sumner Pl., S.W.7 (tel. 01/581-1591), is among the most expensive on the street, but it is also the best. Built as a sumptuous private home in 1842, it is still elegant today thanks to the extensive refurbishment program completed in 1987. It's filled with an array of artwork, both modern and antique. Part of the Alexander seems more like a gallery than a hotel. English hunting scenes alternate with original theater posters of Mistinguette to create an ambience that made S.J. Perelman, the American humorist, return again and again. The 39 rooms contain private baths/showers, color TVs, videos, direct-dial phones, and artworks. Singles cost £60 ($105), and doubles go for £75 ($131.25) to £95 ($201.25). A cottage with a garden entrance, suitable for four to five guests, costs £165 ($288.75). Prices include breakfast and VAT. Tube: South Kensington.

Number Sixteen, 16 Sumner Pl., S.W.7 (tel. 01/589-5232), is an elegant luxury "pension," made up of four early Victorian town houses linked together into a dramatically organized whole, with an elevator. As each house was added, the front and rear gardens expanded, until their flowering shrubs and tulips create one of the most idyllic spots on the street.

The 39 rooms contain an eclectic mixture of English antiques and modern paintings. There's an honor-system self-service bar in one of the elegantly formal sitting rooms, where a blazing fire is lit to take off the cold weather chill. Many of the clients of this place are tied into the arts in some way.

Singles range from £40 ($70) to £60 ($105), with doubles going for £95 ($166.25) to £110 ($192.50). VAT and a continental breakfast served in the rooms are included in the price of a night's stay. Tube: South Kensington.

One Cranley Place, One Cranley Place, S.W.7 (tel. 01/589-7704), is one of the little nuggets of London, a "secret address." Set behind a Regency-style Victorian row house, this well-accessorized hotel offers only ten bedrooms, but each is carefully and tastefully furnished, evoking the aura of an elegant country home. Lying on a little mews, the hotel is owned—but not managed—by a couple from Michigan. They have filled it with summertime colors. A front parlor, for example, is embellished with Turkish kilim weavings, Chinese vases, and a scattering of antiques. A fireplace is lit in the reception, and a stairway takes you to the gallery-windowed alcoves, carpeted hallways, and the bedrooms, which are individually and very successfully decorated. Doubles range from £85 ($148.75) to £130 ($227.50), plus VAT. Breakfast and daytime snacks are served in a blue-and-white country-style kitchen, skylit from above, with views of a well-maintained garden. The location is three blocks from the South Kensington tube station.

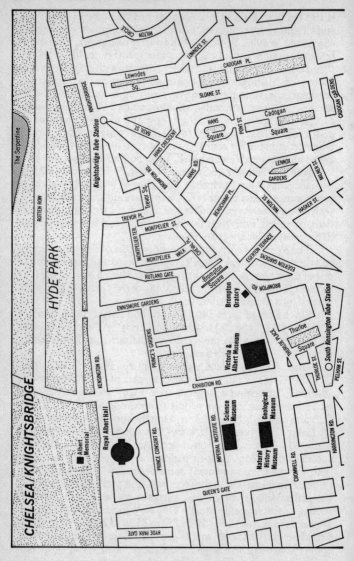

CHELSEA/KNIGHTSBRIDGE

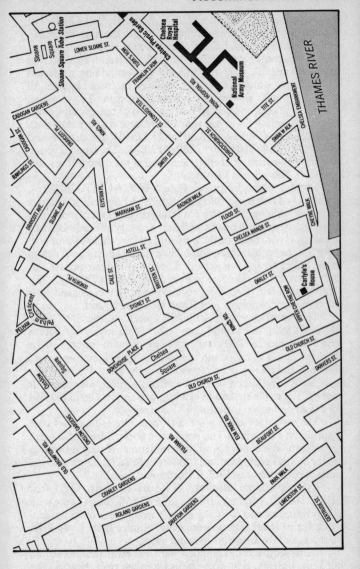

Aster House, 3 Sumner Pl., S.W.7 (tel. 01/581-5888). The smallest hotel on this unusual street of hotels, the Aster has an early Victorian façade. Rachel and Peter Caraplet are the owners, and their guests come from around the world. Peter, an architect, has built L'Orangerie, over the adjacent garage, adding a Machin Conservatory which doubles as a breakfast room and lounge. All 12 of the hotel's rooms have private bath, color TV, mini-bar, direct-dial phone, and central heating. Two of the attractive units are on the ground floor, one with a fireplace and a curtained four-poster. Singles cost £42 ($73.50) to £52 ($91), and doubles and twins go for £58 ($101.50) to £69 ($120.75). The family's young daughter, Christina, is likely to greet you at the door with a wide-eyed grin. Tube: South Kensington.

Number Eight, Emperor's Gate, S.W.7 (tel. 01/370-7516), is a hotel in a cul-de-sac, offering warmth and elegance in a stately Victorian building. Bedrooms in this small hotel are of individual scope and décor, each one named after a county of England. Most of the units have baths or showers, and all have direct-dial phone, color TV, radio, hairdryer, and other modern amenities. A sumptuous buffet breakfast is served. There is a 24-hour private bar, with room service. The rate in a single for B&B is £45 ($78.75). Doubles cost £55 ($96.25). Personal service of a high standard is the keynote of Number Eight. Tube: Gloucester Road.

The **Regency Hotel,** 100–105 Queen's Gate, S.W.7 (tel. 01/370-4595), is a skillful conversion of six lovely old houses which now provide 200 comfortable rooms with private bath or shower, color TV, radio, and direct-dial phone. Elevators service all floors, and there is porter service 24 hours a day. The hotel was completely refurbished in 1986 and offers good value for your money. The tariffs are £66 ($115.50) for a single, £86 ($151.50) for a twin or double, including VAT and service.

The restaurant offers a full à la carte menu, and snacks are available on the terrace. The hotel has a cocktail bar and a small health club. The South Kensington museums are near at hand, as are the South Kensington and Gloucester Road Underground stations to either the West End or Heathrow Airport.

Aston's Budget Studios, 39 Rosary Gardens, S.W.7 (tel. 01/370-0737), combines the elegance of a Victorian home with the convenience and economy of self-catering, in a quiet residential street of South Kensington, only minutes from Hyde Park, Harrods, and the Underground and buses.

Each studio is fully equipped, with bathroom facilities shared but kept clean and tidy. Some units have their own showers. The studios range in size from singles to large family units. Prices, quoted on a per-week basis, are £130 ($227.50) for one person, £95 ($166.25) per person for two, £85 ($148.75) per person for three, and £80 ($140) per person for four. Shelagh King, the hostess, also rents spacious one-bedroom apartments for £500 ($875) per week. Tube: Gloucester Road.

AT WESTMINSTER: In proper Westminster, the seat of the British government since the time of Edward the Confessor, you can have your own well-equipped flat at the following location:

Dolphin Square, Dolphin Square, S.W.1 (tel. 01/834-9134), is one of the largest apartment blocks in Europe. Many residents make it their permanent home, but it's open to transients as well. On the Thames, between Chelsea and Westminster, it lies near the Tate Gallery. Each of the apartments is fully furnished, containing the necessary supply of china, kitchen equipment, and cutlery. Apartments, all with color TV, come in a wide range of sizes. A one-room apartment with a double-bed-sitting room, bathroom, and kitchen goes for £59 ($103.25) per night for two people. For a twin-bedded-room flat with a lounge, bedroom, bathroom, and kitchen, the charge is £82 ($143.50) per night for a couple. Larger apartments at more expensive tariffs are also available. The longer you stay, the better the rate you'll be quoted.

Besides the apartments, guest rooms are also rented at £25 ($43.75) in a single, £38 ($66.50) in a double, plus VAT. Early-morning tea and biscuits are served to persons staying in these facilities. The Dolphin Square Restaurant overlooks the heated swimming pool, which is kept at a constant temperature of 75° Fahrenheit. In addition, there are eight squash courts and a sauna, and there are gardens outside the building. It's best reached by taxi. Tube: Pimlico Station.

If it is a regular, traditional hotel you are seeking, then consider the following.

Stakis St. Ermins Hotel, Caxton Street, S.W.1 (tel. 01/222-7888), a turn-of-the-century red-brick hotel, is ideally located in the heart of Westminster and only a few minutes' walk from Buckingham Palace, the Houses of Parliament, and Westminster Abbey. Its 296 bedrooms all have private bathroom, radio, TV, and individually controlled central heating, with 24-hour room service. In addition, there are 15 banqueting rooms.

The hotel has two restaurants: the Caxton Grill offers an excellent value à la carte menu, while the Carving Table has a set price for lunch and dinner, serving a selection of roast meats and specialties. The lounge bar offers an alternative, serving light snacks 24 hours a day. The rates at the hotel are £81 ($141.75) in a single, rising to £103 ($180.25) in a twin-bedded room. These rates include VAT. Tube: St. James's Park.

IN BAYSWATER: North of Kensington Gardens is an unofficial section of London known as Bayswater. Most of it lies north of Bayswater Road and west of Hyde Park. This section contains a number of B&B hotels.

The **Pembridge Court Hotel,** 34 Pembridge Gardens, W.2 (tel. 01/229-9977), presents a neoclassically elegant cream-colored façade to a residential neighborhood which is making gains toward a rapid gentrification. Its brick-lined restaurant, where full meals with wine cost from £15 ($26.25), are popular and well-recommended attractions, often filled with the owners of neighboring town houses taking a respite from the broken plaster and dusty pipes of their renovations.

Most of the comfortably outfitted bedrooms contain at least one antique, as well as 19th-century engravings and plenty of warmly patterned fabrics. A full English breakfast is included in the price of £45 ($78.75) to £70 ($122.50) in a single, £60 ($105) to £85 ($148.75) in a double. VAT is extra. Each of the 26 bedrooms has its own bath, color TV, direct-dial phone, and hairdryer. The building, which was constructed in 1852 as a private house, is ably administered by Paul Capra. Tube: Notting Hill Gate.

HAMPSTEAD: The old village of Hampstead, sitting high on a hill, is the most desirable residential suburb of London. The village borders a wild heathland, which contains sprawling acres of weeded dells and fields of heather. Yet the Northern Line of the Underground reaches the edges of the heath, making it possible for Londoners to enjoy isolated countryside while living only 20 minutes from city center. These advantages have caused many young artists to discover what Keats could have told them years ago: Hampstead is the place to live. The little Georgian houses have never received so much attention and love as they get now.

Sandringham Hotel, 3 Holford Rd., N.W.3 (tel. 01/435-1569). You'd never guess this is a hotel, because it stands on a residential street in one of the best parts of London. After getting off at the Hampstead tube station, you walk up the hill past interesting shops, pubs, and charmingly converted houses. Shortly, at the Turpin Restaurant, you turn right into Hampstead Square, which leads into Holford Road. A high wall and trees screen the house from the street (if you have a car, you can park in the driveway).

The hotel is a well-built, centrally heated house, and the comfortable rooms often house professional people who want to be near the center of London, yet retain the feel of rural life. The B&B charge is £21.50 ($37.75) in a single, increasing to £36 ($63) in a double if bathless, £41 ($71.75) with private bath, all prices inclusive of VAT.

The pretty breakfast room has been enlarged by the addition of a Victorian conservatory and overlooks a walled garden. From the upper rooms, you have a panoramic view over the heath of the center of London. You'll find a home-like lounge furnished with color TV. Mrs. Maria Dreyer is the owner and manager.

THE Y'S

"Y" Hotel, 112 Great Russell St., W.C.1 (tel. 01/636-8616), may shatter your expectations of a YMCA. This Bloomsbury version is a modern hotel built by the London Central YMCA for men and women of all ages. At the Oxford Street end of Tottenham Court Road, its prices reflect its standard of comfort: £36 ($63) in a single room, and £54 ($94.50) in a double- or twin-bedded room, including VAT and service. Every bedroom has an outside window, central heating, color TV, radio, and private shower, and is comfortably furnished complete with wall-to-wall carpeting. On the premises are squash courts, a gymnasium, a swimming pool, shops, and underground car parking. In fact, the recreational facilities cover three entire floors and include a billiards room, a sauna, and a solarium. But there are no telephones in the bedrooms. Tube: Tottenham Court Road.

The **YWCA Central Club,** Great Russell Street, W.C.1 (tel. 01/636-7512), is a large and attractive Lutyens building. All rooms contain hot and cold running water, and accommodations are offered to women and girls and married persons. Special reduced rates are offered to long-term students. Singles rent for £20 ($35) nightly, doubles for £15 ($26.25) per person, triples for £13 ($22.75) per person, and five-bedded rooms for £11 ($19.25) per person. VAT is included. Reservations should be by mail, enclosing an international money order in the amount of the first night's deposit. Included in the rate is use of the bathrooms, showers, and central heating. The coffeeshop is open from 8 a.m. to 7 p.m. for all meals. The facilities are spacious and dignified, with lounges and writing room, hairdresser, launderette, TV room, and swimming pool. Tube: Tottenham Court Road.

AIRPORT HOTELS

As one of the major gateways to Europe (not to mention England), London's two major airports are among the busiest in the world. Many readers have expressed a desire to be near their point of departure, spending the night in ease before "taking off." With that in mind, I'd suggest the following accommodations, beginning—

AT GATWICK:

The airport's most convenient resting place is the **Gatwick Hilton International Hotel,** Gatwick Airport, Crawley in Surrey (tel. 0293/518080), a deluxe, five-floor hotel of the Hilton chain. A covered footbridge links the hotel to the air terminal only a five-minute walk away. You can also obtain porterage to the airport, and there are trolleys and electric cars if you can't cope with a walk.

The most dramatic part of the hotel is the first-floor lobby, where a glass-covered portico rises through four floors, containing a full-scale replica of the de Havilland Gypsy Moth airplane *Jason,* used by Amy Johnson on her solo flight from England to Australia in 1930. The reception is close by, an area of much greenery, trees, flowering shrubs, and trailing ivy and fig.

There is a well-equipped health club with a sauna, massage room, and swimming pool, along with other temptations available to guests. On the ground floor is a restaurant serving both English and continental dishes. Opening for breakfast at 7 a.m., it serves dinner until 11 p.m. The Jockey Club bar, with its masculine, Edwardian décor, is mainly for drinking, although sandwiches are available. There's also a cozy lounge bar, where light refreshments are available 24 hours a day.

Rooms have the amenities expected of a Hilton: full air conditioning, double-glazed windows, phone, radio, and color TV with a full-length feature film shown daily in addition to normal stations (plus a mini-bar). Laundry and dry cleaning are returned within the day if collected by 9 a.m. The 552 bedrooms, each with private bath or shower, cost from £90 ($157.50) in a single and from £100 ($175) in a double. Family rooms suitable for up to six people rent for £125 ($218.75), executive twins for £125 ($218.75), and junior suites for £155 ($271.25).

The hotel staff provides many services for the business traveler who needs to contact his or her associates in a hurry. Up-to-date flight information is also flashed on the TV screen.

AT HEATHROW:

A favorite stop for travelers is the **Sheraton Skyline,** Bath Road, Hayes, Middlesex (tel. 01/759-2535). Its contemporary plushness and its array of entertainment and dining facilities attract the experienced traveler, who checks in here either to recover from a long-distance flight or else to avoid London's morning traffic before an early flight the next day. This establishment—more of a miniature city than a hotel—has been voted the world's best airport hotel.

Set behind trees, the hotel operates on an international schedule, as business travelers from all over the world check in around the clock. In a luxurious soundproof cocoon, with scores of jets winging overhead, guests enjoy the well-appointed atmosphere.

The hotel was designed around a Tahitian-style atrium where tropical plants and towering palms thrive beneath a translucent roof. The foundations of a cabaña bar are set into the climate-controlled waters of a curvaceous swimming pool. A Caribbean steel band plays nightly. Each of the hotel's 354 well-furnished rooms contains insomnia aids such as color TV with in-house video movies, a massage-style shower, air conditioning, a radio, and room service. Singles cost from £78 ($136.50), and doubles from £88 ($154), plus VAT.

In the Edwardian Colony Bar, a fireplace flickers late into the night, and in its adjacent well-upholstered restaurant, the Colony Room, a large staff of uniformed waiters serves well-prepared food beneath massive ceiling timbers and heavy brass chandeliers. A French café offers light meals and full buffet breakfasts, and in Diamond Lil's, a Montana-style cabaret, showgirls entertain and the fare includes char-broiled steaks and generous drinks. The staff works hard to verify and confirm departures from Heathrow.

COUNTRY HOMES AND CASTLES

Country Homes and Castles, 118 Cromwell Rd., S.W.7 (tel. 01/370-4445), is a program offering overseas visitors the chance to stay in private homes as guests of the owners. There are houses in all parts of Britain, ranging from small cottages, historic manor houses, and ancient Scottish castles to large mansions in their own parkland. The owners vary in their interests, ages, and professions, and every effort is made to send visitors to families it is thought they will particularly enjoy. As it is such a personal service, there are no set tours, but the agency will arrange just one or two nights in a house to fit in with your own travel plans or a complete tour using hotels and country homes and bearing in mind your interests. Prices range from about £150 ($262.50) to £350 ($612.50) per couple per night, including drinks, dinner with wine, accommodations with private baths, and breakfast. All payments are made through the agent to avoid the embarrassment of hosts and guests having to discuss money. The U.S. representative is Sue Duncan, 4092 North Ivy Rd., Atlanta, GA 30342 (tel. 404/231-5837).

CHAPTER V

EATING AND DRINKING

□ □ □

George Mikes, Britain's famous Hungarian-born humorist, once wrote about the culinary prowess of his adopted country: "The Continentals have good food. The English have good table manners."

Quite a lot has happened since.

Basically, of course, some of the English are still woeful cooks, and their table etiquette is as impressive as ever. But with the pressure of tourism and the influx of foreign chefs, the local cuisine picture has brightened considerably. There also exists now a current wave of English-born, bred, and trained chefs who have set a superb standard of cookery, using high-quality ingredients. One food writer called this new breed the "very professional amateur."

In the snackeries of suburbia the vegetables may still taste as if they had a grudge against you, and the soup remains reminiscent of flavored tapwater. But in the central sections of London—where you'll do your eating—the fare has improved immeasurably. This is largely because of intense competition from foreign establishments, plus the introduction of espresso machines, which made English coffee resemble . . . well, coffee.

In the upper brackets, London has always boasted magnificent restaurants, several of which have achieved world renown. But these were the preserve of the middling wealthy, who'd had their palates polished by travel abroad. The lower orders enjoyed a diet akin to parboiled blotting paper. For about a century the staple meal of the working class consisted of "fish 'n' chips," and they still haven't learned how to properly fry either the fish *or* the chips (potatoes).

There are some dishes—mostly connected with breakfast—

at which the English have always excelled. The traditional morning repast of eggs and bacon (imported from Denmark) or kippers (smoked herring, of Scottish origin) is a tasty starter, and the locally brewed tea beats any American bag concoction.

It's with the other meals that you have to use a little caution. If you want to splurge in a big way, you have the London "greats" at your disposal: gourmet havens such as Tante Claire, Le Gavroche, and À l'Ecu de France in Jermyn Street, or half a dozen others.

If these star eateries are too expensive for you, you'll find more moderately priced restaurants such as the Baker & Oven. And then I'll turn to the budget establishments that charge even less for a three-courser.

The prevailing mealtimes are much the same as in the U.S. You can get lunch from about midday onward and dinner until about 11 p.m., until midnight in the Soho area. The difference is that fewer Londoners go in for the "businessperson's lunch." They'll either make do with sandwiches or take a snack in a pub (see the last part of this chapter). The once-hallowed custom of taking afternoon tea for many years became the preserve of matrons unworried about their waistlines. However, in the past few years it is having a renaissance. Viewed as a civilized pause in the day's activities, it's particularly appealing to those who didn't have time for lunch or who plan an early theater engagement. Some hotels, such as the Ritz, feature orchestras and tea-dancing in afternoon ceremonies, usually from 3:30 to 6:30 p.m.

What may astonish you is the profusion of international restaurants. London offers a fantastic array of Italian, Indian, Chinese, French, German, Swiss, Greek, Russian, Jewish, and Middle Eastern dineries, which probably outnumber the native establishments. You'll find them heavily represented in my list.

Most of the restaurants I mention serve the same meals for lunch and dinner, so they're easily interchangeable. Most—but not all—add a 10% to 15% service charge to your bill. You'll have to look at your check to make sure of that. If nothing has been added, leave a 12% to 15% tip.

All restaurants and cafés in Britain are required to display the prices of the food and drink they offer, in a place where the customer can see them before entering the eating area. If an establishment has an extensive à la carte menu, the prices of a representative selection of food and drink currently available must be displayed as well as the table d'hôte menu, if one is offered. Charges for service and any minimum charge or cover charge must also be made clear. The prices shown must be inclusive of VAT.

Finally, there's the matter of location. Once upon a time London had two traditional dining areas: Soho for Italian and Chinese fare, Mayfair and Belgravia for French cuisine.

Today the gastronomical legions have conquered the entire heart of the metropolis, and you're liable to find any type of eatery anywhere, from Chelsea to Hampstead. The majority of my selections are in the West End region, but only because this happens to be the handiest for visitors.

That's enough of the preliminaries. Let's go and dine.

THE TOP RESTAURANTS

The very top restaurants in London rank among those at the top anywhere. Usually they are French, or at least French-inspired. However, many chefs also do remarkable and inventive English dishes by making use of the very fresh produce available in the country. Wine tends to be very expensive in the leading restaurants of London, but, in general, food costs less than it does at comparable restaurants in Paris.

Le Gavroche, 43 Upper Brook St., W.1 (tel. 408-0881), has long stood for quality French cuisine, perhaps the finest in Great Britain. It's the creation of two Burgundy-born brothers, Michel and Albert Roux. Service is faultless; the ambience chic and formal, but not stuffy. The menu changes constantly, depending on the availability of the freshest produce of the season, but, more important, upon the inspiration of the Roux brothers, who began modestly in London at another location and have gone on to fame in the culinary world.

Their wine cellar is among the most interesting in London, with many quality burgundies and bordeaux. Try, if featured, their stuffed smoked salmon and their mousseline of lobster. Most main courses are served on a silver tray covered with a silver dome. The lid is lifted off with great flourish, and the platters, like a stage play, are artistically arranged. You can enjoy an apéritif upstairs while perusing the menu and enjoying the delectable canapés.

A set luncheon is offered at a relatively modest price of £19.50 ($34.25), with a table d'hôte dinner costing £45 ($78.75). To order à la carte in the evening will cost from £50 ($87.50) per person. Lunch is presented from noon to 2 p.m. and dinner from 7 to 11 p.m. Closed on weekends. Tube: Bond Street.

La Tante Claire, 68 Royal Hospital Rd., S.W.3 (tel. 352-6045). The quality of its cuisine is so legendary that this "Aunt Claire" has become one of the grande dames of the capital's gaggle of French restaurants. It's considered a culinary monument of the highest order. The waiting list for an available table continues to make a meal here one of the more sought-after status symbols of London. A discreet doorbell, set into the Aegean-blue-and-white façade, prompts an employee to usher you politely inside. There, birchwood and chrome trim, bouquets of flowers, and a modernized, vaguely Hellenistic décor complements an array of paintings which might have been inspired by Jean Cocteau.

Pierre Koffman is the celebrated chef, creating such specialties as frogs' legs stuffed into ravioli. Every gastronome in London talks about the pigs' trotters stuffed with morels and the exquisite sauces that complement many of the dishes. These include a ragoût of scallops with oysters and truffles, mignonettes of monkfish flavored with saffron, filet of bar with olives and salsify, a ballotine of foie gras with a vinaigrette of leeks, and smothered roast duckling with condiments. For dessert, you might order a medley of divine sorbets or Armagnac ice cream with prunes.

A set luncheon is an amazingly good value at £18.50 ($32.50); however, in the evening, expect to pay around £50 ($87.50) per person. The establishment is open from 12:30 to 2 p.m. and 7 to 11 p.m.; closed Saturday, Sunday, and for three weeks in August. You have a better chance of getting a table if you dine very late. Tube: Sloane Square.

The **Chelsea Room,** Hyatt Carlton Tower, 2 Cadogan Pl., S.W.1 (tel. 235-5411), is a superb restaurant, one of the best in London, lying inside the walls of one of Hyatt's finest international properties (recommended in the previous chapter). The dining room's combination of haute cuisine, stylish clientele, and elegant décor make it a much-sought-after place for lunch or dinner. The location is one floor above the lobby level of the hotel at the end of a paneled hallway reminiscent of something in a private Edwardian house. Your first impression might be of floods of sunlight entering via the curving glass canopy that Hyatt, at huge expense and labor, added to its façade in 1987. The view encompasses the perimeter of fashionable town houses ringing the gardens of Cadogan Place. The color scheme is tasteful and subdued in grays, beiges, and soft greens.

The dining room is run by a winning team: maître cuisinier de France Bernard Gaume, and long-standing maître d'hôtel Jean Quero. Monsieur Gaume has pleased palates at some of the leading and most famous hotels in Europe, including L'Abbaye in Tallories, the Savoy in London, and Hôtel des Bergues in Geneva. His portions are large and satisfying, and presentation shows his extraordinary flair. Highly professional dishes, original offerings, time-tested classics, and very fresh ingredients are his forte. The menu will change by the time of your visit, but to give you an idea, you are likely to be served: baked sea bass in a light sauce with leeks and a garnish of salmon and Russian caviar, roast partridge served on a bed of Savoy cabbage, or small filets of venison in a game sauce with port and a medley of multicolored peppercorns with juniper berries. His desserts require a separate menu, ranging from a light chestnut mousse with ginger sauce to a chilled hazelnut parfait in a light Cointreau sauce. Wedgwood plates with the restaurant's cockerel motif adorn each place setting. The average lunch costs from £22 ($38.50); dinners begin at £40 ($70). The room is open daily from 12:30 to 2:45 p.m. and 7 to 11:15 p.m. except on Sunday when it closes at 10:45 p.m. Tube: Sloane Square.

The Terrace Restaurant, The Dorchester, Park Lane, W.1 (tel. 629-8888). Only the extravagance and privileges of the 1930s could produce a décor this eclectic and opulent. The richness and the color, combined with some of the most refined and sophisticated cuisine in Great Britain, create this superlative restaurant. Best described as "Between the Wars" in décor, using both Middle Eastern and Far Eastern motifs, it originally hosted some of the greatest names of the Big Band era who played to enthralled crowds of jazz enthusiasts. Today, with its lotus-capped columns, rich lacquers, and geometrical screens still intact, it is a stylishly alluring place to dine. Perhaps because of its Europeanized version of a Japanese décor, many representatives of Tokyo's banks hold their business reunions in the dining room, which is open only for dinner every night except Sunday from 6 to 11:30 p.m.

Cooking since he was six years old, the maître chef is Anton Mosimann. From the Swiss village of Solothurn, he went on to work at some of the leading hotels in the world, including the Gstaad Palace and the Hilton Cavalieri in Rome. He supervises not only the Terrace but the Superb Grill Room as well.

A devotee of cuisine naturelle, he was heavily influenced by Japanese cookery. He selects ingredients for their seasonal freshness, and cooks to preserve their texture, color, nutrition, and flavor. Using no rich cream-and-butter sauces, he imaginatively makes use of low-calorie ingredients such as yogurt, fromage blanc, and quark. Try, for example, his steamed sea bass Oriental, warm oysters in champagne sauce, poached filet of beef with mustard sauce, ragoût of lobster, or a warm foie gras with winter greens and green beans. He also prepares a delectable symphony of fruits de mer naturelle. To finish, why not a symphony of sorbets? A regular set dinner costs £35 ($61.25), but my advice is to select his "menu surprise," six little courses of fresh produce at £80 ($140) for two diners.

Simply Nico, 48a Rochester Row, S.W.1 (tel. 630-8061), is the domain of its owner, Nico Ladenis, who is firmly entrenched as one of the great chefs of Great Britain. Mr. Ladenis, the most talked-about chef in London, is also the only one who is a former oil company executive, a trained economist, and a self-taught cook. Raised by Greek and French parents in East Africa, he was educated in England. He welcomes North Americans with an enthusiastic appreciation which at this writing seems increasingly rare. In his culinary finesse, he is assisted by his charming and hard-working wife, Dinah-Jane, whose efficiency permeates every aspect of the carefully timed activity.

Menu items are written in clear, straightforward English which admirably negotiates the intricacies of French equivalents. Meals are profoundly satisfying and often memorable in the very best gastronomic tradition of "post nouvelle cuisine," where the tenets and benefits of classical cuisine are creatively and flexibly adapted to the local super-fresh ingredients.

The menu changes frequently, according to the imagination of Mr. Ladenis. Some of the more experienced patrons (he is said not to suffer fools lightly) leave the menu choice entirely up to him. You might face specialties such as a warm mousse of sole and crab served with a prawn sauce, a pillow of smoked salmon stuffed with prawn mousse, preserved duck leg served with a sauce of caramelized shallots, slices of veal kidneys flavored with mustard and served in a pastry case on a bed of light garlic sauce, or sea bass with a crust of herbs on a bed of spinach with a white wine and vinegar butter. He also prepares an authentic Mediterranean fish soup of red mullet with a saffron-flavored garlic mayonnaise. Desserts are sumptuous.

Reservations are absolutely vital because he could easily fill this restaurant three times or more every night. Lunch is 12:30 to 2 p.m., and at £16.50 ($29) has been called "surely London's greatest lunchtime bargain, considering that this is a two-star restaurant. At dinner there is a two-course meal for £24 ($42), plus a late-night supper at £21 ($36.75). However, the average tab for a not-average meal will be around £40 ($70) per person, and evening hours are 7:30 to 11 p.m., Monday to Friday only. Tube: Victoria.

Ninety Park Lane, Grosvenor House, 90 Park Lane, W.1 (tel. 499-1290), is one of the finest restaurants of London, thanks to the importance attached to it as the premier dining room of the flagship hotel of Trusthouse Forte. You enjoy an apéritif in the paneled and gilded majesty of the restaurant's bar, perhaps perusing the menu as you sip. The dining room is filled with masses of fresh flowers, a scattering of 18th-century oil portraits, and some top-quality English antiques personally owned by members of the Forte family. The ambience is a lot like an English country house, but with a world-class cuisine. Since its much-heralded opening, some of the most famous names in Britain, including members of the royal family and Margaret Thatcher, have dined here. The cuisine has as its consultant Louis Outhier, whose restaurant, L'Oasis in La Napoule, is one of the most awarded in France.

You'll be presented with a long and sophisticated menu, as well as three fixed-price meals, costing £36 ($63) to £46 ($80.50) per person. At lunchtime an elegant three-courser is usually available at £26 ($45.50), but in the evening, if you dine à la carte, count on £50 ($87.50) per person. The cuisine is nouvelle French, but without a lot of unnecessary frills and pretensions that crop up on the menus of less gifted chefs. You might, for example, enjoy seared escalope of foie gras with turnips and apples, Bélon oysters wrapped in salmon with a light mousseline, lamb filet scented with sweet wines and paprika, saddle of venison in a sauce made from blueberries and marc de bourgogne, and a house specialty, Brie stuffed with truffles. For dessert, you can make selections from the most-talked-about trolley in London, which the staff refers to as a "Caravane." Reservations are necessary. Lunch is noon to 2:30 p.m. weekdays, and dinner is offered nightly except Sunday from 7:30 to 10:45 p.m.

Bracewell's, Park Lane Hotel, Piccadilly, W.1 (tel. 499-3621). Sheltered by the thick fortress-like walls of this previously recommended hotel, this is one of chic London's better-kept secrets. The cuisine prepared by English-born chef David Ryan is among the best in the capital, and the décor and the five-star service are worthy of its distinguished clientele. You might begin with a drink among the gilded torchères and comfortable armchairs of Bracewell's Bar. Later you will be ushered into an intimately illuminated room whose deeply grained paneling was long ago removed from a château in France by industrial magnate Pierpont Morgan. In the 1920s it was reinstalled at the Park Lane.

Your meal will be supervised by Oscar Bassam, a maître flambeurs de monde. He once served as maître d'hôtel on the liner *Queen Mary,* and has traveled the world, performing a culinary kind of theater. Ask for his intricate version of crêpes Suzettes, for example, which he makes fresh on a blazing trolley wheeled to your table.

Full meals from Mr. Ryan's repertoire are served daily except Saturday at lunch and all day Sunday from 12:30 to 2:30 p.m. and 7 to 10:30 p.m. A fixed-price menu costs £26 ($45.50) for five courses, £24 ($42) for four courses. À la carte meals are around £30 ($52.50) per person. The specialties are based on the freshest ingredients in any seasons. Examples of Mr. Ryan's talents are reflected by such dishes as slices of lobster encased in puff pastry with herb butter, terrine of wild duck with a reduced sauce of button onions, suprême of turbot topped with pike mousse and a carrot sauce, sliced breast of wild duck (cooked pink) and garnished with orange and basil sauce, and roasted boneless quail filled with foie gras and served on a bed of celeriac with red wine sauce. Reservations are needed. Tube: Hyde Park Corner.

À l'Ecu de France, 111 Jermyn St., S.W.1 (tel. 930-2837), opened as a restaurant in May 1937, specializing then in regional French cooking. During World War II it was frequented by members of refugee governments, having as customers many famous ministers and great war leaders. The restaurant served to secret parties at the War Office, where discretion was an ironclad rule. Today it offers the quintessence of French cuisine, as well as traditional English food. It's not cheap, but you wouldn't expect it to be.

The atmosphere is traditional, without ostentation. Pillars with mirrors reflect the dark walls and discreet lighting. There's a relaxing atmosphere with a touch of elegance. Occupying a prime site in the midst of theaterland, the place is a natural choice for pre-theater dinners or after-show suppers.

A fixed-price pre-theater dinner costs £15.75 ($27.50), including tax and service. It is served from 6 to 7:30 p.m., with the bar opening at 5:30 p.m. A set luncheon, for £16.75 ($29.25), is reasonably priced considering the choice and quality. A set dinner is priced at £26.75 ($46.75). A full à la carte menu is available at all times. A popular choice for an appetizer is the mousse de saumon (salmon) or feuilleté d'escargot Warsawsky (puff pastry case with snails, vegetables, and herbs in a light Pernod sauce). Good main-course dishes are petit tournedo de boeuf "Belle Patricia" (a small filet of beef with strips of various peppers with a madeira sauce) or paupiette de veau sautée "Mere Helga" (roulade of veal filled with a veal and herb stuffing served in a mushroom sauce). A complete meal will cost from £34 ($59.50).

There is a good selection of desserts, including soufflé aux liqueurs and gâteau fromage. Sunday dinner hours are 7 to 10:30 p.m. Weekday hours are 12:30 to 3 p.m. and 6:30 to 11:30 p.m. No lunch is served on Saturday or Sunday. Tube: Piccadilly Circus.

SOME OTHER LEADING RESTAURANTS

Turner's, 87 Walton St., S.W.3 (tel. 584-6711), is named for Brian J. Turner, one of the most accomplished chefs of London, who gained fame at a number of establishments he didn't own, including La Tante Claire and the Capital Hotel. He believes in putting care, effort, and although he didn't say so, love into his food. As one critic aptly put it, his food comes not only fresh from the market that day but "from the heart." He had early roots in Yorkshire, but surely he didn't learn his refined cuisine working in his father's transport "caff" in Leeds.

In London, he paid his dues, so to speak, working in such hotels as the Savoy and Claridge's before achieving his own place in the culinary sun. That sun is now beaming on him in an attractively decorated, rich minimalist setting on a street of fashion and expensive flats. He seems to view cooking as a "performance," and sometimes he'll make an appearance in the dining room, asking about his food and how it is perceived. He's a sensitive man and a sensitive listener as well.

His cooking has been called "cuisine à la Brian Turner," meaning he doesn't seem to imitate anyone, but sets his own goals and standards. Try, for example, his marinated raw scallops with shredded gherkins, sea bass with fresh tomato-and-basil dressing, or a roast rack of lamb with a herb crust. You might begin with a salad of stuffed poached quail, finishing with a gooseberry mousse. A four-course menu is offered for £22.50 ($39.50), but you will more likely spend from £35 ($61.25). A table d'hôte lunch is a superb bargain at £14.50 ($25.50). Hours are Monday to Friday and Sunday for lunch from 12:30 to 2:45 p.m., and nightly for dinner from 7:30 to 11 p.m. Tube: Knightsbridge.

Wiltons, 55 Jermyn St., S.W.1 (tel. 629-9955), is one of the leading exponents of cookery called "as British as a nanny." In spite of its move into new quarters, its developers re-created the lush ambience of the original premises. You might be tempted to have an apéritif or drink in the bar near the entrance, where photos of the royal family are alternated with oil portraits of the original owners. One of them, the legendary Jimmy Marks, or so it is said, used to "strike terror into the hearts of newcomers if he took a dislike to them." However, those days, still fondly recalled by some, are gone forever, and today a wide array of international guests are warmly welcomed by what I consistently find to be the most sensitive serving staff in the West End.

The thoroughly British menu of this restaurant, which opened in 1941, shortly before the Yanks were to arrive en masse in World War II, is known for its fish and game. You might begin with an oyster cocktail and follow with Dover sole, plaice, salmon, or lobster, prepared in any number of ways. In season, you can enjoy such delights as roast partridge, roast pheasant, or roast grouse. The chef might ask you if you want them "blue" or "black," a reference to roasting times. In season, you might even be able to order roast widgeon, a wild, fish-eating river duck. Game is often accompanied by bread sauce. To finish, and if you're to be truly British, you may order a savory such as Welsh rarebit or soft roes, even anchovies. But if that's all too, too much, try the sherry trifle or syllabub. Dinners cost from £35 ($61.25), and reservations are vital. Lunch hours are 12:30 to 1:30 p.m. Monday to Friday, and dinner hours are 6:30 to 10:30 p.m. Monday to Saturday. Tube: Green Park or Piccadilly Circus.

Boulestin, 1A Henrietta St., W.C.2 (tel. 836-7061). This famous old restaurant was founded more than half a century ago by Marcel Boulestin, the first Fleet Street restaurant critic. It's reached by a side door which goes down into the basement beneath a bank. Kevin Kennedy, who is both the manager and the chef, is one of the new British-bred cuisine experts who has style, flair, and imagination in the kitchen.

The chandeliers are still there, and the menu still has many of the old Boulestin dishes, including crab with artichoke, coquilles St-Jacques, and magret de canard. You might also try the tulipe de sorbets maison. But Mr. Kennedy is also free to experiment, and he does so every week, much to the pleasure of his guests.

He offers a set lunch for £18 ($31.50), but dinner could run higher than £30 ($52.50) per person, including some wine. The restaurant is open from 12:30 to 2:30 p.m. and 7 to 11:15 p.m. It's closed for lunch on Saturday, all day Sunday, on bank holidays, and during most of the month of August. Tube: Covent Garden.

Inigo Jones, 14 Garrick St., W.C.2 (tel. 836-6456), is one of the lights of Covent Garden, and although it has been around for some 20 years it's better than ever. It occupies a former stained-glass studio, but some of the carvings and stained glass have been removed, making the place more garden-like than ecclesiastical. The banquettes and chairs are now in a brick color, and the waiters are dressed in black trousers, white shirt, black tie, and white apron.

But what has made the restaurant such a renewed success is the cookery of the chef de cuisine, Paul Gayler, formerly of the Dorchester Hotel. I can't recommend any specialties, because he depends for his inspiration on the daily offerings of the marketplace. However, I will cite only some dishes enjoyed in the past to give you an idea: escalope of salmon glazed in a smoked bacon and dill sauce, breast of new season grouse with a red wine and black currant sauce, and roast "best end" of lamb with fresh herbs. To begin, you might order a chilled parfait of smoked quail with avocado, finishing your meal with lemon cheesecake with pineapple. The selection of sorbets is often flavored with bay leaf, thyme, cinnamon, and clove. The average price for an à la carte meal is £40 ($70), served from 7 to 11:30 p.m. A fixed-price luncheon, costing £16.75 ($29.25), is offered at lunchtime and from 5:30 to 7 p.m. A menu potager (vegetarian menu) costs £29.50 ($51.75) per person. All prices include VAT and service. Hours are 12:30 to 2 p.m. Monday to Friday for lunch and 5:30 to 11:30 p.m. Monday to Saturday for dinner; closed Sunday. It's best to telephone for a reservation. Tube: Covent Garden.

Cavaliers, 129 Queenstown Rd., S.W.8 (tel. 720-6960), has a reputation based on its superb food. In increasingly fashionable Battersea, it was founded by the famous chef Nico Landenis, and served as his home base before he moved. The restaurant has been purchased by David and Susan Cavalier, who moved from their much-praised Pebbles Restaurant in Aylesbury.

In an L-shaped dining room ringed with natural pine and pastel shades of café au lait and pink, you can enjoy such specialties as roast lobster encased in puff pastry with tomato and tarragon, and pot-roasted Highland grouse with orange and thyme pasties. A three-course dinner is offered for £23.50 ($41.25), and a special lunchtime menu goes for £14.50 ($25.50). The restaurant is open for lunch from 12:15 to 2 p.m. and for dinner from 7:15 to 10:30 p.m. Tuesday to Saturday. Because of the location, this establishment is best reached by taxi.

Kingfisher, Halcyon Hotel, 81 Holland Park, W.11 (tel. 727-7288), in the previously recommended hotel, is an exciting dining possibility, and worth the ten-minute taxi ride from the heart of the West End. Peter James has not only created a small hotel of charm and taste, but on the lower level he has installed a restaurant which attracts the rich and famous, including royalty, perhaps Princess Michael. To reach the restaurant, you pass a medley of trompe-l'oeil murals with color and whimsy. You might enjoy an apéritif in the pink-tinted bar before heading for a meal in the tastefully uncluttered restaurant. Lattices and views of a garden create an image of springtime even in winter.

The menu is sophisticated and highly individualized, the work of James Robins, formerly of Blakes Hotel, to which this restaurant bears some resemblance, at least in its superb food. One food critic wrote that a menu by Robins "reads like a United Nations of cuisine." The menu is based on the inspiration of the chef and the shopping, as only the freshest ingredients are used. You might begin with a crab, coriander, and ricotta ravioli, before going on to roast breast of guinea fowl with noodles, prunes, and leek or salmon baked in pastry with pesto. On one recent luncheon date, I was served steamed sea bass with ginger and fennel that was perfectly prepared. Desserts are worth saving room for, as reflected by a ginger parfait with mango coulis or a dark-chocolate pudding with coffee-bean sauce. A three-course set luncheon costs £17 ($29.75), dinner begins at £25 ($43.75), and hours are daily from 12:30 to 2:30 p.m. and 7:30 to 10:45 p.m. Reservations are necessary.

Scotts, 20 Mount St., W.1 (tel. 629-5248), is considered the most noted restaurant in the world for oysters, lobster, and caviar. It is the most expensive fish restaurant in London. In addition to its regular spacious restaurant and cocktail bar, it has a special caviar bar and an oyster bar. Its origins were humble, going back to a fishmonger in 1851 in Coventry Street. However, its fame rests on its heyday at Piccadilly Circus when it often entertained Edward VII and his guests in private dining rooms. It has been at its present reincarnation since 1967, enjoying a chic address in the neighborhood of the swank Connaught Hotel and Berkeley Square. Its décor, with its terracotta walls, has been called "Assyrian Monumental," the wall panels hung with horsey prints.

The restaurant's longtime chef, John Bertram, believes in British produce, and he handles the kitchen with consummate skill and authority. You get top-notch quality and ingredients, but at a price—around £40 ($70) per person. Lobster is prepared "three ways," and you might also order smoked Ellingham eel. The eel comes from Suffolk where it is "swum" (that is, kept alive) until it's ready for smoking. Dover sole is prepared "any way." The English prefer it "on the bone," considering filet fish for sissies. A favorite beginning is terrine de canard, and more down-to-earth dishes, such as fish cakes, appear regularly or at least weekly on the luncheon menu. Meals are served from 12:30 to 3 p.m. and 6 to 10:45 p.m. On Sunday only dinner is offered, from 7 to 10 p.m. Tube: Green Park.

Suntory, 72 St. James's St., S.W.1 (tel. 409-0201), is the most elite, expensive, and best Japanese restaurant in London. Owned and operated by the Japanese distillers and brewers, it offers a choice of dining rooms. First-time visitors seem to prefer the Teppan-Yaki dining room downstairs, where iron grills are set in each table and you share the masterful skills of the high-hatted chef, who is amazingly familiar with a knife. You can also dine in other rooms on fare such as sukiyaki and tempura, perhaps selecting sushi, especially the fresh raw tuna fish delicately sliced. You can also enter one of the private dining rooms, but only if shoeless.

Waitresses in regional dress serve you with all the highly refined ritualistic qualities of the Japanese, including the presentation of hot towels. You may prefer a salad of shellfish and seaweed or a superb squid. Appetizers are artful and delicate, and even the tea is superior. Japanese businessmen on an expense account like the hushed tone of the place, the elegant décor that is said to evoke the quality of a Japanese manor house.

Set menus cost £20 ($35), £27 ($47.25), and £35 ($61.25), the latter featuring lobster. The least expensive way to dine here is to order the £12 ($21) set lunch. It is open Monday to Saturday from 12:30 to 1:30 p.m. and 7 to 9:30 p.m. Tube: Green Park.

MODERATELY PRICED RESTAURANTS

The **Bombay Brasserie,** Courtfield Close, adjoining Bailey's Hotel, S.W.7 (tel. 370-4040). By anyone's expectations, this is the finest, most popular, and most talked-about Indian restaurant in London. Established in 1982, with a cavernous trio of rooms, it is staffed with one of the capital's most accommodating teams of Indian-born waiters, each of whom is willing and very able to advise you on the spice-laden delicacies that thousands of years of Indian culinary tradition have developed. Lattices cover the windows, dhurrie rugs the floors, and sepia photographs of imperial Britain at its Asian height adorn the walls.

You might enjoy a drink amid the wicker chairs of the pink-and-white bar before heading in to dinner. The atmosphere there has often been compared to Singapore Raffles. My favorite of the two dining rooms curves like a half moon beneath a glass-covered ceiling to create an Edwardian conservatory filled with trompe-l'oeil murals, Indian sculptures, hanging vines, and verdant ficus. A buffet lunch costs around £10 ($17.50), and in my opinion, considering its quality, this is one of the best food values in London. It's served daily from 12:30 to 3 p.m. and is especially popular on Sunday, so reservations are important. À la carte meals, costing from £15 ($26.25) each, are served nightly from 7:30 p.m. to midnight.

One look at the menu, and you're launched on "A Passage to India," a grand culinary tour of the subcontinent: tandoori scallops, fish with mint chutney, chicken Tikka (a dish from the Hindukush mountains), sali boti (mutton with apricots, a famous Parsi wedding dish), and whole meals for vegetarians. One corner of the menu is reserved for Goan cookery, that part of India that was seized from Portugal in 1961. The cookery of North India is represented by Mughlai specialties. Reflecting royal traditions of the Mughul emperors, it includes the famous Muslim pillau specialty, chicken biryani. Under the category "Some Like It Hot," honoring the old Marilyn Monroe movie, you'll find such dishes as mirchi korma Kashmiri style, a favorite of a frequent customer, Faye Dunaway. Tube: Gloucester Road.

The Lindsay House, 21 Romilly St., W.1 (tel. 439-0450), bases many of its dishes on 18th-century English recipes. Other platters have been called Tudor and nouvelle. Everyone from royalty to film stars, from diplomats to regular people show up here, including an array of discerning Americans. The owners, Roger Wren and Malcolm Livingston, who already run some of the most fashionable restaurants in London, including the English House and the English Garden, decided to open this eating house in the heart of Soho. They selected a 19th-century house badly in need of renovation, and converted it tastefully and dramatically with rich colors and fabrics, a medley of greens and reds. Welcoming fireplaces and fresh flowers give it class and style, probably more than it possessed in its heyday. Even the toilets are "decorated," forming an attraction in their own right.

Fortunately, the food lives up to the décor. For what is called "first dishes," you might begin with potted spinach with herbs (studded with chicken livers, ham, and tongue, and served with a Cumberland sauce) or Hannah Glasse's stewed "scollops" with oranges, based on an old recipe. To follow, you might try roast rack of Southdown lamb or a traditional fish pie with cubes of halibut, salmon, scallops, and quail eggs in a creamy sauce. Summer puddings are often featured—packed with traditional fruits such as strawberries, red currants, and raspberries, all served with a raspberry "cullis" with Devonshire clotted cream. You might also order floating islands, which were one of England's best 18th-century confections. Light poached meringues were floated in a rose-scented custard.

The restaurant offers a set lunch for £13.50 ($23.75), but you can spend as much as £30 ($52.50) per person for dinner. The restaurant, which is on an upstairs floor, is open for lunch from 12:30 to 2:30 p.m., and for dinner from 6 p.m. to midnight. On Sunday, lunch is from 12:30 to 2 p.m.; dinner, from 7 to 10 p.m. Tube: Leicester Square or Tottenham Court Road.

Launceston Place Restaurant, la Launceston Pl., W.8 (tel. 937-6912), has a kind of urban chic, lying in an affluent, almost village-like neighborhood, a place where many Londoners would like to live if only they could afford it. The restaurant is a series of uncluttered Victorian parlors illuminated in the rear with a skylight at lunch. It is architecturally stylish, with art nouveau lithographs and paintings. The owners, Simon Slater and Nicholas Smallwood, know what they're doing. They learned their trade at the world-famous Hard Rock Café, which they ran, but Launceston Place evokes no memory of that. Lying off Gloucester Road, it stands next to Lady Eden's School, which is known for training what used to be called—and still is around here—debutantes.

Since its opening in the spring of 1986, Launceston Place has been known for its food. You get a classic British cuisine, including such dishes as steamed mussels in cider with spring onions, liver with red onion marmalade and "bubble and squeak," smoked haddock mousse, a casserole of pheasant with wild mushrooms, roast guinea fowl with figs and port, or rack of lamb with elderberry and apple jelly.

A set menu, served from 12:30 to 2:30 p.m. and 7 to 8 p.m., costs only £10.50 ($18.50), a remarkable food value. Otherwise, à la carte dinners cost from £20 ($34) per person, and hours are 12:30 to 2:30 p.m. and 7 to 11:30 p.m. It is closed Sunday and for lunch on Saturday. Tube: Gloucester Road.

The Rib Room, Hyatt Carlton Tower, 2 Cadogan Pl., S.W.1 (tel. 235-5411). Many of the residents of the well-heeled neighborhood surrounding this five-star hotel drop in just for drinks and to enjoy the warmly intimate russet-colored décor. It sits on the ground floor of Hyatt's premier European hotel, behind glass windows allowing light to stream in from the ample spaces of Cadogan Place. A team of decorators successfully created an richly textured décor of rust-colored marble, deeply grained hardwoods, subtle lighting, and yard after yard of glossy brass trim. The food served here includes the very finest of Scottish beef along with fresh fish.

Both the preparation and the service are excellent. You might ask for one of the seafood trays, including the "Billingsgate," containing two kinds of oysters, clams, shrimps, and crab, among other offerings. Hot and cold appetizers range from French onion soup to fresh asparagus. But the traditional specialties include roast prime rib of Aberdeen Angus, New Yorker sirloin, roast rack of English lamb with rosemary, and a special mixed grill, with lamb cutlet, filet steak, veal kidney, and a medallion of veal and bacon. Meals cost from £22 ($38.50) and are served Monday to Saturday from 12:30 to 2:45 p.m. and 7 to 11:15 p.m., on Sunday to 10:45 p.m. Tube: Sloane Square.

Al Hamra, 31 Shepherd Market, W.1 (tel. 493-1954), is the premier Lebanese restaurant in London. You get good value, impeccable service, and food that delights the palate. As for the staff, Beruit's loss was London's gain. Nostalgic refugees—those who managed to get out with their money—come here for a taste of the old country, and they rarely leave disappointed. To begin with, you are faced with a dazzling selection of mezes, or appetizers. There are at least five dozen, both hot and cold, ranging from the inevitable hummus (chick peas) to such delights as shinklish (cheese salad of Lebanon) or batrakh (fish roe, garlic, and olive oil). A salad of fresh vegetables, including tomatoes and cucumbers, is placed on each table, and you are to help yourself. You can eat your way through so many different and tantalizing flavors and taste sensations that it's difficult to go on to the main course.

If you do, you can select such dishes as grilled quails in garlic sauce and excellent grilled meats on a skewer. Typical of Middle Eastern cuisine, lamb is heavily featured. One English food critic highly praised the lamb testicles, but you may happily settle for the kousa mahsi (zucchini stuffed with minced lamb and rice). The bread, baked on the premises, is an important part of the dining here. Likewise, the Lebanese who frequent the place like the honeyed sweets, but a member of the staff assured me that these desserts are "adjusted" for English diners—that is, they are prepared with less sugar than is customary. Try, also, the trout in a hot spicy sauce, which is invariably good. Hours are noon to midnight daily, and the cost is £15 ($26.25) per head, which is very reasonable, considering the quality of the fresh ingredients and the time-consuming preparation they take. Sometimes it's very difficult to get a table, so call early for a reservation. Tube: Green Park.

For a very special meal in truly British surroundings, try **Winstons Restaurant and Wine Bar,** 24 Coptic St., W.C.1 (tel. 580-3422), named in honor of Winston Spencer Churchill. Winstons offers good food and wine in a unique traditional but informal way. The restaurant is set in an original 18th-century Bloomsbury house full of Churchill mementos, with the first-floor dining room being elegantly decorated in Edwardian club style. Your meal might begin with a Stilton or Brie wrapped in pastry and deep-fried, served with fresh cranberries, followed by Scotch salmon, steak, or filet of beef Wellington. Desserts include the old favorite English apple pie or mouthwatering treacle orange and walnut tart. The average price for a meal, including wine, is £20 ($35). The restaurant is open for lunch from 11 a.m. to 3 p.m. Monday to Friday and for dinner from 5:30 to 11:15 p.m. Monday to Saturday. On the ground floor, the wine and piano bar offers a unique Churchillian meeting place with an extensive wine list. The establishment, which is closed Sunday, is fully air-conditioned. Tube: Tottenham Court Road.

Au Jardin des Gourmets, 5 Greek St., W.1 (tel. 437-1816), is an "Ile de France" off Soho Square, where devotees of the Gallic cuisine gather for their pâté maison. There is an à la carte menu with a comprehensive selection offered by the manager, Franco Zola. The soups are exceptionally good, chilled cucumber and mint soup and soupe à l'oignon gratinée among them. House specialties include carré d'agneau, roast breast of duck in red wine with fresh cranberries, and a hot seafood dish in wine sauce. Vintage wines are available, but you can also order by the glass. The average price of a meal, including a half bottle of the house wine, is £23 ($40.25) per person. However, a set lunch or dinner is offered for just £13.50 ($23.75). The restaurant is open from 12:30 to 2:15 p.m. and 6:30 to 11:30 p.m.; closed Sunday. Tube: Tottenham Court Road.

Manzi's, 1–2 Leicester St., off Leicester Square, W.C.2 (tel. 734-0224), is London's oldest seafood restaurant. Famous for fish, Whitstable and Colchester oysters, and other seafood specialties, Manzi's has a loyal patronage, drawn to its moderately priced fare and fresh ingredients. In season, you can order half a dozen of the legendary Whitstable oysters. If you'd like something less expensive, I suggest a prawn cocktail, even fresh sardines. If it's a luncheon stopover, you might happily settle for the crab salad. Main-course specialties include Dover sole and grilled turbot. The house also has a good selection of wines and sherries.

You can dine either in the simply decorated ground-floor restaurant or in the Cabin Room upstairs, any time from noon to 2:40 p.m. and in the evening until last orders are taken at 11 p.m. A meal will cost around £18 ($31.50), plus the cost of the house wine. Steaks are also available. Tube: Leicester Square.

Hilaire, 68 Old Brompton Rd., S.W.7 (tel. 584-8993), is a jovially cramped restaurant, housed in what was originally built as a Victorian storefront. Ceiling fans, immaculate napery, applegreen walls, fresh flowers, and twin Corinthian columns form the framework for elegant French specialties.

There is no à la carte menu here, since both lunch at £14 ($24.50) and dinner at £22 ($38.50) are offered at a fixed price. A typical lunch might include clams baked in garlic butter, mousseline of sole with a chive sauce, bread-and-butter pudding, and coffee. Bryan Webb prepares a mixture of classical French and cuisine moderne that has made this one of the most stylish restaurants in London. Menu items include homemade rillettes of duckling, chicken-liver mousse with a sweet onion sauce, calves' brains with capers, roast end of lamb with grilled kidneys and béarnaise sauce, fresh fish of the day, and filet of veal with morels, followed by a choice of luscious desserts.

Reservations are suggested for full meals, which are served from noon to 2:30 p.m. and 7:30 to 11:30 p.m. An apéritif bar, a cluster of extra tables, and a pair of semiprivate alcoves are in the lower dining room. Tube: South Kensington.

San Lorenzo, 22 Beauchamp Pl., S.W.3 (tel. 584-1074). This is the kind of fashionable, young, modern place that the unique artist, Jonathan Routh, might attend for an evening. Of course, his paintings might be on exhibit, but he'd surely like the food too. He's known for illustrating a book of what might have happened *if* Queen Victoria had visited Jamaica. He also painted the Sardinia home of the owner-managers of this chic rendezvous, Mara and Lorenzo Berni.

A 1987 debutante, San Lorenzo already seems firmly established on the London scene, not only among artists and writers, but among models and photographers as well. In back is a two-level dining room capped with a glass canopy which is pulled back on warm, sunny days.

Reliability is the keynote of the cuisine, that and good-quality produce, often seasoned with fresh herbs. Nearly everything you order seems delectable, from the homemade fettuccine with salmon to the carpaccio, and certainly the risotto with fresh asparagus. You can also order traditional regional Italian dishes such as salt cod with polenta or a bollito misto, going on to fried calamare or partridge in a white wine sauce. The veal piccata is exceptionally good. Meals, costing from £20 ($35), are served from 12:30 to 3 p.m. and 7:30 to 11:30 p.m. Monday to Saturday. Always make a reservation, and even then it may be hard to get a table when you show up. Tube: Knightsbridge.

The Georgian Restaurant, Harrods Department Store, Knightsbridge, S.W.3 (tel. 730-1234, ext. 3467), lies on the top floor of this fabled emporium, under elaborate ceilings and Belle Époque skylights. It is one of the neighborhood's most appealing lunchtime restaurants. Breakfast, lunch, and afternoon tea are served. One of the rooms, big enough for a ballroom, contains a pianist, whose music trills between the crystals of the chandeliers.

A member of a battalion of polite waitresses will bring you the first course of a fixed-price lunch, costing £14 ($24.50) per person. The second course is served from a sprawling buffet filled with cold meats and an array of fresh salads. Guests who want a hot meal can head for the carvery section where a uniformed crew of chefs dishes up such food as Yorkshire pudding with roast beef, poultry, fish, and pork. Desserts are brought to the table by your waitress. Harrods's afternoon tea, costing £6.50 ($11.50) per person, is one of the most popular events. Breakfast is served from 9:30 to 11 a.m. and lunch from noon to 2:30 p.m. Tea time is 3:30 to 5:30 p.m., but guests start lining up before 3 p.m. Sandwiches and pastries are served from the "Grand Buffet," which shuts down at 5:15 p.m. Everything is closed on Sunday. Tube: Knightsbridge.

Joe Allen's, 13 Exeter St., W.C.2 (tel. 836-0651), is a fashionable restaurant attracting theater people. It lies north of the Strand in the vicinity of the Savoy Hotel. The restaurant, serving an American and international cuisine, is a sister to other branches in Paris, Los Angeles, Toronto, and New York. The décor is inspired by the New York branch, with theater posters, gingham tablecloths in red-and-white check, and a blackboard menu offering such specialties as black-bean soup, barbecued spareribs, a regular spinach salad, a bowl of chili, calves' liver and onions, and carrot cake. A simple meal will begin at £10 ($17.50), although you can spend far more, of course, perhaps £20 ($35), depending on how much you order to drink. Joe Allen's is open from noon to 1 a.m. Monday through Saturday, till midnight on Sunday. Tube: Covent Garden or Embankment.

Langan's Brasserie, Stratton Street, W.1 (tel. 491-8822), is a relaxed, café-style restaurant modeled after a Parisian brasserie. Although the chef is English, the food and atmosphere are very French. Langan's is the brainchild of restaurateur Peter Langan, in partnership with actor Michael Caine and the chef de cuisine, Richard Shepherd, and has become a chic spot since it opened in 1976. The potted palms and overhead fans created a faded '30s atmosphere; you expect the evening instrumentalists to break into "As Time Goes By" at any moment. Langan's is open for lunch Monday to Friday from 12:30 to 3 p.m. and for dinner from 7 p.m. to midnight Monday through Friday. On Saturday, hours are 8 p.m. to 12:45 a.m. and the restaurant is shut all day on Sunday. Complete dinners, including wine, VAT, and service, come to about £25 ($43.75) per person. Upstairs is a more intimate dining room with silver service, although the same prices are charged. The Venetian décor was the work of Patrick Proctor, the artist. Tube: Green Park.

Drones, 1 Pont St., S.W.1 (tel. 235-9638), was labeled by one newspaper columnist as "the unofficial club for bright people, at least half of whom seem to know each other." The late David Niven and friends launched this two-floor restaurant some years ago, and its reputation for charm and chic has spread. Reservations are imperative, preferably a day in advance.

There is no elaborate menu, no fancy sauces, just simple but good food. At lunch have the Droneburger, a favorite. For dinner, the calves' liver with bacon is superb (have it cooked pink if you prefer it). As an appetizer, the mousse de saumon (salmon) fumée au caviar is worthy, as is the foie gras fraiche truffée. Main-dish specialties are veal pojarsky ciboulette, duck with orange, chicken suprême with mushrooms, and a fresh crab salad. Chocolate mousse and soufflé au Grand Marnier vie for your attention in the dessert department. The menu is wisely limited and seldom changes, although plats du jour are featured. A meal, not including your wine selection, costs from £18 ($31.50).

You sit on bentwood armchairs with green velvet cushions at white wrought-iron tables. The simple white walls are perfect foils for oil paintings and framed copies of children's comics and magazines. Try to get a table downstairs. If you're lingering at the bar while waiting for a table (a likely possibility), take a look at the collection of movie-star photographs.

Open seven days a week, Drones serves lunch from 12:30 to 3 p.m. and dinner from 7:30 p.m. to midnight. Tube: Sloane Square.

Restaurants Afloat

Perhaps the most charming oddities on the London dining scene are the nautical eateries that have sprung up. They range from converted barges to craft the size of Mississippi steamers and may either be permanently docked or mobile, but invariably offer good cuisine in intriguingly different surroundings. Since they stick to the placid Thames or the canal system there is no chance of your appetite's being disturbed by seasickness.

R.S. (for restaurant ship) *Hispaniola.* Moored on the Thames at Victoria Embankment, Charing Cross, this large and luxurious air-conditioned ship offers a splendid view of the heart of London from Big Ben to St. Paul's, armchair comfort at the tables, and two cocktail bars for other brands of comfort. Meals are served on both the upper and lower decks, and at night the sparkling lights along the banks turn the entire area into a romantic setting. The menu offers many meat and vegetarian dishes, and the cost without service is £12.50 ($22) for lunch, £18 ($31.50) for dinner. Lunch is served Monday to Friday and on Sunday from noon to 2 p.m. On Sunday and Monday dinner is served from 7 to 10 p.m., to midnight Tuesday to Saturday. For reservations, telephone 839-9011. Tube: Embankment.

My Fair Lady, a cruise-while-you-dine establishment, anchors at 250 Camden High St., N.W.1, about two miles from central London. Traditionally decked out, this motor-driven barge noses through the Regent's Canal for three hours, crossing the zoo, Regent's Park, passing through Maida Hill tunnel until it reaches Robert Browning's Island at Little Venice, where a popular singer-guitarist joins you for the return journey.

While cruising you eat an excellent three-course meal for £18 ($31.50) and enjoy the passing scene along the banks. Lunch is served on Sunday only, for £13 ($22.75), with the cruise starting at 1 p.m. The dinner trip departs at 8 p.m. For reservations and information, telephone 485-4433 or 485-6210.

The English House, 3 Milner St., S.W.3 (tel. 584-3002), is a tiny restaurant in the heart of Chelsea, where dining is like being a guest in an elegant private house. Created and designed by Michael Smith with his flair for color and fabric, the décor of the English House provides both spectacle and atmosphere. Blues and terracotta predominate. The walls are clad in a printed cotton and are a traditional English design of autumn leaves and black currants. The fireplace creates a home environment, and the collection of interesting and beautiful furniture adds to the background. Attention has been paid to detail, and even the saltcellars are Victorian in origin.

The food is British with such succulent offerings as home oak-smoked pigeon breast, Old English steak pie with pickled walnuts, and Welsh rarebit, made by a new recipe based on the time-honored ingredients: beer, mustard, cheese, and egg yolks. The chef's daily choices are included in a special luncheon menu at £9.75 ($17) for two courses and coffee. À la carte dinners average £25 ($43.75), all prices inclusive of VAT and service. The restaurant is open daily for lunch from 12:30 to 2:30 p.m. (to 2 p.m. on Sunday), and for dinner from 7:30 to 11:30 p.m. (to 10:30 p.m. on Sunday).

The English Garden, 10 Lincoln St., S.W.3 (tel. 584-7272), is another design creation of Michael Smith, who did the English House, previewed above. The décor is pretty and light-hearted. The Garden Room on the ground floor is whitewashed brick with panels of large stylish flowers. The attractive pelmets are in vivid flower colors with stark white curtains. Rattan chairs in a Gothic theme and candy-pink napery complete the scene. With the domed conservatory roofs and banks of plants, the atmosphere is relaxing and happy.

The menu is extensive and includes plenty of salads and fish. Interesting dishes are a checkerboard of freshwater fish (an intricately patterned mousse of salmon, carp, and pike), collops of beef with plum brandy, and lemon flummery, a deceptively rich confection of lemon and eggs, adapted from an 18th-century recipe, served with ratafia biscuits. The chef's daily choices are included in a special luncheon menu at £12.50 ($22) for three courses and coffee. À la carte dinners average £24 ($42), all prices including VAT and service. A comprehensive wine list is available, and an excellent French house wine is always obtainable. The restaurant is open daily for lunch from 12:30 to 2:30 p.m. (to 2 p.m. on Sunday), and for dinner from 7:30 to 10 p.m.

Drakes, 2a Pond Pl., S.W.3 (tel. 584-4555), bears a resemblance to the hall of a grand Tudor house, with its bare brick walls, brass chandelier, tapestries, and fine oil paintings of ducks. It has a visible kitchen where you can see baby lamb, game, and ducklings being spit-roasted over a charcoal grill. All main dishes are complemented by fine, fresh English produce. Typical English favorites such as Dover sole, smoked salmon, and roast beef with Yorkshire pudding are always available. There is a 100-bin wine list to represent the most outstanding wine regions, and you can also enjoy an apéritif in the comfortable lounge while you make your menu selections.

Drakes is open for dinner seven days a week and for lunch on Sunday. A three-course evening meal averages £25 ($43.75), with VAT and service included. Hours are 6:30 to 11 p.m. (7 to 10:30 p.m. on Sunday). Sunday lunch is served from 12:30 to 3 p.m. The general manager, Campbell Porter, is on hand to help visitors in choosing from the extensive menus. Drakes is fully air-conditioned and has a no-smoking area. Tube: South Kensington.

Coconut Grove, 3–5 Barrett St., W.1 (tel. 486-5269), lies in Mayfair, at the end of St. Christopher's Street, just off Oxford Street. Bright and lively, the restaurant has an art deco mood with subtle pastel shades and large palm trees enhancing the ambience. The restaurant has two levels: the ground floor favored by high-profile, trendy customers, and the basement, preferred for business or more intimate lunches or dinners. A chef's specialty of the day accompanies the large and varied menu. A dozen or so salads are offered, including avocado and bacon, spinach, and chicken and walnut. Vegetarian dishes are an important part of the menu, particular favorites being vegetable pancakes, guacamole, and crûdités. You might like the Coconut Grove fresh pasta or the broiled halibut with ratatouille. The cost of a dinner for two is $18 ($31.50) to £22 ($38.50), including wine or cocktails. Sunday brunch is also served. Coconut Grove is open seven days a week from noon to 1 a.m.

Adjoining the restaurant is the Polo Bar, serving superb cocktails. During the summer months, tables are placed outside the bar on the pavement overlooking St. Christopher's Place walkway. Tube: Bond Street.

Odin's, 27 Devonshire St., W.1 (tel. 935-7296), was the first creative statement of a London restaurateur, Peter Langan, who later became enormously successful with Langan's Bistro, next door, and the more famous Langan's Brasserie in Mayfair. Amid an eclectic décor of gilt-touched walls, art deco armchairs, Japanese screens, ceiling fans, evocative paintings, and immaculate napery, you can enjoy well-prepared specialties of the owner-chef, Christopher German. The menu offers an excellent wine list and selections from many culinary traditions. Selections change every day, depending on the shopping and the availability of super-fresh ingredients. You can begin your meal with pigeon breast in puff pastry, marinated salmon with lemon, prawn bisque, or a chicken-liver mousse. Main courses include a filet of turbot with prawns from Dublin Bay, steamed Dover sole with ginger and pink peppercorns, wild salmon with sorrel sauce, and a Scottish sirloin with garlic and breadcrumbs. A set lunch costs from £13.50 ($23.75), while dinner goes for £30 ($52.50) per person. Lunch is served from 12:30 to 2:30 p.m., and dinner from 7 to 11:30 p.m. The restaurant is closed every Saturday for lunch and all day Sunday. Tube: Regent's Park.

Langan's Bistro, 26 Devonshire St., W.1 (tel. 935-4531), has been a busy fixture on the London restaurant scene since the mid-60s, ever since Peter Langan founded it near the headquarters of BBC Publications. Set next to Odin's Restaurant (see above), the bistro is less expensive than the better-known Langan's Brasserie in Mayfair. You'll find it behind a buttercup-yellow storefront in a residential neighborhood. Inside, almost every square inch of the high ceiling is covered with fanciful clusters of Japanese parasols. Rococo mirrors accent the black walls, setting off surrealistic paintings and old photos guaranteed to create a warmly nostalgic kind of excitement.

The French-inspired menu changes frequently, and only the best and freshest seasonal ingredients are used in the tempting specialties. These include smoked monkfish with tomato fennel and Pernod sauce, veal with Pommery mustard and tarragon, and pork with prunes and brandy. On one occasion I enjoyed sautéed calves' liver with cranberries and kumquats. The desert extravaganza is known as "Langan's chocolate pudding." Full meals begin at £20 ($35) and are served from 12:30 to 2:30 p.m. and 7 to 11:30 p.m. The restaurant is closed Saturday at lunchtime and all day on Sunday. Tube: Regent's Park.

Simpson's-in-the-Strand, 100 The Strand, W.C.2 (tel. 836-9112), is more of an institution than a restaurant. Next to the Savoy Hotel, it has been in business since 1828. All this very Victorian place needs is an Empire. It has everything else: Adam paneling, crystal, and an army of grandly formal waiters hovering about. On most first-time visitors' lists, there is this notation: "See the changing of the guard, then lunch at Simpson's." It's that popular, so make a reservation. Of course, the inevitable complaints arrive, such as "My cabbage was as gray as the London fog." Women once found it somewhat of a male bastion when it was known as Grand Cigar Divan, but that reputation is more memory than reality today.

There is one point on which most diners agree: Simpson's serves the best roasts (joints) in London. One food critic wrote that "nouvelle cuisine here means anything after Henry VIII." Huge roasts are trolleyed to your table and you can have slabs of beef carved off and served with traditional Yorkshire pudding. The classic dishes are roast sirloin of beef, roast saddle of mutton with red-currant jelly, roast Aylesbury duckling, and steak, kidney, and mushroom pie. Remember to tip the tail-coated carver. For dessert, you might order the treacle roll and custard or else Stilton with a vintage port. Meals cost £18 ($31.50) to £22 ($38.50). Service is Monday to Saturday from noon to 2:45 p.m. and from 6 to 9:45 p.m. From 6 to 7 p.m., an early-evening dinner is offered for £12.50 ($22), with three courses and coffee, including VAT and service. Tube: Covent Garden.

Shezan, 16 Cheval Pl., off Montpelier Street, S.W.7 (tel. 589-0314), is one of the most sophisticated Pakistani restaurants I've ever dined in, and one of the best. In a cul-de-sac behind Harrods, Shezan is a brick-and-tile establishment, where the preparation, cookery, and presentation are excellent. Although the setting is deceptively modern, the cooking is based on recipes known for generations. Meals here are a pleasurable, pampered experience. Order, if possible, one of the exquisite dishes from the tandoor ovens, such as murgh tikka lahori (marinated chicken). I also like the diced lamb cooked in butter with tomatoes and spices. It's called bhuna gosht. The kebabs are, of course, regularly featured, and many diners come here just to order the spicy, tasty tandoori charcoal barbecues and grills. The tandoori breads are a special treat, especially the nan-e-babri, a white-flour bread. Count on spending about £18 ($31.50) for a magnificent, exotic repast. However, a set lunch costs only £10.50 ($18.50). Lunch is served daily except Sunday from noon to 2:30 p.m., and dinner is from 7 to 11:30 p.m. Tube: Knightsbridge.

Keats, Downshire Hill, Hampstead, N.W.3 (tel. 435-1499), is called "a small serious restaurant for committed gourmets." Not more than a stone's throw from Keats's house, it's out in Hampstead and is the finest dining choice you can uncover in that residential suburb. Proprietor Aron Misan takes pride that only the finest ingredients go into his dishes. Some items are actually flown in. The large and varied menu lists the classic French cuisine strong on meat and fish. But Mr. Misan has even more pride in his wine cellar, where the best choice is among the clarets. Expect to pay about £20 ($35), not including wine. Keats is open for lunch from noon to 2:30 p.m. Monday to Friday and for dinner from 7:30 to 11:15 p.m. Monday to Saturday; closed Sunday. Reservations are a must. Tube: Belsize Park.

Le Cellier du Midi, 28 Church Row, N.W.3 (tel. 435-9998), is something of a paradox—a basement French bistro which is crisp, light, and comfortable—off Hampstead Heath Street. It's decorated with Victorian knickknacks, and bunches of garlic and onions hanging from the roof beams. Rough wooden tables are covered with red cloths. The kitchen offers classic French cooking with the day's specialties shown on the blackboard.

For £16 ($28), you're given a four-course meal which may seem paradoxical: a fixed-price repast ordered à la carte. You get your choice of appetizers, perhaps choosing escargots de Bourgogne, délice de champignons à l'estragon (a fresh-mushroom mousse served hot with tarragon sauce), or a terrine of fresh crabmeat and crab pâté served cold with a cucumber sauce. Main courses include beef filet, lamb, duck, veal, chicken, or fish, served with vegetables or salad, and then comes a selection of desserts. Coffee and wine are extra of course, but VAT, cover charge, and service are included in the price. Le Cellier is open daily for dinner from 7 to 11:30 p.m. It is wise to reserve, particularly on weekends. This place is well recommended for the quality of its cuisine and its general ambience. Tube: Hampstead.

Brinkley's, 47 Hollywood Rd., S.W.10 (tel. 351-1683). Once, in this neighborhood, the best cuisine you could hope to find was "bangers and mash." But today some of the most fashionable members of young London gravitate here, drawn by shops selling some of the most exclusive and costly goods in town. Brinkley's has a small garden terrace in back, although London's gray skies usually encourage diners to head for the lower dining room instead. There, one of the waiters will serve a three-course, fixed-price meal for £16 ($28), although if you go after 10 p.m., the cost for the same meal is only £13 ($22.75). The menu changes regularly, but is likely to include such appetizers as a hot terrine of wild mushrooms, fish pâté with watercress sauce, and saffron-flavored fish soup. Main courses might feature a breast of chicken with fresh mussels and herbs, fresh lamb kidneys with sweetbreads, marinated venison steak with truffle sauce, and several temptingly prepared fish dishes. Only dinner is served, and reservations are necessary. Tube: Earls Court.

La Croisette, 168 Ifield Rd., S.W. 10 (tel. 373-3694), lies in an unlikely neighborhood in southwest London. Yet because of its French décor, you might believe you're in the south of France once you go inside. You enter a turn-of-the-century apéritif bar, then descend a wrap-around iron staircase into an intimate dining room inspired by Cannes. The £22 ($38.50) set menu offers an amazingly wide choice of seafood. For example, your first course might include one of five different kinds of oysters, three preparations of mussels, five of scallops, or else frogs' legs provençale, six appetizer salads, and many more. Most visitors opt for the plateau des fruits-de-mer, where all the bounty of the sea's shellfish is served from a cork platter dripping with garlands of seaweed and fresh crustaceans. A handful of meat dishes, notably lamb, is offered for meat lovers, but by far the strongest tempters are the imaginative array of red snapper, sea bass, stingray, monkfish, or sole. The establishment is closed all day Monday and every Tuesday at lunch. Lunch is served otherwise from 12:30 to 2:30 p.m., and dinner from 7 to 11:30 p.m. Tube: Earls Court.

Reads, 152 Old Brompton Rd., S.W.5 (tel. 373-2445), is known for serving food that is "English with imagination." The décor is smartly sophisticated, with apricot-colored walls, potted trees, and bamboo chairs. There are also silkscreen depictions of birds and flowers. The cookery has individuality, and dishes are light and stylish, with swift, attentive service. The best bargain is the £11.50 ($20.25) lunchtime menu served from 12:30 to 2:30 p.m. Monday to Saturday. The menu changes daily, but is likely to include parsnip soup flavored with orange, a ragoût of monkfish, salmon, red fish, and plaice, or homemade venison sausages with rosemary and juniper berries. A table d'hôte dinner menu is more elaborate, including, for example, pumpkin soup with curry and homemade yogurt, loin of Highland venison, or wild Exe salmon. On Sunday you get a traditional roast of Angus beef with Yorkshire pudding. Hours then are noon to 3 p.m. Otherwise dinner is served Monday to Saturday from 7:30 to 11 p.m. Tube: Gloucester Road.

Ciboure, 21 Eccleston St., S.W.1 (tel. 730-2505). The artfully simple décor mingles elements of hi-tech with clear colors, unusual flowers, and imaginative lighting. Even the menu is abbreviated and enlightened, offering flavorful combinations of food whose ingredients are impeccably fresh. The vegetables, too often neglected in England, are perfectly cooked and beautifully served by the polite French waiters. In many ways this is one of my favorite restaurants in London. You'll find it on the periphery of Belgravia, behind a façade which some of the most discriminating diners in London search out. A set lunch is offered for £13

($22.75), and à la carte dinners go for around £30 ($52.50) per person. An after-the-theater fixed-price menu is priced at £13 ($22.75). Specialties include a papillote of barbue aux légumes fondants, spring lamb with a duxelles of mushrooms, filets of red snapper with a rosemary cream sauce, roast duck with a compote of limes, a tartelette of pigeon with ratatouille, and chicken breast with a coriander sauce and mango. Lunch is served daily except Saturday from noon to 2:30 p.m.; dinner, from 7 to 11:30 p.m. Reservations are strongly suggested, and the restaurant is closed on Sunday. Tube: Victoria Station.

London's Chinese accent has long passed from the Limehouse in the East End. It moved first to Soho and then to Covent Garden in the shape of **Poons of Covent Garden**, 41 King St., W.C.2 (tel. 240-1743). The restaurant is run by Wai-Lim (Bill) and his wife, Cecilia Poon. Mr. Poon's great-great-grandfather cooked for the Chinese emperors, and succeeding generations of the family have all interested themselves in traditional Chinese cookery. The décor is an island see-through kitchen which has been the subject of some controversy. I personally like it, as it's fascinating to stand and watch the chefs go through their intricate steps. The house specializes in wind-dried meat and sausage, which is quite different in flavor from smoked. Two of the most recommendable courses include Poons special crispy duck and Poons special wind-dried meat with seasonal greens. For a beginning, you might select the shark-fin broth or the bird's-nest soup. Other preferred specialties include Poons sweet-and-sour pork based on an original recipe and the special crispy chicken (one half).

If you're a dedicated gourmet of Chinese cuisine, as are many people these days, you'll find Poons willing to prepare for you some rare and delectable specialties, providing you give them 24 hours' notice. Ever had stewed duck's feet with fish lips? Cecilia Poon is usually on hand to explain the niceties of the menu and to discuss the ingredients of any particular dish. They also do a set lunch at £7.80 ($13.75). Pre-theater dinners are served for £5.50 ($9.75) and £8.80 ($15.50). An à la carte meal averages £15 ($26.25), with a table d'hôte menu costing £16.50 ($29). The restaurant is open from noon to midnight daily except Sunday. Tube: Covent Garden.

Pomegranates, 94 Grosvenor Rd., S.W.1 (tel. 828-6560), is a basement restaurant with amber lighting. The owner, Patrick Gwynn-Jones, has traveled far and collected recipes for dishes throughout the world. Asian and Indonesian delicacies vie for space on the menu along with European and North American

Wine and Dine at the Tate

The **Tate Gallery Restaurant,** Millbank, S.W.1 (tel. 834-6754), is particularly attractive to wine fanciers, offering what may be the best bargains for superior wines to be found anywhere in the country. Tom Machen, formerly the restaurant manager, now devotes his full time and attention to building up the wine list and keeping the prices amazingly reasonable, even low. He allows a markup on wines ranging from 40% to about 65%, rather than the 100% to 200% added to the wholesale price in other restaurants. You'll be charged from £5.50 ($9.75) for a bottle of house wine to around £50 ($87.50) for Château Lafite Rothschild '76. The prices here are lower even than they are in retail wine shops. Wine connoisseurs frequently come here for lunch and never look at a painting.

However, if you're looking for food instead of (or in addition to) wine, the restaurant, open only for lunch, from noon to 3 p.m. Monday to Saturday, specializes in English cuisine. You can choose "umbles paste" (a pâté), "hindle wakes" (cold stuffed chicken and prunes), "pye with fruyt ryfshews" (fruit tart topped with meringue), or perhaps just one of "Joan Cromwell's grand sallets," made of raisins, almonds, cucumbers, olives, pickled beans, and shrimp, among other ingredients. Or you might prefer more customary dishes, which manager Paul King also provides: steak, omelets, ham, roasts of beef and lamb, fish, and the traditional steak, kidney, and mushroom pie. An average lunch costs from £16 ($28). It's advisable to make a reservation, and if you wish, you can ask to be placed in a no-smoking section. Tube: Pimlico. Bus: 88.

dishes: Mexican baked crab with avocado and tequila, kare-kare (Filipino oxtail with peanuts), and English game pie, along with freshly cooked vegetables and bread (baked twice daily). The décor is purely European, with mirrors and well-laid tables. Set lunches cost £12 ($21), £15 ($26.25), and £17.50 ($30.75), although the à la carte average, including wine, is likely to be from about £22 ($38.50) up. House wines are reasonable in price, and there is in addition a good wine list. The establishment is open for lunch from 12:30 to 2 p.m. Monday to Friday, and for dinner from 7:30 to 11:15 p.m. Monday to Saturday. It's best reached by taxi.

THE BUDGET RESTAURANTS

Now we turn to the budget-priced restaurants, grouped geographically as follows:

IN SOHO: The jumble of streets and alleys known as Soho lies slightly northeast of the theater district, and is packed with cabarets, bars, and a fantastic assortment of foreign restaurants. An analogy might be drawn between Soho and New York's Greenwich Village, or San Francisco's Fisherman's Wharf. It's a place for special meals, mostly medium- to budget-priced.

Gay Hussar, 2 Greek St., W.1 (tel. 437-0973), has been called "the best Hungarian restaurant in the world." Frankly, I find the food better here than at some of the most famous restaurants in Budapest. The "last of the great Soho restaurants," it is owned by Victor Sassie, an Englishman who trained in Budapest and is much loved in restaurant circles for keeping alive the old cuisine of Central Europe. He runs an intimate, cozy rendezvous where diners can begin with a chilled wild cherry soup or perhaps a hot spicy redfish soup in the style of Szeged, in Hungary's southern Great Plain. Main courses are likely to include stuffed cabbage, roast saddle of carp, half a perfectly done chicken served in a mild paprika sauce with a cucumber salad and noodles, and of course, veal goulash with egg dumplings. For dessert, select either a raspberry-and-chocolate torte or else lemon-cheese pancakes. A set lunch costs £12 ($21), with dinners costing from £18 ($31.50). Meals are served daily except Sunday from 12:30 to 2:30 p.m. and 5:30 to 11 p.m. Tube: Tottenham Court Road.

Chuen Cheng Ku, 17 Wardour St., W.1 (tel. 437-1398), is one of the finest eateries in Soho's "New China." A large restaurant on several floors, Chuen Cheng Ku is noted for its Cantonese food and is said to have the longest and most interesting menu in London. Specialties are paper-wrapped prawns, rice in lotus leaves, steamed spareribs in black-bean sauce, shredded pork with cashew nuts, all served in generous portions. Dim sum (dumplings) are served from 11 a.m. to 6 p.m. The Singapore noodles, reflecting one of the Chinese-Malaysian inspirations, are thin rice noodles, sometimes mixed with curry and pork or shrimp with red and green peppers. A set lunch or dinner costs from £13 ($22.75) per person. Featured à la carte dishes include fried oysters with ginger and scallions, sliced duck with chili and black-bean sauce, and steamed pork with plum sauce. An average à la carte dinner goes for £10 ($17.50). A service charge of 10% is added to all accounts. The restaurant is open daily from 11 a.m. to 11 p.m. Tube: Piccadilly Circus or Leicester Square.

The Baker & Oven

This "Simon the Pieman" setting is not only unusual, but worthy in its actual food offerings. **The Baker & Oven,** 10 Paddington St., W.1 (tel. 935-5072), is appropriately named: around the turn of the century it was a real bakery. Nowadays the dining room has been installed in the basement, and narrow tables have been set inside the brick-lined ovens.

To commence your meal, try the country-style pâté or a good savory bowl of onion soup. Among the house specialties are the jugged hare and the roast Aylesbury duckling with stuffing and applesauce. Desserts are in the classic English tradition, especially the hot apple pie with thick country cream. Meals cost from £12 ($21), plus the cost of your drink. Hours are noon to 3 p.m. and 6:30 to 11 p.m. Closed Saturday for lunch, Sunday, and bank holidays. Tube: Baker Street.

The **Dumpling Inn,** 15a Gerrard St., W.1 (tel. 437-2567), despite its incongruous name and even more incongruous décor (Venetian murals, apparently left behind by its predecessor), is a cool and rather elegant hostelry, serving a totally delectable brand of Peking cuisine. Also known as Mandarin cooking, this is haute cuisine à la Chinoise, as distinct from the much more common and familiar Cantonese kitchen. A Chinese proverb attesting to the food's subtle intricacy says: "It takes three generations to learn how to eat." Mandarin cuisine dates back almost 3,000 years and owes some of its special piquancy to the inclusion of various Mongolian ingredients, such as Hot Pot.

The inn boasts a legion of near-fanatical regulars who wouldn't dream of touching any other brand of celestial fare. They come for the shark-fin soup, for the beef in oyster sauce, the seaweed and sesame seeds prawns on toast, duck with chili and blackbean sauce, and the fried sliced fish with sauce. Naturally, the specialty is dumplings, and you can make a meal from the dim sum list. Chinese tea is extra. The average meal costs from £15 ($26.25). The portions are not large, so you can order a good variety without fear of leftovers. Service is leisurely, so don't dine here before a theater date. It's advisable to reserve a table. Hours are noon to 11:45 p.m. Monday to Saturday, from noon to 11:30 p.m. on Sunday. Tube: Piccadilly Circus.

COVENT GARDEN: London's former flower, fruit, and vegetable market dates from the time when the monks of Westminster Abbey dumped their surplus home-grown vegetables there. In 1670 Charles II granted the Earl of Bedford the right to "sell roots and herbs, whatsoever" in the district. Although long gone to a new location, the old market still makes a good choice for dining.

Porter's English Restaurant, 17 Henrietta St., W.C.2 (tel. 836-6466), is owned by the Earl of Bradford, who is a frequent visitor. It has a friendly, informal, and lively atmosphere in comfortable surroundings. Open daily from noon to 3 p.m. and 5:30 to 11:30 p.m., it specializes in classic English pies, including steak and kidney, lamb and apricot, chicken and asparagus, and steak, oyster, and clam. The traditional roast beef with Yorkshire pudding is served on weekends. With whipped cream or custard, the "puddings" come hot or cold, including bread-and-butter pudding and a steamed syrup sponge. Count on a bill of around £12 ($21). The bar does quite a few exotic cocktails, and you can also order Westons Farmhouse Draught cider by the half pint, even English wines or traditional English mead. Tube: Covent Garden.

BELGRAVIA: If you've been shopping in Knightsbridge, it won't be out of your way to lunch or dine in Belgravia, the adjacent upmarket section of London.

Upper Crust in Belgravia, 9 William St., S.W.1 (tel. 235-8444), is recommended by visitors and local business people alike. This very English restaurant, with a friendly staff, is an atmospheric place, evocative of a farmhouse setting. Its owners, the butchers Wainwright & Daughter, guarantee a goodly supply of high-quality game, fish, and meat. You can order true British fare here, including fisherman's pie or steak and pickled walnut pie, and for dessert, perhaps Yorkshire pudding stuffed with sweet mincemeat. The restaurant serves breakfast from 10 a.m. to noon, lunch from 11:30 a.m. to 3 p.m. when a two-course meal costs from £7.50 ($13.25), tea from 2:30 to 6 p.m., and dinner from 6 to 11:30 p.m., averaging around £12 ($21). Tube: Knightsbridge.

IN KENSINGTON: Chances are, you'll find yourself in this popular district for lunch. If so, I highly recommend—

Clarke's, 124 Kensington Church St., W.8 (tel. 221-9225), is named after English chef Sally Clarke, who is considered one of the finest in London, and hers is one of the hottest restaurants here. She trained in California at Michaels in Santa Monica and the River Café in Venice (California, that is). Sally Clarke is justifiably proud of this excellent Anglo-French restaurant. Everything is bright and modern, with wood floors, discreet lighting, and additional tables in the basement. Here you get a set menu with a very limited choice, but the food is so well prepared "in the new style" that diners rarely object. A set two-course lunch costs £13.50 ($23.75); a table d'hôte dinner, £23 ($40.25). Bargain tip: Go after 10 p.m. when the set dinner is reduced in price to £17 ($29.75). Lunch hours are 12:30 to 2 p.m. and dinner or supper from 7:30 to 11 p.m. Monday to Friday; closed Saturday and Sunday. You might begin with appetizers such as a hot cream soup of roasted red peppers with parmesan and rosemary breadsticks, then follow with pork filet marinated in sesame oil, ginger, and mint, which is grilled and served with a light mint sauce. Desserts are likely to include a strawberry and vanilla ice cream trifle. Tube: Notting Hill Gate or High Street Kensington.

ON CARNABY STREET: While shopping for those designer jeans on Carnaby Street, you can drop in at the following selection for lunch. It's especially recommended if you didn't fit into those slim-waisted pants.

Crank's in London, Marshall Street, W.1 (tel. 437-2915), makes dining on vegetarian-health food a pleasure. In fact it's the leader in London restaurants dedicated to natural foods, prepared ingeniously so that every bite is not only brim full of vitamins, but is a "culinary voyage to give you vim and vigor." Meals cost from £7 ($12.25). The location is just off Carnaby Street.

The decoration is reassuring: natural wood, wicker-basket lamps, bare pine tables, and handmade ceramic bowls and plates. It's self-service: you carry your own tray to one of the tables on the stepped-up level. Crank's is a "temple" of stone-ground flour used for the making of bread and rolls. It's especially noted for its uncooked vegetable salad, and there's always a hot stew of savory vegetables (and secret seasonings), served in a hand-thrown stoneware pot with a salad. You can have two sizes of salads, selecting from any of the contents of five salad bowls, each an original production.

Homemade cakes, such as honey cake, gingerbread, and cheesecake, are featured. Tiger's milk? Of course. In an adjoining shop, bakery goods, nuts, and general health-food supplies are sold. The restaurant is open Tuesday to Saturday from 10 a.m. to 11 p.m., closing at 8:30 p.m. on Monday. It's a popular place, as much with nonvegetarians as with vegetarians, and is well worth a visit. Tube: Piccadilly Circus.

Crank's also has a 100-seat restaurant and take-away at 9–11 Tottenham St., W.1 (tel. 631-3912). Tube: Tottenham Court Road or Warren Street. Another branch operates in Covent Garden, specializing in take-out food, a small food-and-juice bar, and, downstairs, a whole-grain shop.

MAYFAIR: In the center of Mayfair, opposite Browns Hotel stands the **Gaylord Mayfair,** an elite Indian restaurant at 16 Albemarle St., W.1 (tel. 629-9802). Actually there are two Gaylords in London, but this is the newer one. It has established an enviable reputation among local connoisseurs of Indian cuisine. Some, in fact, consider it the finest of its breed by a long shot. One reason for this is that the Gaylord offers samplings of several regional cooking styles, so that you can feast on Kashmiri and Mughlai as well as on the usual tandoori delicacies. The décor is on a par with the fare. The entire restaurant blazes in purple and gold, from the ornate Oriental lamps hanging over each table to the gold-studded door and glass ceiling (specially imported from India). The pervasive palatial air was designed to put patrons in the proper banqueting mood.

The menu is downright dazzling in its variety. The few items I have managed to sample can convey only a feeble idea of the culinary encyclopedia available. The best idea here is to follow my example and order as many of the smaller dishes as you can, so that you can taste a variety. To do this, of course, you will need to go with friends.

Try the keema nan (leavened bread stuffed with delicately flavored minced meat) and certainly the little spiced vegetable pasties known as samosas. For a main course, you might choose goshtaba (lamb "treated and beaten beyond recognition"), or the murg musallam (diced chicken sautéed with onions and tomatoes). If you don't happen to like curry, the staff will help you select a meal of any size totally devoid of that spice, although flavored with a great many others. You'll find the manager helpful in guiding you through the less familiar Kashmiri dishes. Just follow his tips and you're headed for a culinary adventure. A tandoori mix or other meat set meal costs £10.50 ($18.50); a vegetarian fixed-price menu goes for £9.25 ($16.25). The Gaylord is open daily for lunch from noon to 3 p.m. and for dinner from 6 to 11:30 p.m. (to 11 p.m. on Sunday). Tube: Green Park.

The **Chicago Pizza Factory,** 17 Hanover Square, W.1 (tel. 629-2669), specializes in deep-dish pizza covered with cheese, tomato, and a choice of sausage, pepperoni, mushrooms, green peppers, onions, and anchovies. The regular-size pizza is enough for two or three dinners, and the large one is suitable for four or five people. The restaurant was introduced to London by a former advertising executive, Bob Payton, an ex-Chicagoan.

The atmosphere is pleasant and friendly even though they're

quite busy. It's one of the few places where a doggy bag is willingly provided. There are smoking and no-smoking tables. The menu also includes stuffed mushrooms, garlic bread, salads, and home-made cheesecakes served with two forks. The cost begins at £8 ($14) for a meal.

The restaurant also has a large bar with a wide choice of cock-tails, including a specialty known as St. Valentine's Day Massacre. U.S. beers are also sold. A video over the bar shows continuous American baseball, football, and basketball games. The 275-seat restaurant is full of authentic Chicago memorabilia, and the wait-resses wear *Chicago Sun-Times* newspaper-sellers' aprons. The Fac-tory is just off Oxford Street behind Woolworth's, opposite John Lewis and within easy reach of Regent Street as well. The Factory is open Monday to Saturday from 11:45 a.m. to 11:30 p.m. Tube: Bond Street.

Hard Rock Café, 150 Old Park Lane, W.1 (tel. 629-0382), is a down-home southern-cum-midwestern American roadside din-er with good food at reasonable prices, taped music, and service with a smile. Almost every night there's a line waiting to get in, as this is one of the most popular places in town with young people. It's also the favorite of visiting rock stars, film stars, and tennis players from America. They give generous portions of all their food items, and the price of a main dish includes not only a salad but fries.

Naturally, you can get corn on the cob, and their specialties include a smokehouse steak, filet mignon, and a T-bone special. They also do char-broiled burgers and hot chili. The dessert menu is equally tempting, including homemade apple pie, thick cold shakes, and "real American homemade country ice cream." There's also a good selection of beer. They are open seven days a week charging from £8 ($14) and up for a complete meal. Food is served from noon to 12:30 a.m. Monday to Thursday and on Sun-day, to 1 a.m. on Friday and Saturday. *People* magazine called this place "the Smithsonian of rock 'n' roll." Tube: Green Park or Hyde Park Corner.

THE CITY: When the English talk about "The City," they don't mean London. The City is the British version of Wall Street, but not only is it an important square mile of finance and business, it contains many sights. Here is the "Old Lady of Threadneedle Street" (the Bank of England), the Stock Exchange, and Lloyd's of London, the great insurance center. Typical English food—shepherd's pie, mixed grills, roast beef—is dished up here.

In past centuries, **Cheshire Cheese,** a venerable alehouse at 145 Fleet St., E.C.4 (tel. 353-6170), was the hangout of Samuel

Johnson—his favorite table is still on the first floor—where he dined with his friends and entertained them. Today it's as popular as ever, offering solid English fare of good quality. The atmosphere is thoroughly enchanting: shining mahogany walls and sawdust on the floor.

A favorite plate is the steak, kidney, mushroom, and game pie, quite filling. Equally popular is the roast beef with Yorkshire pudding, at the same price. Also the noble pork chop is preferred by many. For dessert, "ye famous pancake" is favored. A meal costs from £10 ($17.50). Lunch is served from noon to 2:30 p.m.; dinner, from 6 to 8:30 p.m. Tube: St. Paul's.

The **Barbican Centre,** The Barbican, Silk Street, E.C.2 (tel. 638-4141), offers a choice of eating and drinking establishments in several price ranges. On Level 5, the Waterside Café is a self-service restaurant, offering a range of hot meals, salads, sandwiches, pastries, tea, and coffee, along with wine and beer. It is open from 10 a.m. to 8 p.m. daily Monday to Saturday (from noon on Sunday and public holidays). Hot meals include roast chicken with bacon, or you may prefer to make a selection from the salad bar, with meals costing from £8.50 ($15). It offers views over the lake, and in summer, there are seats on the terrace. On Level 7, The Cut Above is a carvery restaurant which features roast joints, along with an array of cold meats, fish, and salads. Meals cost from £15 ($26.25), plus VAT and service. It is open daily from noon to 3 p.m. and 6 p.m. until the last orders are taken half an hour after the last performance at the Barbican Hall Theatre. On Level 6, you might also want to patronize Wine on Six, which has an extensive list of bottled and draft wines and beers, accompanied by a variety of cold meats, fish, and salads, along with specialty breads and cheese. Light meals with drinks cost from £6.50 ($11.50). It is open from 5:30 p.m. before concerts Monday to Saturday. There are bars, along with coffee and snack bars, in the foyers of the Barbican Hall Theatre and Cinema One. Tube: Moorgate.

AT ST. KATHARINE YACHT HAVEN:

A good way to spend a Sunday, when most of the restaurants in the West End shut down, is to take the Tube to the Tower of London and from there walk to St. Katharine's Dock, a development created out of the old London dock area where the "bacon and egg ships" from Holland used to tie up.

Tower Thistle Hotel, St. Katharine's Way, E.1 (tel. 481-2575). At the Carvery Restaurant at this modern hotel built overlooking the Thames, you can enjoy all you want of some of the most tempting roasts in the Commonwealth.

For example, you can select (rare, medium, or well done) from standing ribs of prime beef with Yorkshire pudding, horseradish sauce, and the drippings; or from tender roast pork with cracklings accompanied by a spiced bread dressing and apple sauce; or perhaps the roast spring Southdown lamb with mint sauce. Then you help yourself to the roast potatoes, the green peas, the baby carrots. Perhaps you'll prefer a selection of cold meats and salads from the buffet table. No one counts, even if you go back for seconds or thirds.

Before going to the carving table you will be served either a shrimp cocktail, a bowl of soup, or a cold slice of melon. Afterward you can end the meal with a selection from the dessert trolley (I especially recommend the fresh-fruit salad, ladled out with thick country cream poured over). You also receive a large cup of American-style coffee. Lunch costs £12.50 ($22), going up to £13.50 ($23.75) at dinner. Hours are daily from 12:15 to 2:30 p.m. and 6 to 10 p.m.

Before or after dinner you might want to visit the Thames Bar, which has a nautical theme and a full panoramic view of its namesake, along with Tower Bridge and the river traffic. There is a small balcony outside for drinks in summer. Take bus 15.

ALONG THE THAMES: One of London's oldest riverside pubs, **The Prospect of Whitby,** 57 Wapping Wall, E.1 (tel. 481-1095), was founded originally in the days of the Tudors. In a traditionally pubby atmosphere, with a balcony overlooking the river, the Prospect has many associations: it was visited by Dickens, Turner, and Whistler searching for local color. Come here for a tot, a noggin, or whatever it is that you drink. The Pepys room honors the diarist, who may—just may—have visited the Prospect back in rowdier days, when the seamy side of London dock life held sway here.

Downstairs you can enjoy a beer and snacks. Or you can go upstairs to the restaurant to dine more formally. Among the tempting appetizers are pâté country style or a hearty soup. Well-recommended main courses include chicken Kiev and escalope of veal Cordon Bleu. Meals run about £14 ($24.50) per person. If you're planning to have lunch upstairs, you'll have to call for a reservation if you want a table in the bow window overlooking the river. There's also live music almost every evening from 8:30 p.m.

The street-level pub is open from 11 a.m. to 3 p.m. and 5:30 to 11 p.m. six days a week and from noon to 2 p.m. and 7 to 10:30 p.m. on Sunday. The upstairs restaurant's hours are noon to 2 p.m. and 7 to 10:15 p.m. daily. No lunch is served on Saturday and no dinner on Sunday evening.

Take the Metropolitan Line to Wapping Station. When you emerge onto Wapping High Street, turn to your right and head down the road along the river. Wapping Wall will be on your right, running parallel to the Thames. It's about a five-minute walk. (It was around the area of Wapping Wall that lesser pirates were executed by tying them to rings in the wall at low tide and then letting the tide come up and finish the job.)

The **Anchor,** 1 Bankside, Southwark, S.E.1 (tel. 407-1577), is steeped in atmosphere, standing near what used to be the infamous debtors' prison, Clink (hence, the expression putting one "in the clink"). The original Anchor burned down in 1676 but was rebuilt and survived the bombs of World War II. Much of the present tavern, however, is aptly described by the management as "Elizabeth II."

After getting off at the tube stop, you pass by Southwark Cathedral through a warehouse district that looks at night like Jack the Ripper country till you reach the riverside tavern. There's a viewing platform—especially popular during the day—right on the Thames.

You'll find a number of bars named after the historical associations of the inn (Thrale Room, Dr. Johnson's Room, the Globe Bar, the Clink Bar, and the Boswell Bar). In addition, you can dine either upstairs or down in such "parlours" as the Globe Bar, the Chart Rooms, or the Georgian pine-paneled Shakespeare Room. The food is good, and meals begin at £15 ($26.25) in the Chart Rooms. Sunday lunch costs £8.95 ($15.50). From May to October, there is an outdoor barbecue area.

The Anchor is open from noon to 2 p.m. for lunch and from 7 to 10 p.m. for dinner Monday through Saturday. On Sunday, lunch is from noon to 2 p.m.; dinner, 7 to 9 p.m. Tube: London Bridge.

AND OTHERS

The establishments that follow fall into no particular category, but all are well worth recommending.

Bloom's, 90 Whitechapel St., E.1 (tel. 247-6001), is London's most famous Jewish restaurant. But to reach it, you have to take the tube to Aldgate East, a station in the unfashionable East End. This large, bustling restaurant is in back of a delicatessen. The cooking is strictly kosher. Sunday lunchtime is extremely busy, so I suggest that you try it out on some other occasion.

The cabbage borscht is the traditional opening course, although you may prefer a chicken blintz. Main-dish specialties run to sauerbraten and salt beef (corned). For dessert, the apple strudel is a favorite. Expect to spend from £12 ($21) for a meal. The restaurant is closed Saturday, but open on other days from 11:30 a.m. to 10 p.m. On Friday, it's open only from 11 a.m. to 3 p.m.

Bloom's has a second restaurant at 130 Golders Green Rd., N.W.11 (tel. 455-1338). The Whitechapel facility has a license to serve drinks and specializes in Israeli wines.

Although Middle Eastern establishments of every breed have been flourishing in London for years, the **Persepolis,** 39 Kensington High St., W.8 (tel. 937-3555), was the first Persian restaurant I encountered. And if this is a representative sample of Iranian cooking, let's have more of it.

The Persepolis is sleek and modern, minus even the slightest touch of Oriental "kitsch." A small, subtly lit place, it features dark-wood tables and chairs and picture windows viewing the street. The only distinctive Persian features are wrought friezes on the walls showing winged lions and spade-bearded ancient kings illuminated by colored lanterns. You get two menus: one in flowery Persian script, the other in English.

Appetizers include homemade creamy yogurt with either chopped mint-flavored cucumber or chopped spinach flavored with fried onions. For a main dish, you might choose chicken with grated walnuts and pomegranate purée served over rice, or perhaps chopped lamb and beans cooked with leeks and parsley. Baklava and halva shekari (a sesame-seed concoction) are among the desserts. Most specials cost £8 ($14) to £12 ($21), including VAT. The restaurant is open daily from 11:45 a.m. to 11 p.m. except Sunday evening. Tube: High Street Kensington.

At the corner of Queensway and Bayswater Road you'll find a little slice of Hungary, complete with paprika flavors and Gypsy music. The **Mignon,** 2 Queensway, W.2 (tel. 229-0093), is one of the oldest Magyar hostelries in London and has retained undiminished popularity in the face of considerable younger competition. It occupies an ideal corner position, the dining room windows offering simultaneous views of Hyde Park and Queensway.

The interior has pleasantly rustic touches: the cooking corner, where you can watch the chef toiling, is roofed like a peasant hut and hung with Hungarian wine flasks and kitchen utensils. Wrought-iron lanterns illuminate the scene. At night, a Danubian four-piece combo provides the right air of nostalgia by means of a bass, an accordion, a Hungarian violin, and a cimbalom, which looks like a zither and sounds like a harpsichord, specializing in the characteristic—slightly triste, frequently fiery—strains that stamp the Magyar brand of rhythm.

The food has the correct degree of palate-tingling spice that demands wine or beer accompaniment. I recently had a meltingly tender veal goulash with dumplings, cucumber salad, a glass of imported lager, and black coffee, and the check came to £15 ($26.50), including the cover charge. Alternatively I can recommend the paprika schnitzel (a spicier derivation of the Viennese product), followed by the rich chocolate mousse.

The Mignon is open daily except Monday from midday to 3 p.m. then from 6 p.m. to 1:30 a.m., although last food orders must go in by midnight. Tube: Queensway.

A REAL BRITISH BREAKFAST

The fame of the British breakfast has spread around the world. For a breakfast at its best, try the **Fox and Anchor,** 115 Charterhouse St., E.C.1 (tel. 253-4838). Charterhouse Street leads into a lovely tree-lined square where most of the buildings that survived the bombs in 1941 date back to the 16th century. At the other end of the short, narrow street is the famous Smithfield meat market. The pub has been serving the traders from the market since World War II, starting at 6 a.m. and finishing at 11 a.m.

The breakfasts are gargantuan, especially if you order "the full house," which will have at least eight different items on your plate, including sausage, bacon, mushrooms, kidney, eggs, and a fried slice of bread to mention just a few, along with unlimited tea or coffee, toast and jam. For the lot, expect to pay £4.50 ($8). If you fancy a drop of ale to wash it down, you can order a glass from 6 to 9 a.m.

Or perhaps you want a more substantial meal? Then toast and jam, a T-bone steak with mushrooms, chips, tomatoes, and salad will cost about £10 ($17.50). Add a Black Velvet (champagne and Guinness) and the day is yours.

One word of warning: Most of the breakfasters are from the market, immaculate in their white coats but occasionally spotted with blood. It's part of the scene, and I doubt if you'd notice if I hadn't mentioned it. Tube: Farringdon.

TIME OUT FOR TEA

During the 18th century the English from every class became enamoured of a caffeine-rich brew finding its way into London from faraway colonies. Tea-drinking became the rage of London. The great craftsmen of England designed furniture, porcelain, and silver services for the elaborate ritual, and the schedule of aristocrats became increasingly centered around teatime as a mandatory obligation. Even Alexander Pope found it expedient to be witty publicly as he satirized teatime as something uniquely English.

The most dramatic way to enjoy this custom is to experience tea at the Ritz Palm Court. That's in the **Ritz Hotel,** Piccadilly, W.1 (tel. 493-8181); tube to Green Park.

The hotel has afternoon tea dances where gentlemen are requested to wear a jacket and tie and ladies are encouraged to wear hats, those little ones with veiling. Tea is served at 3:15 and 4:30 p.m. You must phone and reserve a table, and count on spending £16 ($28) per person. Tube: Green Park.

Le Meridien Piccadilly, Piccadilly, W.1 (tel. 734-8000). From 3 to 6 p.m. daily, the bleached-oak perimeters of the vast and lavishly decorated hall of this previously recommended hotel welcome nonresidents for the very British tradition of tea. Here, perhaps more than at any other London hotel, it comes with a certain Gallic flair. But that may be only perceived thanks to the resident harpist, the masses of flowers, and the formal service. A complete tea, accompanied by a selection of sandwiches and tarts, costs from £8 ($14) per person. The menu lists a bewildering array of exotic teas, several of which you may never have tried. Tube: Piccadilly Circus.

DINING OUTSIDE LONDON

In a red-brick early-Victorian vicarage near Reading in Berkshire sits one of the finest dining rooms in the London environs. It's **L'Ortolan,** The Old Vicarage, Church Lane, Shinfield (tel. 0734/88-3783), which is worth the search and effort to get there. A Singapore-born English chef, John Burton-Race, achieved renown when he was the sous-chef of the famous Raymond Blanc. Now, along with his French wife, Christine, he runs this engaging place, after it was deserted by another famous chef, Nico Ladenis, who returned to London.

This once was an out-of-the-way hamlet: now the world comes to the door of the latest venture of the Burton-Race team. The restaurant, named for a game bird, seems to breathe both material warmth and a seriousness about gastronomy which implies almost at once that this is one of the culinary citadels of England. You might be offered a table in my favorite alcove: the glass-enclosed conservatory whose neo-Gothic Plexiglas curves expand an unusually lovely well decorated room.

The cuisine is self-styled as "contemporary classic." The menu changes constantly, based on seasonal produce and inspirations of the chef. However, you are likely to be served elaborate dishes such as monkfish in a saffron and mussel sauce, squid stuffed with scallop mousse and flavored with basil sauce, or stuffed deboned oxtail with a quenelle of wild mushrooms that is perfectly delectable in every way. Or perhaps you'll be there on a day he serves ravioli stuffed with langouste and a langouste mousse poached in a langouste bouillon and topped off with a langouste coulis, making for a langouste medley that's highly complex but superb. A set lunch costs £17.50 ($30.75), and a set dinner, £25 ($43.75), but you are likely to spend far more, of course. Hours are 12:15 to 2:15 p.m. and 7:15 to 10:30 p.m. The restaurant is closed Sunday evening and all day Monday, and reservations are essential.

A PATTERN OF PUBS

The English public house—also known variously as the "local," the "watering hole," the "boozer," or the pub—is such a significant national institution that it has to get a bracket for itself. The pub represents far, far more than merely a place in which to drink.

For millions of Englishmen—and thousands of Englishwomen—it's the regular lunchtime rendezvous. For an even larger number, it also doubles as a club, front parlor, betting office, debating chamber, television lounge, or refuge from the family. It is not, by and large, a good "pickup" spot, but it's very nearly everything else.

The London establishments cover the entire social spectrum of the city, from the sleekest haunts to the plainest proletarian strongholds, from overstuffed Victorian plush palaces to neo-Scandinavian-décor dreams. The range of entertainment is equally wide: from graveyard silence to epileptic rock bands, nude female performers, and even lunchtime and evening theater performances. Also popular in London are "drag" shows featuring female impersonators.

English pubs have a simultaneously greater and narrower scope than their foreign equivalents, the French bistro, the American bar, and the German Wirtshaus. Their entertainment repertoire is larger than you'd find in Stateside bars. They cater to a wider range of social groups than their German counterparts. And the edibles they supply are more varied than those of a Parisian bistro.

Yet they fulfill their pleasant functions only during certain stingily measured periods, and the time you most feel in need of them is frequently the time they close their doors. With certain local variations, London's pubs are permitted to open only from 11:30 a.m. to 3 p.m., then from 5:30 p.m. (7 p.m. on Sunday) to 11 p.m. (10:30 p.m. on Sunday). English wiseacres will remind you that *certain* pubs (like those around city markets) open and close earlier and you could thus *theoretically* extend your imbibing periods. But who wants to chase around town searching for a spot to have a quiet noggin in? However, during the lifetime of this edition, pub hours are expected to be changed by Parliament.

And don't let anyone persuade you that Britain's barbaric licensing laws are based on any traditional religious scruples. They aren't. All of them were introduced during the country's industrialization, and their one and only purpose was to get working people into their beds early enough to arrive bright-eyed at their factory benches next morning. Their social and financial betters were at liberty to drink themselves bowlegged until the wee hours in some private clubs, where the same liquors sold at triple prices.

That situation has remained unchanged through a couple of world wars and several socialist governments. Late-night restaurants and nightclubs will serve drinks at juiced-up prices until 2:30 in the morning. Hotel bars serve them to their residents entirely at the management's discretion. Only the poor, ordinary English wage-earner remains excluded. He or she still has to mount the water wagon at 11 p.m. sharp.

Now having got that off my chest, I can proceed with some particulars on pubs.

To start with, they're eminently respectable institutions, which unescorted women tourists can frequent without the faintest hesitation.

London pubs serve almost every known drink concoction (with the possible exception of a really dry Martini), but their stock in trade is beer. And here you should be warned that standard English draft beer is (a) weak, and (b) most often served "with the chill off" . . . meaning lukewarm. To get something near your accustomed temperature level, ask for a "cold lager," and put the accent on "cold."

Pub food varies as much as the décor. Most of them concentrate on lunches, and while a great many stick to a rather meager menu of sandwiches, sausages, and dubious "meat pies," some put on luncheon spreads that would have warmed old Dr. Johnson's gluttonous heart.

At last count, there were some 5,000 pubs in metropolitan London, so the following survey represents no more than a few random samplings of the field. Perhaps you could try an exploration safari of your own: move on to possibly greener pastures next door after one drink. If repeated at length, the process evolves into a "pub crawl," possibly Britain's most popular national pastime.

ON FLEET STREET: Since Fleet Street is newspaper country and swarming with journalists, it's not surprising that it has pubs the way some streets have cats. My favorite is the following:

Dating back to 1549, **Ye Olde Cock Tavern,** 22 Fleet St., E.C.4 (tel. 353-3454), boasts a long line of ghostly literary comrades, such as Dickens, who have favored this ancient pub with their presence in life. Downstairs, you can order a pint as well as snackbar food. You can also order steak-and-kidney pie or a cold chicken-and-beef plate with salad. Light meals cost from £4 ($7). At the Carvery upstairs, a meal costs from £12 ($21) and includes a choice of appetizers, followed by all the roasts you can carve—beef, lamb, pork, or turkey. The Carvery serves only lunch, from noon to 3 p.m., and the street-level pub's hours are 11:30 a.m. to 2:30 p.m. and 5 to 9:30 p.m. The place is closed Saturday and Sunday. Tube: Temple or Chancery Lane.

THE CITY: Associated with Sir Christopher Wren, **Ye Olde Watling,** 29 Watling St., E.C.4 (tel. 248-6252), was built after the Great Fire of London in 1666. On the ground level is a mellow pub, with an intimate restaurant upstairs which serves lunch from noon to 2:15 p.m. Monday through Friday. Under oak beams and at trestle tables you can have a good choice of English food, with such traditional dishes as homemade steak-and-kidney pie, shepherd's pie, roast beef and Yorkshire pudding, and pork chops in cider. Also on the menu are chili con carne and lasagne. Prices include two vegetables. You'll be charged around £4.50 ($8) for a meal. Tube: Mansion House.

NEAR CLERKENWELL: Once frequented by Dr. Sam Johnson, the **Olde Mitre** is hidden in Ely Court, E.C.1 (tel. 405-4751), a narrow little entryway linking Ely Place, which leads off Charterhouse Street at Holborn Circus, and Hatton Garden, home of London's diamond trade. Another entrance is beside 8 Hatton Garden. This tavern was first built in 1546 by the Bishop of Ely for his palace servants. The sign hanging outside the present building bears a drawing of a bishop's mitre, and the sign above the door bears the date. The carefully rebuilt pub consists of small rooms with dark oak paneling, ancient settles, and jugs hanging from the low beams. In good weather, you may be lucky enough to find a seat in the tiny courtyard between the pub and the Church of St. Etheldreda. Interesting relics in the pub include a preserved chunk of a cherry tree around which Queen Elizabeth I is said to have danced the maypole when the tree marked the dividing line between the part of the garden belonging to Sir Christopher Hatton and that which was the property of the bishop. A metal bar at the entrance of Ely Court was placed there to prevent horsemen from riding into this tiny space. Light bar meals are available in the tavern for £2.50 ($4.50) and up. Hours are 11 a.m. to 3 p.m. and 5:30 to 11 p.m.; closed Saturday and Sunday. Tube: Farringdon.

SOHO: Popularly known as the French House, **Maison**

Berlemont, 49 Dean St., W.1 (tel. 437-2799), is run by Gaston Berlemont, who was born in the building in 1914. It was the unofficial headquarters of the French resistance in exile in London during the war. Nostalgic Frenchmen still come here, talking about the old days and purchasing outstanding *vins* by the glass, beginning at £1 ($1.75). The pub has a plain exterior and the décor is not remarkable. However, the hospitality of the patron is laudable. A lot of authors and theater and film people are also attracted to "The French." It's open from 11 a.m. to 3 p.m. and 5:30 to 11 p.m. Tube: Tottenham Court Road, Piccadilly Circus, or Leicester Square.

ST. JAMES'S: A short walk from Piccadilly Circus is the **Red Lion,** 2 Duke of York St., St. James's Square, S.W.1 (tel. 930-2030). Ian Nairn compared its spirit to that of Edouard Manet's painting *A Bar at the Folies-Bergère* (see the collection at the Courtauld Institute Galleries). Try to avoid peak hours. The owners, Michael and Elfriede Brown, offer pub lunches at noon, with traditional fish 'n' chips on Friday. Roasts are regularly featured. A simple meal costs £3.50 ($6.25) and up. Everything is washed down with Ind Coope's fine ales in this little Victorian pub with its posh turn-of-the-century decorations—patterned glass, deep-mahogany curlicues—that recapture the gin-palace atmosphere. It's open six days a week from 11 a.m. to 3 p.m. and 5:30 to 11 p.m., on Sunday from noon to 2 p.m. and 7 to 10:30 p.m. Single women can be at ease here. Tube: Piccadilly Circus.

LEICESTER SQUARE: One of the most famous Victorian pubs in London is the **Salisbury,** 90 St. Martin's Lane, W.C.2 (tel. 836-5863). Its glittering cut-glass mirrors reflect the faces of English state stars (and hopefuls) sitting around the curved buffet-style bar, having a cold joint snack. A plate of the roast leg of pork on the buffet, plus a salad, costs from £4 ($7). The Salisbury is ably run by Dave Suter. If you want a less prominent place to dine choose the old-fashioned wall banquette with its copper-topped tables and art nouveau décor. The light fixtures, veiled bronze girls in flowing robes holding up clusters of electric lights concealed in bronze roses, are appropriate. In the saloon, you'll see and hear the Olivier of yesterday and tomorrow. Open from 11 a.m. to 3 p.m. and 5:30 to 11 p.m. Monday to Saturday, from noon to 2 p.m. and 7 to 10:30 p.m. on Sunday. Tube: Leicester Square.

TRAFALGAR SQUARE: A perennial favorite is the **Sherlock Holmes,** 10 Northumberland St., W.C.2 (tel. 930-2644), the gathering spot for "The Baker Street Irregulars." Upstairs you'll find a re-creation of the living room at 221B Baker St. and such "Holmesiana" as the cobra of *The Speckled Band* and the head of the *Hound of the Baskervilles*. The downstairs is mainly for drinking, but upstairs you can order complete meals with wine. Main dishes are familiar and reliable, including veal Cordon Bleu or perhaps Dover sole meunière. You select a dessert from the trolley. Meals begin at £9.50 ($16.75). There's also a good snackbar downstairs, with cold meats, salads, cheese, and wine sold by the glass if you wish. Hours are 11 a.m. to 3 p.m. and 5:30 to 11 p.m. Monday to Friday, noon to 3 p.m. and 7 to 11 p.m. on Saturday, and noon to 2 p.m. and 7 to 10:30 p.m. on Sunday. Tube: Charing Cross.

CHELSEA: In a fashionable residential district of London, the **King's Head and Eight Bells,** 50 Cheyne Walk, S.W.2 (tel. 353-1820), is a historic Thames-side pub. It's popular with stage and TV personalities as well as writers. Many distinguished personalities once lived in this area. A short stroll in the neighborhood will take you to the former homes of such personages as Carlyle, Swinburne, and George Eliot. Press gangs used to roam these parts of Chelsea seeking lone travelers who were abducted for a life at sea. The snackbar has been upgraded to Cordon Bleu standards at pub prices. The best English beers are served here, as well as a goodly selection of wines and liquors.

A large plate of rare roast beef is a favorite selection, followed by a choice of salad from the salad bar: celery and raisins, rice, beansprouts, for instance. Other tasty dishes include homemade game pie, if featured, or steak-and-kidney pie. Everything is displayed on a large old table in the corner. Meals cost from £6 ($10.50). Open daily from 11 a.m. to 3 p.m. and 5:30 to 11 p.m., it's a long, long walk from the Sloane Square tube stop.

BLOOMSBURY: Opposite the British Museum, the **Museum Tavern,** 49 Great Russell St., W.C.1 (tel. 242-8987), is a turn-of-the-century pub with all the trappings: velvet, oak paneling, and cut glass. It's right in the center of the London University area, and popular with writers and publishers. Very crowded at lunchtime, it is popular with researchers at the museum, and it is said that Karl Marx wrote in the pub over a meal. At lunch you can order real, good-tasting, low-cost English food. Such standard fare is offered as shepherd's pie, beef in beer with two vegetables, and a fish pie. There's also a cold buffet, including herring, Scottish eggs, and veal-and-ham pies, as well as salads and cheese. Count on spending from £5 ($8.75) for a meal. The tavern is open Monday to Saturday from 11 a.m. to 3 p.m. and 5:30 to 11 p.m., Sunday noon to 2 p.m. and 7 to 11:30 p.m. Tube: Holborn or Tottenham Court Road.

IN HAMPSTEAD: Hampstead is a residential suburb of London, and a desirable one. It stands high on a hill, its chic village houses bordering a wild heathland. Keats used to live here. For a pub in Hampstead, take the Northern Line of the Underground to the edge of the heath. Once there, drop in at—

Spaniards Inn, Spaniards Lane, N.W.3 (tel. 455-3276), is a Hampstead Heath landmark, opposite the old tollhouse, a bottleneck in the road where people had to pay the toll to enter the country park of the bishop of London. The notorious highwayman, Dick Turpin, didn't pay. He leaped over the gate on his horse when he was in flight from the law. The pub was built in 1630, and it still contains some antique benches, open fires, and cozy nooks in its rooms with their low, beamed ceilings and oak paneling. Old muskets on the walls are mute survivors of the time of the Gordon Riots of 1780, when a mob stopped in for drinks on their way to burn nearby Kenwood House, property of Lord Mansfield. The innkeeper set up so many free drinks that when the Horse Guards arrived, they found many of the rioters *hors de combat* from too much libation and relieved them of their weapons.

The pub serves traditional but above-average food. A light repast begins at £2.50 ($4.50). Hot dishes are served until half an hour before closing at lunchtime and until 9:30 p.m. Pub hours are 11 a.m. to 3 p.m. and 5:30 to 11 p.m. Monday to Saturday, from noon to 2 p.m. and 7 to 10:30 p.m. on Sunday. In summer, customers can sit at slat tables on a terrace in a pleasant garden beside a flower-bordered lawn, with an aviary. Byron, Shelley, Dickens, and Galsworthy patronized the pub. Even Keats may have quaffed a glass here.

Jack Straw's Castle, North End Way, N.W.3 (tel. 435-8374). This weather-board pub is on the summit of the heath, about 443 feet above sea level. The nearby Whitestone Pond was used in the war as an emergency water tank, and previously Shelley used to sail paper boats on the pond. The pub was rebuilt and enlarged in the 1960s on the site of the original. Jack Straw was one of the leaders of the peasants who revolted along with Wat Tyler in 1381 against what was, basically, a wage freeze. Prices were allowed to rise.

The pub was created in Jack's old home, now a bustling place with a large L-shaped bar and quick-snack counter where there are cold salads, meats, and pies, plus three hot dishes with vegetables served every day. You can eat in the bar or on the large patio overlooking part of the heath.

The upstairs Carving Room, offering three courses for £12 ($21), is open from noon to 2:30 p.m. and 6:30 to 10:30 p.m. Monday to Friday, from 6:30 to 10:30 p.m. on Saturday, and from noon to 2 p.m. and 7 to 10 p.m. on Sunday. Pub hours are 11 a.m. to 3 p.m. and 5:30 to 11 p.m. Monday to Saturday, from noon to 2 p.m. and 7 to 10:30 p.m. on Sunday. After leaving the Underground station, the pub is a five-minute walk up the hill, where you can enjoy the good fresh air.

BELGRAVIA: Protected from the noise of the traffic, **The Grenadier,** Wilton Row, S.W.1 (tel. 235-3074), tucked away in a mews, is one of London's numerous reputedly haunted pubs. Apart from the ghost, the basement also houses the original bar and skittle alley used by the Duke of Wellington's officers on leave from fighting Napoleon. The scarlet front door of the one-time officers' mess is guarded by a scarlet sentrybox and shaded by a vine. The bar is nearly always crowded. Luncheons and dinners are offered daily, even on Sunday. In the stalls along the side you can order leek-and-potato soup, baked Virginia ham, and apple pie and cream. Snacks are available at the bar if you don't want a full meal. Lunch or dinner in the small restaurant averages around £15 ($26.25) to £18 ($31.50). Naturally, filet of beef Wellington is a specialty. Tube: Knightsbridge.

ST. KATHARINE'S DOCK: If you're strolling through this new development, created out of the old London dock area, you'll surely come upon the following tavern:

Dickens Inn by the Tower, St. Katharine's Way, E.1 (tel. 488-2208), is a carefully reconstructed 19th-century warehouse. Incorporating the original redwood beams, stock bricks, and ironworks, it is a balconied pub/restaurant on three levels. I prefer it for its bar snacks. Keeping regular pub hours on the ground level is the Tavern Room, where you can order cockles, smoked mackerel, or a ploughman's lunch, among other offerings. In the restaurant, the choice is seafood or traditional English meat dishes. Prices begin at £2.50 ($4.50) for one of the snacks, around £4 ($7) for the hot dish of the day accompanied by a vegetable. A three-course meal in the restaurant begins at around £15 ($26.25). The inn is open from 12:30 to 3 p.m. and 6:30 to 10:30 p.m. It's sometimes closed on Sunday.

ELEPHANT & CASTLE: South of the Thames, the following pub is easily reached by Underground train to Elephant & Castle. From the station where you get off, it's a five-minute walk.

Goose and Firkin, 47 Borough Rd., S.E.1 (tel. 403-3590), is a pub that brews its own beer. The owner of this enterprise is David Bruce, who worked as a brewer for one of the big companies for many years until his chance came to buy the pub which is known as the Goose and Firkin. He has now expanded his operation to include ten other London pubs. A large mirror proclaims "Bruce's Brewery, established 1979."

David brews three special strengths: Goose, at 95p ($1.65) for a pint; Borough Bitter, at £1.05 ($1.85) a pint; and Dogbolter, £1.20 ($2.10) a pint. For special occasions, he produces a variety of strong ales with names such as Earthstopper, Kneetrambler, Gobstopper, and for Christmas, Slay Belles, all costing £2.50 ($4.50) a pint. Be warned: these latter brews are, as the names imply, extremely potent.

Food is also available in this lovely old London pub. Each day there is a different hot dish. Or else you can order extra-large baps (bread buns) filled with your choice of meat and salad. Meals cost from £2.50 ($4.50). The pub is managed by Niki and Alan Brunn, and the brewer is Pete Jamson. Most evenings, there is a pianist playing all the old numbers in a good old "knees up" style.

WINE BARS

One of the most significant changes in English drinking habits has been the emergence of the wine bar. Many Londoners now prefer to patronize wine bars instead of their traditional pubs, finding them cleaner, the food better, and the ambience more inviting. Wine bars come in a wide range, some of them becoming discos at night. The oldest and most traditional wine bars are in—

THE CITY: Dating from 1663, **Olde Wine Shades,** 6 Martin Lane, Cannon Street, E.C.4 (tel. 626-6876), survived the Great Fire of 1666 and Hitler's bombs. It is the oldest wine house in the City. Near the Monument, it is decorated with oil paintings and 19th-century political cartoons. Dickens used to patronize it. There is a restaurant downstairs, but you can order light meals upstairs, including Breton pâté and French bread with ham "off the bone." You can order jacket potatoes filled with cheese, venison pie with a salad garnish, or a large beef salad. Meals cost from £7.50 ($13.25). Hours are 11:30 a.m. to 3 p.m. and 5 to 8 p.m. Men must wear jackets, collars, and ties. The place is closed Saturday, Sunday, and bank holidays. Tube: Monument.

Mother Bunch's Wine House, Arches F & G, Old Seacoal Lane, E.C.4 (tel. 236-5317), lies underneath the arches of Ludgate Circus. In atmospheric vaults, you can enjoy a "well-stocked larder," especially the best of baked hams and game pie. Sherry, madeira, and port are served from the wood. Often fea-

tured are smoked ham off the bone and game pie. Meals begin at
£10 ($17.50). The wine house is open from 11:30 a.m. to 3 p.m.
and 5:30 to 8:30 p.m. Monday to Friday. Tube: Blackfriars.

SOUTH OF PICCADILLY: Among the many wine bars in London, **Greens Restaurant and Oyster Bar,** 36 Duke St., S.W.1
(tel. 930-4566), is a good choice for the excellence of its menu, the
charm of its staff, and its central location. A busy place, it has a clut-
tered entrance leading to a crowded bar, where you can stand at
what the English call "rat-catcher counters" if the tables are full,
there to sip fine wines and, from September to May, enjoy oysters.
Other foods to encourage the consumption of the wines are
quail's eggs, king prawns, smoked Scottish salmon, crab, and baby
lobsters. If you choose to go on into the dining room, you can select from a long menu, with a number of fish dishes or such grilled
foods as calves' liver and bacon, kedgeree, and Green's fish cakes
with parsley sauce. Desserts include Duke of Cambridge tart,
black-currant sorbet, and banana fritters. Meals cost from £20
($35). Greens is open for lunch daily and for dinner daily except
Sunday. Hours are 12:30 to 2:45 p.m. (Sunday brunch from
11:30 a.m. to 3:30 p.m.) and 6:30 to 10:30 p.m. It's best to reserve a table if you're not planning to arrive early in the evening.
Tube: Piccadilly Circus or Green Park.

NEAR LEICESTER SQUARE: In the theater district, **Cork
and Bottle Wine Bar,** 44–46 Cranbourn St., W.C.2 (tel.
734-7807), is just off Leicester Square. New Zealander Don
Hewitson, the owner, has been called "the kiwi guru of the modern wine-bar movement." He devotes a great deal of love and care
to this establishment and has revitalized the food, with a wide
range of hot dishes, so that this is not a typical glass of wine and
slice of pâté type of bistro.

The most successful dish is a raised cheese-and-ham pie. In
just one week the bar sold 500 portions of this alone. It has a
cream-cheesy filling, and the well-buttered pastry is crisp, not your
typical quiche. Don also offers a machon lyonnaise, a traditional
worker's lunch in Lyon. He imports his own saucisson from a
charcuterie in Lyon, serving it hot with warm potato salad, a
mixed green salad, spicy Dijon mustard, and French bread. You
can also order an "American gourmet salad," consisting of let-
tuce, tomato, avocado, green beans, and croutons, in a spicy red
Stilton dressing. Meals cost from £12 ($21).

Don has expanded the wine list, and he doubts if anyone in
the U.K. has a better selection of beaujolais cru and wines from
Alsace. He also stocks a good selection of California labels. The bar

is open Monday to Saturday from 11 a.m. to 3 p.m. and 5:30 to 11 p.m. On Sunday, hours are noon to 2 p.m. and 7 to 10:30 p.m. Tube: Leicester Square.

MAYFAIR: A good choice is **Downs Wine Bar,** 5 Down St., W.1 (tel. 491-3810), near the elegant Athenaeum Hotel in the heart of Mayfair. On a fair day, you'll find a handsome and sophisticated crowd of people here, occupying one of the sidewalk tables, a continental atmosphere. Every evening from 8:30, you can descend a spiral staircase to an admission-free disco. Nearly 100 wines are available, each bottled in its country of origin. Hot dishes are available, including Stroganoff, stuffed potatoes, soups, burgers, and such specials as rack of lamb with garlic. Meals cost from £10 ($17.50).

The upstairs dining room is decorated in a modern style with chrome and cane chairs, along with banquettes. Hours are noon to 3 p.m. and 5:30 p.m. to midnight six days, from noon to 2:30 p.m. and 7 to 10:30 p.m. on Sunday. Tube: Green Park.

Bubbles, 41 North Audley St., W.1 (tel. 499-0600), is an interesting wine bar near the American Embassy, owned by David and Susan Nichol and Susan's sister, Jean Hewitson. David offers numerous wines by the bottle and glass, including an American selection. All three owners take a special interest in the food. David was a chef and restaurant owner in New Zealand before coming to London. He specializes in ballotines and terrines, including a ballotine of duck stuffed with veal and spinach and a game terrine.

Try Susan's well-known chicken salad or roast leg of English lamb cooked rare. There is a lovely selection of both French and English cheese, as well as tempting desserts, including New Zealand Pavlova with cream. They have a charcoal grill on which they grill Lincolnshire sausages and steaks, done as you like them. Meals begin at £11 ($19.25). Hours are 11 a.m. to 3 p.m. and 5 to 11 p.m. Monday to Friday. Only lunch, from 11 a.m. to 3 p.m., is served on Saturday. Tube: Marble Arch.

Shampers, 4 Kingly St., W.1 (tel. 437-1692), is a venture of New Zealander Don Hewitson of Cork and Bottle Wine Bar near Leicester Square, who has perked up the wine bar movement with his excellent selection of wines and the imaginatively prepared food. You have a choice of seats either upstairs or down. Or perhaps you'll elect to perch on a stool alongside the bar. I prefer the cozy ambience of the downstairs.

A meal for one person with wine comes to about £12 ($21). Salads are a star, and look for the hot dish of the day, possibly including grilled marinated rabbit with mustard sauce. The sources of wines range from California to Germany to Australia. This might make Shampers an especially good place to stop if you're shopping in the area. Hours are Monday to Friday from 11 a.m. to 3 p.m. and 5:30 to 11 p.m. The bar also serves lunch on Saturday. Tube: Oxford Circus.

NEAR VICTORIA STATION: On one of London's most popular streets for budget hotels, **Ebury Wine Bar,** 139 Ebury St., S.W.1 (tel. 530-5447), is convenient for dining or drinking. This wine bar and bistro attracts a youthful clientele to its often crowded but always atmospheric precincts. Wine is sold either by the glass or bottle. A cold table is offered daily, and you can always get an enticing plat du jour, such as beef braised in beer, preceded perhaps by orange-and-carrot soup. The menu invariably includes grilled steaks and lamb cutlets. All the food is prepared fresh daily, with meals costing from £10 ($17.50). The wine bar is open seven days a week for lunch and dinner, serving from 11 a.m. to 3 p.m. and 5:30 to 11 p.m. (on Sunday, hours are noon to 2:45 p.m. and 6 to 10:30 p.m.). Tube: Victoria Station.

Methuselah's, 29 Victoria St., S.W.1 (tel. 222-1750). Don Hewitson, a New Zealander, is credited with changing the face of London wine bars, and all of them that have shown his magic touch over the years are recommended in this guide. Opposite New Scotland Yard, his latest venture is popular with MPs from the House of Commons. Mr. Hewitson not only has an excellent cellar of wines, but he also believes in providing a sophisticated menu to back it up, along with attractive surroundings. He called his food "Bourgeois," and it shows a devotion to Provence. The day's specialties are written on the blackboard. There is a ground-floor bar, along with two cellar buffet and wine bars, plus a more formal dining room, the Burgundy Room, on the mezzanine. Meals cost from £10 ($17.50) and are served Monday to Friday only from 11:30 a.m. to 3 p.m. and 5:30 to 11 p.m. Tube: Victoria.

KNIGHTSBRIDGE: Said by some people who know about such matters to be the finest wine bar in London, **Le Metro Wine Bar,** 28 Basil St., S.W.3 (tel. 589-6286), around the corner from Harrods Department Store, draws a fashionable crowd to its precincts in the basement. You can order special wines by the glass instead of by the bottle, thanks to a cruover machine which stands proudly in a position of honor behind the bar. This machine keeps the wine in perfect condition even after it is opened. As the wine is drawn, the vacuum is replaced by an inert gas which prevents oxidization.

The wine bar food is supervised by John Elliot, one of the finest chefs in London (he works out of the Capital Hotel). It's owned by David and Margaret Levin. The food served at Le Metro is good, solid, and reliable, and it's also prepared with flair. The dishes might include fried chicken liver with salad, a lamb stew with croutons, braised shin of veal, and roast preserved duck. You might begin with a pâté of smoked mackerel. Meals cost from £10 ($17.50). It is open from noon to 10:30 p.m. Monday to Friday, from noon to 6 p.m. on Saturday; closed Sunday. Tube: Knightsbridge.

Bill Bentley's, 31 Beauchamp Pl., S.W.3 (tel. 589-5080), stands right on Beauchamp Place, the fashionable restaurant- and boutique-lined block. A small Georgian house, it is cozy and intimate, with a little patio out back. The wine list is varied and reasonable, including a good selection of bordeaux.

As its menu with its 19th-century male figures slurping oysters suggests, Bill Bentley's is really an oyster restaurant. The selection of first courses is superior to most restaurants in that it offers everything from giant prawns with Provence herbs to a shellfish bisque or Loch Fyne herring marinade.

Meat dishes are fairly limited, but include succulent grilled sirloin steak. However, the fish is outstanding, including Bill Bentley's fish cakes, and, of course, filets of lemon sole. The chef always prepares an assortment of fresh vegetables of the day, along with fine salads (try the watercress and orange), as well as a selection of desserts, mousses, and ice creams (perhaps you'd prefer to end your meal with a selection from the cheese board).

If you order oysters, count on spending from £15 ($26.25) for a meal. Hours are 11:30 a.m. to 3 p.m. and 5:30 to 11 p.m. weekdays; on Saturday from 6:30 to 11 p.m.; closed Sunday. Tube: Knightsbridge.

CHELSEA: A recent facelift has put **Blushes Café,** 52 King's Rd., S.W.3 (tel. 589-6640), in the pink, through the efforts of proprietors Geoffrey Thorpe and Stephen Lynn to bring a continental flavor to the establishment, basement cocktail bar, café, and all. Food from Italian to French to Mexican to Oriental countries is offered, with meals costing from £12 ($21). You can order breakfast from 7:30 a.m. to noon, then lunch (offered all day) and afternoon teas. The place closes at midnight. Live jazz is featured. Tube: Sloane Square.

CHAPTER VI

THE SIGHTS OF LONDON

□ □ □

The moment you have to categorize the marvels of a sightse-ers' paradise like London, you find yourself in a predicament. What on earth do you put where?

Is Madame Tussaud's a museum or a show, when it happens to be both? Is the Commonwealth Institute educational, cul-tural, or entertainment, when it's all three?

It's almost as bad as trying to index "Love."

The system I'm following is therefore somewhat loose around the edges. One group spills over into the next, the awe-some nudging the banal, grandeur hobnobbing with irreverence. The sole purpose of my classification is to make the sightseeing process as digestible as possible for such a hunk.

In the first half of this chapter, for instance, you get an array of attractions sharing only one common denominator: they have to be seen in daytime. Most of them are free or viewable at a very nominal fee. But during the tourist season they are inclined to get rather thronged, so be prepared to participate in the hallowed English ritual of "queuing up."

Further on in the chapter I'll cover museums, for which London is justly famous, and also organized tours.

Toward the end of the chapter I'll head over to riverside sights along the Thames and also touch on London sports.

DAYTIME ATTRACTIONS

BUCKINGHAM PALACE: At the end of the Mall, a superbly smooth road running from Trafalgar Square, this massively grace-ful building is the official residence of the Queen.

You can tell if Her Majesty is at home by whether the Royal

Standard is flown at the masthead. You can't, of course, drop in for a visit (and getting an official invite isn't easy, even for ambassadors), but you can do what thousands of others do . . . peep through the railing into the front yard.

The palace was built as a red-brick country house for the notoriously rakish Duke of Buckingham. In 1762 it was bought by King George III, who—if nothing else—was prolific. He needed room for his 15 children. From then on the building was expanded, remodeled, faced with Portland stone and twice bombed (during the Blitz). Today it stands 360 feet long in a 40-acre garden and contains 600 rooms.

Every summer morning at 11:30, Buckingham Palace puts on its most famous spectacle, the . . .

Changing of the Guard

This ceremony, which lasts half an hour, is perhaps the finest example of military pageantry extant. The new guard, marching behind a band, comes from either the Wellington or Chelsea Barracks and takes over from the old in the forecourt of the palace.

The troops are supplied by the Guards Division, Britain's elite equivalent of the United States Marines. They wear their traditional black bearskins and scarlet tunics, the different regiments distinguished by the plumes worn on the headdress: white for the Grenadiers, red for the Coldstreams, blue for the Irish, green and white for the Welsh. The Scots wear no plumes.

The drill movements are immensely intricate and performed with a robot precision that makes the ceremony seem like a kind of martial ballet, set to rousing music.

But don't get the idea that these are toy soldiers. The Guards date back to 1642, and since then they have fought on every battlefield Britain ever disputed, an endless gory chain stretching from Scotland in 1650 to Korea three centuries later. And those scarlet tunics were originally designed to hide bloodstains on their wearers.

At 11:30 a.m. on weekdays and at 10 a.m. on Sunday, another guard-changing takes place a few minutes' walk away, on the far side of St. James's Park, at the Horse Guards Parade, Whitehall, S.W.1. These ceremonies are curtailed in winter, between October 1 and March 31. During those months, the official schedule is that the changing of the guard takes place on even calendar days in October, December, and February, and on odd calendar days in November, January, and March. Telephone 730-3488 for information on the ceremony if the weather makes it uncertain. Tube: St. James's Park or Green Park.

This is performed by the even more spectacular Household

Cavalry, in waving plumes and silver breastplates, mounted on black horses. The units concerned, the Life Guards and the Blues and Royals, are now armored regiments, but for peacetime ceremonies they still wear the uniforms in which they charged Napoleon's green-coated hussars.

Three other places in London also get ritual Guards protection: the Tower of London, St. James's Palace, and the Bank of England, the latter as a result of the 18th-century "No-Popery" riots, during which anti-Catholic mobs threatened to tear the town apart; they had to be subdued by means of 20,000 troops and some 300 were left dead.

TOWER OF LONDON: This forbidding, gray-brown giant with the sinister moats and even more sinister ravens could be the stone symbol of London's past. Even today, centuries after the last head rolled from Tower Hill, a shivery atmosphere of impending doom lingers over the mighty walls.

The Tower is actually an intricate pattern of different structures, built at various times and for varying purposes, most of them connected with expressions of royal power.

The oldest is the **White Tower,** put up by the Norman William the Conqueror in 1078 to keep the native Saxon population of London in check. Later rulers added other towers, more walls, and fortified gates, until the building became like a small town within a city.

Until the reign of James I, the Tower was also one of the royal residences. But above all, it was a prison for distinguished captives . . . usually their last.

Two of Henry VIII's unfortunate wives, Anne Boleyn and Catherine Howard, were locked up there before being taken out to the scaffold, as was Lady Jane Grey. The first Elizabeth spent a nightmare stretch in the Tower before she became queen, not knowing whether the next dawn would bring the headsman. She survived to become England's greatest monarch, but apparently never quite got over those nights.

That didn't stop her from dispatching her foremost lover, the Earl of Essex, to the same prison and block she dreaded when he became silly enough to plot rebellion. The scaffold is gone, but a stone slab indicates the spot where it stood.

The **Bloody Tower** still stands where, according to the unproven story dramatized by Shakespeare, the two little princes were murdered by the henchmen of Richard III. And where Sir Walter Raleigh spent 13 years before his date with the executioner.

Only one American was ever locked in the Tower—a South Carolina merchant named Henry Laurens, who was also president

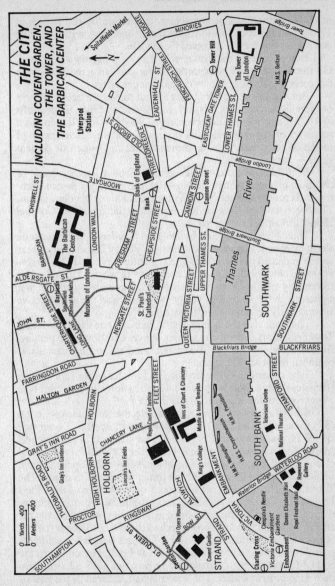

THE CITY
INCLUDING COVENT GARDEN,
THE TOWER, AND
THE BARBICAN CENTER

Spitalfields Market

MINORIES

Tower Bridge

LEADENHALL ST

ALDGATE

HOUNDSDITCH STREET

N

Tower Hill

The Tower of London

EASTCHEAP GATE TOWER

H.M.S. Belfast

Liverpool Station

OLD BROAD ST

FENCHURCH STREET

LOWER THAMES ST.

Bank of England

THREADNEEDLE

Bank

London Bridge

River

MOORGATE

CHEAPSIDE STREET

CANNON STREET

Cannon Street

CHISWELL ST

GRESHAM STREET

LONDON WALL

UPPER THAMES ST.

Southwark Bridge

Thames

The Barbican Center

BARBICAN

SOUTHWARK

ALDERSGATE ST

QUEEN VICTORIA STREET

SOUTHWARK STREET

CHARTERHOUSE STREET

Barbican
Smithfield
(Central Markets)

LONG LANE

Museum of London

NEWGATE STREET

St. Paul's Cathedral

JOHN ST.

Blackfriars Bridge

BLACKFRIARS

FARRINGDON ROAD

FLEET STREET

STAMFORD STREET

HALTON GARDEN

HOLBORN

Royal Court of Justice

Inns of Court & Chancery

Middle & Inner Temples

Television Centre

SOUTH BANK

H.M.S. Chrysanthemum / H.M.S. President

H.M.S. Wellington

National Theatre

GRAY'S INN ROAD

CHANCERY LANE

King's College

WATERLOO ROAD

Gray's Inn Gardens

HIGH HOLBORN

EMBANKMENT

Waterloo Bridge

Hayward Gallery

THEOBALD'S ROAD

Lincoln's Inn Fields

Cleopatra's Needle

Queen Elizabeth Hall

KINGSWAY

VICTORIA

Royal Festival Hall

PROCTOR

ALDWYCH

STRAND

Charing Cross

Victoria Embankment Gardens

Yards 400

Meters 400

SOUTHAMPTON

GT. QUEEN ST.

Royal Opera House

BOW ST.

Covent Garden

Covent Garden

STRAND

Embankment

of the Continental Congress. Captured at sea by the British in 1780, Laurens had 18 months behind those gray walls, until he was exchanged for the defeated Cornwallis.

Every stone of the Tower tells a story—mostly a gory one. On the walls of the **Beauchamp Tower** you can actually read the last messages scratched in by despairing prisoners.

But the Tower, besides being a royal palace, fortress, and prison, was also an armory, treasury, menagerie, and for a few months in 1675, an astronomical observatory. In the White Tower you'll see rows of the original suits of armor worn by generations of medieval scrappers: ornate, cumbersome, and—for our dimensions—extremely small.

In the **Jewel House** lie England's Crown Jewels—some of the most precious stones known—set into the robes, sword, scepter, and crowns donned by each monarch at his or her coronation. They've been heavily guarded ever since the daredevil Colonel Blood almost got away with them.

The Tower is guarded by Yeoman Warders (plus electronic alarm systems). On state occasions, they carry halberds and wear scarlet and gold uniforms designed in Tudor times. At 10 p.m. every night, they elaborately lock the Tower in what is known as the Ceremony of the Keys. After that—until the arrival of the first sightseers in the morning—only the guards and the ghosts move around in those haunted battlements.

There are also the ravens. Six of them, all registered as official Tower residents and fed an exact six ounces of rations each per day. According to legend, the Tower will stand as long as those black, ominous birds remain there.

Take either the Circle or District Line to Tower Hill station (the site is only a short walk away). Or on a sunny day, why not take a boat instead, leaving from Westminster Pier?

Admission to the Tower, including the Jewel House, is £4 ($7) for adults, £2 ($3.50) for children from April to December; £4 ($7) for adults and £1.50 ($2.65) for children in January and March. In February, when the Jewel House is closed for the annual cleaning and maintenance, admission is £3 ($5.25) for adults, £1.50 ($2.65) for children. Those under 5 are admitted free. The Tower and all its buildings are closed on New Year's Day, Good Friday, the Christmas holidays, and on Sunday from November through February. The gates open at 9:30 a.m. weekdays all year and at 2 p.m. on Sunday from March to the end of October (closed Sunday the remainder of the year). The last tickets are sold at 5 p.m. March to the end of October and at 4 p.m. November to the end of February, with actual closing being at 5:45 p.m. in summer, 4:30 p.m. in winter. The Tower Wharf, entered by the East or

West Gate, is open daily except Christmas Day from 7 a.m. weekdays, from 10 a.m. on Sunday. Closing times vary depending on the season but never earlier than 6:30 p.m.

Tours of approximately an hour in length are given by the Yeoman Warders at about 30-minute intervals, starting from the Middle Tower near the main entrance. The tour includes the Chapel Royal of St. Peter ad Vincula. The last guided walk starts about 3:30 p.m. in summer, 2:30 p.m. in winter. For further information about opening times and visiting privileges, telephone 709-0765, ext. 235.

HOUSES OF PARLIAMENT: These are the spiritual opposite of the Tower, the stronghold of Britain's democracy, the assemblies that effectively trimmed the sails of royal power. Both Houses (Commons and Lords) are in the formerly royal Palace of Westminster, the king's residence until Henry VIII moved to Whitehall.

Although I can't assure you of the oratory of a Charles James Fox or a William Pitt the Elder, the debates are often lively and controversial in the House of Commons (seats are at a premium during crises). The chances of getting into the House of Lords when it's in session are generally better than they are in the more popular House of Commons, where even the Queen isn't allowed. The old guard of the palace informs me that the peerage speak their minds more freely and are less likely to adhere to party line than their counterparts in the Commons.

The general public is admitted to the Strangers' Gallery in the House of Commons on "sitting days," normally from about 4:15 p.m. on Monday to Thursday and from about 9:30 a.m. on Friday. You have to join a public queue outside the St. Stephen's entrance on the day in question. Often, there is considerable delay before the head of the public queue is admitted. You can speed matters up somewhat by applying at the American Embassy or the Canadian High Commission for a special pass, but this is too cumbersome for many people. Besides, the embassy has only four tickets for daily distribution, so you might as well stand in line. It's usually easier to get in after about 6 p.m.

The head of the queue is normally admitted to the Strangers' Gallery of the House of Lords after 2:40 p.m. from Monday to Wednesday (often at 3 p.m. on Thursday).

The present House of Commons was built in 1840, but the chamber was bombed and destroyed by the German air force in 1941. The 320-foot tower that houses Big Ben, however, remained standing and the celebrated clock continued to strike its chimes, the signature tune of Britain's news broadcasts. "Big

Ben," incidentally, was named after Sir Benjamin Hall, a cabinet minister distinguished only by his long-windedness.

Except for the Strangers' Galleries, the two Houses of Parliament and Westminster Palace are presently closed to the public. Tube: Westminster.

Across the road from Westminster rises—

WESTMINSTER ABBEY: With its square twin towers, superb archways, and Early English Gothic splendors, the abbey is one of the greatest examples of ecclesiastical architecture on earth. But it is far more than that: it is the shrine of a nation, symbol of everything Britain stood for and stands for, the edifice in which most of her rulers were crowned and many lie buried, along with the nameless bones of the Unknown Warrior.

King Edward the Confessor, whose bones lie there, rebuilt the abbey in 1065 just before his death. The next year, 1066, saw both the last of the Saxon kings, Harold who died at the Battle of Hastings, and the first of the Normans, William the Conqueror, crowned in the abbey. Little now remains of King Edward the Confessor's abbey, as rebuilding in the Gothic style was started by King Henry III and completed shortly before the dissolution of the monasteries by King Henry VIII, but it has remained the Coronation Church.

Next to the tomb of Edward III stands the Coronation Chair, with the ancient Scottish relic known as the Stone of Scone beneath the seat. Just before the present Queen Elizabeth's coronation, some Scottish nationalists kidnapped the stone, but were persuaded to return it in time for the crowning.

The entire abbey is crammed with such treasures, some truly priceless, some curious. There are the strange waxworks, showing the wax images of important personalities which were carried in their funeral processions, including Lord Nelson and the Duchess of Richmond, who achieved immortality by posing as the figure of Britannia you see on British pennies.

There is Poet's Corner, with monuments to the British greats from Chaucer to Dylan Thomas and one American, Henry Wadsworth Longfellow. Also you'll find the graves of such familiars from U.S. history books as Major André and Gen. John Burgoyne. A memorial stone for Sir Winston Churchill was laid in 1965.

Adults pay £1.80 ($3.15) and children 40p (70¢) to visit the Royal Chapels, the Royal Tombs, the Coronation Chair, and the Henry VII Chapel. Hours are Monday to Friday from 9:20 a.m. to 4:45 p.m. and on Saturday from 9:20 a.m. to 2:45 p.m. and 3:45 to 5:45 p.m. On Wednesday, the Royal Chapels are open with free admission from 6 to 7:45 p.m. This is the only time photography is allowed in the abbey. On Sunday the Royal Chapels are closed, but the rest of the church, at Broad Sanctuary, S.W.1, is open between services. Up to six super-tours of the abbey are conducted by the verger every weekday, beginning at 10 a.m. For information and reservations, phone 222-7110. Tube: Westminster.

MADAME TUSSAUD'S: This building on Marylebone Road, N.W.1, at Baker Street Station (tel. 935-6861), is not so much a wax museum as an enclosed entertainment world. A weird, moving, sometimes terrifying collage of exhibitions, panoramas, and stage settings, as well as a snackbar and gift shops, it manages to be most things to most people, most of the time.

Madame Tussaud learned her art in France, attended the court of Versailles, and personally took the death masks from the guillotined heads of Louis XVI and Marie Antoinette, which you'll find among the exhibits. Her original museum was founded in Paris in 1770 and moved to England in 1802. Since then, her exhibition has been imitated in every part of the world, but never with anything like the realism and imagination that marks the genuine Madame Tussaud's in London. The exhibition is a legion of famous and infamous personalities fashioned to uncanny likeness. Madame herself modeled the features of Benjamin Franklin, whom she met in Paris. All the rest—from George Washington to John F. Kennedy, from Mary, Queen of Scots to Sylvester Stallone—receive the same painstaking finish that makes you want to swear you can see them breathing.

The best-known portion is the **Chamber of Horrors.** There, in a kind of underground dungeon, stands a genuine gallows (from Hertford prison), with other instruments, and victims, of the death penalty. The shadowy presence of Jack the Ripper lurks in the gloom as you walk through a Victorian London street; George Joseph Smith can be seen with the tin bath in which he drowned the last of his three brides; and Christie conceals another murdered body behind his kitchen wall. Dr. Crippen, the poisoner, and his accomplice, Ethel le Neve, stand trial in the dock, and Mrs. Pearcey raises a poker to a crying baby in its pram. Many of their peers are displayed nearby, and present-day criminals are portrayed within the confines of prison. As you walk among them, their eyes follow you—they move—or do they?

My favorite showpiece is the **Battle of Trafalgar,** fought out daily on the ground floor. You step right into the lower gun deck of Nelson's flagship *Victory,* and you're in the midst of it: among the half-naked sweating gun crews, the blinding white smoke, the acrid smell of gunpowder and burning rigging, the cracklings of flames, screams of the wounded, and deafening thunder of brass cannon (the gunfire on the sound track is the real thing). Then, with sounds of battle still in your ears, you descend into the gloom below the waterline, where Nelson—the victor—lies on his deathbed.

Next door to Madame Tussaud's is the copper-domed **Planetarium.** A huge, complex apparatus projects the night skies onto the dome, showing and dramatizing space movements and events by means of lighting effects, music, sounds, and narration. Programs (sample title: "Once in a Lifetime," featuring Halley's Comet) are given regularly throughout the day from 11 a.m. to 4:30 p.m.

In another exhibition, wax figures of Ptolemy, Copernicus, Galileo, Newton, and Einstein appear in imposing three-dimensional structures representing their revolutionary discoveries in astronomy. Exciting effects include sound, light, and projection.

Admission to Madame Tussaud's is £4.30 ($7.50) for adults, £2.80 ($4.90) for children under 16. The Planetarium costs £2.50 ($4.50) for adults, £1.60 ($2.80) for children under 16.

A combined ticket for admission to both Madame Tussaud's and the Planetarium costs £5.60 ($9.75) for adults, £3.40 ($6) for children under 16. Both places are closed only on Christmas Day.

ST. PAUL'S CATHEDRAL: Partly hidden by nondescript office buildings on Ludgate Hill, yet shining through by the sheer power of its beauty, stands London's largest and most famous church, St. Paul's Churchyard, E.C.4 (tel. 236-4128). Built by Sir Christopher Wren in place of the cathedral burned down during the Great Fire of 1666, St. Paul's represents the ultimate masterpiece of his genius.

The golden cross surmounting it is 365 feet above ground; the golden ball on which it rests measures 6 feet in diameter, and looks like a marble from below. Surrounding the interior of the dome is the **Whispering Gallery,** an acoustic marvel in which the faintest whisper can be clearly heard on the opposite side.

The interior of the church looks almost bare, yet houses a vast number of monuments linked with Britain's history. The Duke of Wellington (of Waterloo fame) has his tomb there, as have Lord Nelson and Sir Christopher Wren. At the east end of the cathedral is the **American Memorial Chapel,** honoring the 28,000 U.S. servicemen who fell while based in Britain in World War II.

The cathedral (tube to St. Paul's) is open daily from 8 a.m. to 6 p.m. The crypt and galleries, including the Whispering Gallery, are open only from 11 a.m. to 4:15 p.m. weekdays. Guided tours, lasting 1½ hours and including the crypt and parts of St. Paul's not normally open to the public, take place at 11 and 11:30 a.m. and 2 and 2:30 p.m. when the cathedral is open (except Sunday), costing £3.50 ($6.25) for adults and £1.60 ($2.80) for children.

St. Paul's is an Anglican cathedral with daily services held at 8 a.m. and 5 p.m. On Sunday, services are at 10:30 a.m., 11:30 a.m., and 3:15 p.m. For more information, telephone 248-2705. In addition, you can climb to the very top of the dome for a spectacular 360° view of all of London, costing £1 ($1.75) per person.

KENSINGTON PALACE: Once the residence of British monarchs, Kensington Palace has not been the official home of reigning kings since the death of George II in 1760, although it is now the London home of the Prince and Princess of Wales. The palace had been acquired less than 100 years before by William of Orange as an escape from the damp royal rooms along the Thames. Since the end of the 18th century, the palace has been a residence for various other members of the royal family. It was here in 1837 that a young Victoria was roused from her sleep with the news that her uncle, William IV, had died and that she was now Queen of England. Here, too, the late Queen Mary was born. In Victoria's bedroom and anteroom you can view a nostalgic collection of Victoriana, including some of her childhood toys and a fascinating old dollhouse.

In the apartments of Queen Mary II, wife of William III, you can admire a striking piece of furniture, a 17th-century writing cabinet inlaid with tortoise shell. Paintings from the Royal Collection literally line the walls of the apartments.

A special attraction is the Court Dress Collection, which shows restored rooms from the 19th century, including Queen Victoria's birthroom and a series of room settings with the appropriate court dress of the day, from 1760 to 1950.

The palace is open to the public from 9 a.m. to 5 p.m. Monday through Saturday and from 1 to 5 p.m. on Sunday. Admission is £2.20 ($3.75), for adults and £1.10 ($1.90) for children. The palace gardens are open daily to the public for leisurely strolls around the Round Pond. One of the most famous sights here is the controversial Albert Memorial to Victoria's consort, one of the most lasting tributes to the questionable artistic taste of the Victorian era. For more information about the palace, telephone 937-9561.

You reach the palace by taking the tube to either Queensway or Bayswater on the north side of the gardens, or High Street Kensington on the south side. You'll have to walk a bit from there, however.

THE COMMONWEALTH INSTITUTE: This vast, colorfully designed pavilion on Kensington High Street, W.8 (tel. 603-4535), is a center of information on the 48 countries of the modern Commonwealth. There are exhibitions on each country, and you can capture some of the atmosphere and flavor of places as different as Sri Lanka and Papua New Guinea, Canada and Kenya, India and Jamaica. Admission is free. There is a program of Commonwealth art events: dance, drama, music, and poetry; art galleries, a restaurant and licensed bar, a bookshop; and an information and education resource center. Hours are 10 a.m. to 5:30 p.m. Monday to Saturday; on Sunday from 2 to 5 p.m. Tube: High Street Kensington; bus 9 from Piccadilly Circus, also bus 27, 28, 31, 33, or 73.

DICKENS'S HOUSE: From the mighty to the modest: at 48 Doughty St. in Bloomsbury stands the simple abode in which Charles Dickens wrote *Oliver Twist* and finished the *Pickwick Papers* (his American readers actually waited at the docks for the ships that brought in each new installment). The place is almost a shrine of Dickensiana, containing his study and reading desk, his manuscripts, and personal relics.

Take the tube to Russell Square. The house is open Monday to Saturday from 10 a.m. to 5 p.m. Admission is £1.50 ($2.65) for adults, 75p ($1.30) for students, 50p (90¢) for children.

BANQUETING HOUSE: The feasting chambers in the Palace of Whitehall are probably the most sumptuous eateries on earth. Unfortunately, you can't dine there unless you happen to be a visiting head of state. Designed by Inigo Jones and decorated with—among other things—original paintings by Rubens, these banqueting halls are dazzling enough to make you forget all about food. Among the historic events that took place here was the beheading of one of its most enthusiastic trenchermen, King Charles I. Also, the restoration ceremony of Charles II, which took place here, marked the return of monarchy after Cromwell's brief Puritan-republican Commonwealth. It's open Tuesday to Saturday from 10 a.m. to 5 p.m. and on Sunday from 2 to 5 p.m.; closed Monday, and on Good Friday. Admission is 70p ($1.25) for adults, 35p (60¢) for children. For more information, telephone 212-4179. Tube: Trafalgar Square.

THE CABINET WAR ROOMS: Visitors today can see the bombproof bunker, that suite of rooms, large and small, just as they were left by Winston Churchill in September 1945 at the end of World War II. Many objects were removed only for dusting, and the Imperial War Museum studied photographs to replace things exactly as they were, including notepads, files, and typewriters, right down to pencils, pins, and clips.

You can see the **Map Room** with its huge wall maps, the Atlantic map a mass of pinholes. Each hole represents at least one convoy. Next door is Churchill's bedroom-cum-office, reinforced with stout wood beams. It has a very basic bed and a desk with two BBC microphones on it for his broadcasts of those famous speeches that stirred the nation.

The **Transatlantic Telephone Room,** to give it its full title, is little more than a broom cupboard, but it had the Bell Telephone Company's special scrambler phone by the name of Sig-Saly. From here, Churchill and Roosevelt conferred. The scrambler equipment was actually too large to house in the bunker, so it was placed in the basement of Selfridges Department Store on Oxford Street. The actual telephone was still classified at the end of the war and was removed.

The entrance to the War Rooms is by Clive Steps at the end of King Charles Street off Whitehall near Big Ben, S.W.1 (Tube: Westminster). The rooms are open every day from 10 a.m. to 5:50 p.m. (last admission at 5:15 p.m.). They may be closed at short notice on certain state occasions. Admission is £2.80 ($4.90) for adults, £1.50 ($2.65) for children. For further information, phone 930-6961.

THE STOCK EXCHANGE: The Exchange is, in terms of the number of stocks and shares listed, the largest in the world. From the Visitors' Gallery, you can watch the dealers on the trading floor below you, and guides are in attendance to give talks and to explain the functions and operations of the stock market. After each talk, there is a film in the adjoining cinema, which gives an insight into the financial world. The Visitors' Gallery entrance is on Old Broad Street, E.C.2, and the nearest Underground station is Bank. For the film, reservations are necessary, to be made by getting in touch with the Publicity Department (tel. 588-2355).

LLOYD'S OF LONDON: The historic headquarters of the worldwide insurers, 1 Lime St., E.C.3 (tel. 623-7100), opened its doors to visitors in 1986, and already thousands of people have come to see the workings of the world's biggest insurance market in its new headquarters in the financial district of London. A Visitors' Gallery on the fourth floor contains a multimedia display depicting the market's history and a reconstruction of the 17th-century coffeehouse of Edward Lloyd, where it all started. Guides explain how risks are placed and about the worldwide intelligence service operated for Lloyd's. A gallery lets you look down into an atrium to the underwriting room below which is centered by the rostrum bearing the famous Lutine Bell, sounded when a ship disaster occurred at sea. The Visitors' Gallery is open Monday to Friday from 10 a.m. to 5:30 p.m. and is reached by outside glass elevators. Admission is free. There is a room where afternoon tea is served, as well as a gift shop. Tube: Bank, Monument, or Aldgate.

———————

This has been a very cursory glance at London's daytime attractions, skimming over only a fraction of what the city has to offer.

There are many more: the **Guildhall,** King Street, where the Corporation of London does its official banqueting; **Samuel Johnson's House,** 17 Gough St., where the formidable Doc plus six secretaries composed his famous dictionary; the grim **Old Bailey,** Newgate Street, the central criminal court where you can watch the most dignified form of justice being meted out; the **Temple,** Middle Temple Lane, the hub of the country's legal system; **Carlyle's House,** 24 Cheyne Row, Chelsea, where the authoritative and opinionated author of *The French Revolution* lived for 49 years; the church of **St. Martin-in-the-Fields,** the **Bank of England,** the **Palace of St. James, Keats's House** . . . I could go on for the entire length of this book.

However, since daytime activities should include the outdoors, I've had to leave some space for . . .

THE PARKS OF LONDON: They deserve an entire chapter to

themselves . . . the greatest, most wonderful system of "green lungs" of any large city on the globe. London's parklands are not as rigidly artificial as those of Paris, yet are maintained with a loving care and lavish artistry that puts their American equivalents to shame.

Above all, they've been kept safe from land-hungry building firms and city councils, and still offer patches of real countryside right in the heart of the metropolis. Maybe there's something to be said for inviolate "royal" property, after all. Because that's what most of them are.

Largest of them—and one of the biggest in the world—is **Hyde Park.** With the adjoining Kensington Gardens, it covers 636 acres of central London with velvety lawns interspersed with ponds, flowerbeds, and trees. At the northwestern tip, near Marble Arch, is Speakers Corner.

Hyde Park was once a favorite deer-hunting ground of Henry VIII. Running through the width is a 41-acre lake known as the Serpentine, where you can row, sail model boats, or swim, provided you're not accustomed to Florida water temperatures. Rotten Row, a 1½-mile sand track, is reserved for horseback riding and on Sunday attracts some skilled equestrians.

Kensington Gardens, blending with Hyde Park, border on the grounds of Kensington Palace. Kensington Gardens also contain the famous statue of Peter Pan, with the bronze rabbits that toddlers are always trying to kidnap. It also harbors the Albert Memorial, that Victorian extravaganza.

East of Hyde Park, across Piccadilly, stretch **Green Park** and **St. James's Park,** forming an almost unbroken chain of landscaped beauty. This is an ideal area for picnics, and you'll find it hard to believe that it was once a festering piece of swamp near the leper hospital. There is a romantic lake, stocked with a variety of ducks and some surprising pelicans, descendants of the pair that the Russian ambassador presented to Charles II back in 1662.

Regent's Park covers most of the district by that name, north of Baker Street and Marylebone Road. Designed by the 18th-century genius John Nash to surround a palace of the prince regent which never materialized, this is the most classically beautiful of London's parks. The core is a rose garden planted around a small lake alive with waterfowl and spanned by humped Japanese bridges. In early summer the rose perfume in the air is as heady as wine.

Regent's Park also contains the Open Air Theater (see the entertainment chapter) and the London Zoo (see the children's section). Also—as at all the local parks—there are hundreds of deckchairs on the lawns in which to sunbathe. The deckchair attendants who collect a small fee are mostly college students on summer vacation.

The hub of England's—and perhaps the world's—horticulture is the **Royal Botanic Gardens, Kew,** by the Thames southwest of the city. These splendid gardens have been a source of delight to visitors, scientific and otherwise, for more than 200 years. The staff deals annually with thousands of inquiries, covering every aspect of plant science.

Immense flowerbeds and equally gigantic hothouses grow species of shrubs, blooms, and trees from every part of the globe, from the Arctic Circle to tropical rain forests. Attractions vary with the seasons. There's also the permanent charm of Kew Palace, home of King George III and his queen, which was built in 1631 and is open for inspection.

Take the District Line tube to Kew Gardens. Admission to the gardens is 50p (90¢). Admission to the palace is 80p ($1.40) for adults, 40p (70¢) for children. The palace is open April to September from 11 a.m. to 5:30 p.m. daily. The gardens may be visited daily except Christmas and New Year's Day from 9:30 a.m. Closing varies from 4 p.m. to 6:30 p.m. on weekdays, 8 p.m. on Sunday and public holidays.

Syon Park

Just nine miles from Piccadilly Circus, on 55 acres of the Duke of Northumberland's Thames-side estate, is one of the most beautiful spots in all of Great Britain. There's always something in bloom. Syon Park was opened to the public in 1968. A nation of green-thumbed gardeners is dazzled here, and the park is also educational, showing amateurs how to get the most out of their gardens. The vast flower- and plant-studded acreage betrays the influence of "Capability" Brown, who laid out the grounds in the 18th century.

Particular highlights include a six-acre rose garden, a butterfly house, and the Great Conservatory, one of the earliest and most famous buildings of its type, built 1822–1829. There is a quarter-mile-long ornamental lake studded with waterlilies and surrounded by cypresses and willows, even a large gardening supermarket, and the **Motor Museum,** with the Heritage Collection of British cars. With some 90 vehicles, from the earliest 1895 Wolseley to automobiles of the present day, it has the largest collection of British cars anywhere.

Syon was the site of the first botanical garden in England, created by the father of English botany, Dr. William Turner. Trees include a 200-year-old Chinese juniper, an Afghan ash, Indian bean trees, and liquidambars. The gardens are open all year (except for Christmas and Boxing Day). The gates open at 10 a.m. and close at 6 p.m.; in winter (after October 31) the gates close at 4 p.m. Admission is £1.50 ($2.65) for adults, 80p ($1.40) for children.

On the grounds is **Syon House,** built in 1431, the original structure incorporated into the Duke of Northumberland's present home. The house was later remade to the specifications of the first Duke of Northumberland in 1762–1769. The battlemented façade is that of the original Tudor mansion, but the interior is from the 18th century, the design of Robert Adam. Basil Taylor said of the interior feeling: "You're almost in the middle of a jewel box."

In the Middle Ages, Syon was a monastery, later suppressed by Henry VIII. Katherine Howard, the king's fifth wife, was imprisoned in the house before her scheduled beheading in 1542.

The house is open from April until the end of September daily except Friday and Saturday from noon to 5 p.m. (last entrance at 4:15 p.m.). If you want to visit the house as well as the park, ask for the combined ticket, costing £2 ($3.50) for adults, £1 ($1.75) for children. For information, phone 560-0882.

MUSEUMS

London has more than 50 museums and exhibitions, and this count does not include the score of local museums run by suburban municipalities, nor the show houses connected with famous personalities, nor the various palaces and mansions that are museums in their own right.

If I tried to mention them all, I couldn't squeeze in much more than an expanded telephone listing for each. They include the **Percival David Foundation of Chinese Art,** the **National Maritime Museum,** a **Piano and Musical Museum,** the **Rotunda Museum** of firearms, the **Wellcome Institute of the History of Medicine,** the **Queen's Gallery,** showing Her Majesty's personal art collection, the **Jewish Museum,** the **Institute of Contemporary Arts.** . . . et cetera, et cetera, ad infinitum.

You can look up any of these if their specialty happens to coincide with yours. Here I have space only for a selection of the bigleaguers, establishments that are internationally famous or unique or both. There are quite enough of these to keep you occupied for most of a rainy summer.

THE BRITISH MUSEUM: Great Russell Street, W.C.1 (tel. 636-1555). This immense museum, set in scholarly Bloomsbury, grew out of a private collection of manuscripts purchased in 1753 with the proceeds of a lottery. It grew and grew, fed by legacies, discoveries, and purchases, until it became one of the world's largest museums, containing literally millions of objects.

It is utterly impossible to swallow this museum in one gulp, so to speak. You have to decide on a particular section, study it, then move on to another, preferably on another day.

The Egyptian room, for instance, contains the Rosetta Stone, whose discovery led to the deciphering of hieroglyphics; the Duveen Gallery houses the Elgin Marbles (a priceless series of sculptures from the pediments, metopes, and the frieze of the Parthenon); the Nimrud Gallery has the legendary Black Obelisk, dating from around 860 B.C.

The treasure trove embraces the contents of Egyptian royal tombs (including bandaged mummies), the oldest land vehicle ever discovered (a Sumerian sledge), fabulous arrays of 2,000-year-old jewelry, cosmetics, weapons, furniture and tools, Babylonian astronomical instruments, and winged lions in the Assyrian Transept that once guarded Ashurnasipal's palace at Nimrud.

The museum is open Monday to Saturday from 10 a.m. to 5 p.m. and on Sunday from 2:30 to 6 p.m. It is closed on Good Friday, December 24, 25, and 26, New Year's Day, and the first Monday in May. Admission is free. Tube: Holborn or Tottenham Court Road.

The **Museum of Mankind,** 6 Burlington Gardens, W.1 (tel. 437-2224), contains the Ethnography Department of the British Museum, showing art and culture material from tribal societies. Hours are the same as at the Bloomsbury museum. There is no charge for admission. Tube: Piccadilly.

THE BRITISH LIBRARY: Some of the treasures from the collections of the British Library (tel. 636-1544), one of the world's greatest libraries, are on display in the exhibition galleries in the east wing of the British Museum building. In the Grenville Library are displayed Western illuminated manuscripts. Notable exhibits are the Benedictional (in Latin) of St. Ethelwold, Bishop of Winchester (963-984), the Luttrell Psalter, and the Harley Golden Gospels of about 800.

In the Manuscript Saloon are manuscripts of historical and literary interest. Items include two of the four surviving copies of King John's Magna Carta (1215) and the Lindisfarne Gospels (an outstanding example of the work of Northumbrian artists in the earliest period of English Christianity, written and illustrated about 698). Almost every major literary figure, such as Dickens, Jane Austen, Charlotte Brontë, and Yeats, is represented in the section given over to English literature. Also on display are historical autographs including Nelson's last letter to Lady Hamilton and the journals of Captain Cook.

In the King's Library, so-called because this is where the library of King George III is housed, the history of the book is illustrated by notable specimens of early printing, including the Diamond Sutra of 868, the first dated example of printing, as well as the Gutenberg Bible, the first book ever printed from movable type, 1455.

In the center of the gallery is an exhibition of fine bookbindings dating from the 16th century. Beneath Roubiliac's 1758 statue of Shakespeare is a case of documents relating to the Bard, including a mortgage bearing his signature and a copy of the First Folio of 1623. The library's unrivaled collection of philatelic items, including such things as the 1840 Great British Penny Black and the rare 1847 Post Office issues of Mauritius, are also to be seen.

The library regularly mounts special temporary exhibitions, usually in the Crawford Room off the Manuscript Saloon.

NATIONAL GALLERY: Extending along the northwest side of Trafalgar Square W.C.2, this stately neoclassical building (together with the **National Portrait Gallery** behind it) contains an unrivaled collection of paintings, covering every great European art school over seven centuries.

It does not represent painting after 1920 (there are other galleries for that), but for sheer skill of display and arrangement it surpasses even its counterparts in Paris, New York, Madrid, and Amsterdam.

All the British greats are gathered here—Turner, Constable, Hogarth, Gainsborough, Reynolds—and shown at their finest. The Rembrandts include two of his immortal self-portraits (at age 34 and 63), while Peter Paul Rubens has adjoining galleries.

The Italian Renaissance shows Leonardo da Vinci's *Virgin of the Rocks,* Titian's *Bacchus and Ariadne,* Giorgione's *Adoration of the Kings,* and unforgettable canvases by Bellini, Veronese, Botticelli, Tintoretto, and Michelangelo.

Then there are the Spanish giants: El Greco's *Agony in the Garden,* and portraits by Goya and Velázquez; the Flemish-Dutch school with Vermeer, Pieter de Hooch, two of the Brueghels, and van Eyck; an immense array of French works stretch into the late 19th-century impressionists and post-impressionists, with Degas, Renoir, Cézanne, Manet, and Monet.

A particularly charming item is the peep-show cabinet by Hoogstraten in one of the Dutch rooms . . . like spying through a keyhole.

The museum is open Monday to Saturday from 10 a.m. to 6 p.m., on Sunday from 2 p.m. to 6 p.m.; admission is free. An excellent brochure, almost indispensable for touring the gallery, can be purchased upon entering. Tube: Charing Cross or Leicester Square.

TATE GALLERY: Millbank, S.W.1 (tel. 821-1313). Fronting the Thames near Vauxhall Bridge in Pimlico, the Tate looks like a smaller and more classically graceful relation of the British Museum. Considered the most prestigious gallery in Britain by many, it houses the national collections covering traditional British art from the 16th century on, plus an international array of moderns.

The Tate thus falls into two separate portions: traditional and contemporary. Since it is difficult to take in all the exhibits, I suggest that you concentrate on whichever section interests you more.

The older works include some of the best of Hogarth, Turner, Blake, Stubbs, Gainsborough, Reynolds, and Constable; the moderns, Picasso, Braque, Matisse, Beardsley, Salvador Dali, Munch, Chagall, Modigliani, Bacon . . . you name it, it's there.

There are also the sculptures, including masterpieces by Epstein, Henry Moore, Rodin, and Maillol (an example is Rodin's *The Kiss*—attacked by the grubby-minded as "obscene" when first shown).

The range of exhibits reaches into the realm of pop art and minimal art, and the most fascinating part of the gallery is frequently the "current exhibition." Admission to the general gallery is free, but for special exhibitions a charge is made.

Downstairs is the restaurant (see Chapter V), with murals by Rex Whistler, and a self-service coffeeshop.

The major Clore Gallery extension adjoining the Tate houses the Turner Bequest of more than 19,000 watercolors and nearly 300 oil paintings.

Take the tube to Pimlico. Buses 77A and 88 stop outside. The gallery is open Monday to Saturday from 10 a.m. to 5:50 p.m. and on Sunday from 2 to 5:50 p.m.

VICTORIA AND ALBERT MUSEUM: Cromwell Road, S.W.7 (tel. 589-6371). Despite its ponderous label, this museum in South Kensington is one of the liveliest and most imaginative in London. It's named after the queen and her consort, but not run in their spirits.

The general theme here is the decorative arts, but the theme is adhered to in a pleasantly relaxed fashion.

There are, for instance, seven "cartoons" (in the artistic, non-Disney sense of the term) by Raphael, painted for Pope Leo in 1516. An entire gallery of medieval art covers every aspect from carvings of Christ in wood to silver candlesticks and ivory caskets, plus a newly opened 20th-century gallery devoted to special exhibitions on contemporary design, fashion, and images.

Islamic art is represented by stunning carpets from Persia and intricate arabesques from every part of the Muslim world. In complete contrast, there are suites of English furniture and ornaments dating back to the 16th century, and a superb collection of portrait miniatures, including the one Hans Holbein made of Anne of Cleves for the benefit of Henry VIII, who was again casting around for a suitable wife.

Among the treasures displayed are the Eltenberg Reliquary (Rhenish, second half of the 12th century); the Early English Gloucester Candlestick; the Byzantine Veroli Casket; the Syon Cope, made in the early 14th century; a marble group, *Neptune with Triton*, by Bernini; and another rare portrait miniature by Hans Holbein the Younger of Mrs. Pemberton.

Take the tube to South Kensington. The museum is open Monday through Thursday, and Saturday from 10 a.m. to 5:50 p.m. and on Sunday from 2:30 to 5:50 p.m. Closed Fridays. No admission is charged, but a small donation is suggested.

MUSEUM OF LONDON: In London's Barbican district near St. Paul's Cathedral, the museum at 150 London Wall, E.C.2 (tel. 600-3699), allows visitors to trace the history of London from prehistoric times to the present through relics, costumes, household effects, maps, and models. Exhibits are arranged so that you can begin and end your chronological stroll through 250,000 years at the main entrance to the museum. You can see the death mask of Oliver Cromwell, but the pièce de résistance is the Lord Mayor's coach, built in 1757 and weighing in at three tons. This gilt-and-red, horse-drawn vehicle is like a fairytale coach. Visitors can also see the Great Fire of London in living color and sound; reconstructed Roman dining rooms with the kitchen and utensils; cell doors from the Newgate Prison made famous by Charles Dickens; and most amazing of all, a shop counter with pre–World War II prices on the items.

The museum overlooks London's Roman and medieval walls and, in all, has something from every era before and after— including little Victorian shops and re-creations of what life was like during the Iron Age in what is now the London area. Anglo-Saxons, Vikings, Normans—they're all here, arranged on two floors around a central courtyard. With quick labels for museum sprinters, more extensive ones for those who want to study, and still deeper details for scholars, this museum is an enriching experience. At least an hour should be allowed for a full but quick visit. Free lectures on London's past are sometimes given during lunch hours. Inquire at the entrance hall.

You can reach the museum by going up to the elevated pedestrian precinct at the corner of London Wall and Aldersgate, five minutes from St. Paul's. The museum is open from 10 a.m. to 6 p.m. Tuesday to Saturday, from 2 to 6 p.m. on Sunday; closed Monday. Admission is free. There is a restaurant overlooking a garden. Tube: St. Paul's or Barbican.

IMPERIAL WAR MUSEUM: Lambeth Road, S.E.1. This, one of the few sights situated south of the Thames, is a block the size of an army barracks, greeting you with the two separate 15-inch guns from the battleships *Resolution* and *Ramillies*.

The large domed building, built in 1815, was the former Bethlem Royal Hospital for the insane, or "Bedlam." Perhaps this is the right place to house the relics of the two World Wars. War may be lunacy, but there's no doubt that it has a macabre fascination all its own, like a rattlesnake among flowerbeds.

A wide range of weapons and equipment is on display, along with models, decorations, uniforms, posters, photographs, and paintings. You can see a Mark V tank, a Battle of Britain Spitfire, a German one-man submarine, and the rifle carried by Lawrence of Arabia, as well as the German surrender document and Hitler's political testament. While preparations are underway for the redevelopment of the museum, the galleries have been reorganized on a chronological basis covering the two World Wars and more recent conflicts. In addition, regular exhibitions are being shown during redevelopment.

The museum is reached by tube to Lambeth North or Elephant & Castle, and is open Monday to Saturday from 10 a.m. to 5:50 p.m., on Sunday from 2 to 5:50 p.m. Admission is free. Public film shows take place on weekends at 3 p.m. and on certain weekdays during school holidays and on public holidays. Various special exhibitions are mounted at different times. The museum is closed on Good Friday, Christmas Eve, Christmas Day, Boxing Day, New Year's Day, and May bank holiday.

COURTAULD INSTITUTE GALLERIES: Woburn Square, W.C.1, contain the following collections: the Lee collection of old masters; the Gambier-Perry collection of early Italian paintings and sculptures, ivories, majolica, and other works of art; the great collection of French impressionist and post-impressionist paintings (masterpieces by Monet, Manet, Degas, Renoir, Cézanne who is represented by eight paintings, Van Gogh, Gauguin) brought together by the late Samuel Courtauld; the Roger Fry collection of early 20th-century English and French painting; the Witt collection of old master drawings; the Spooner collection of English watercolors, and the recent bequest of the Princes Gate collection of superb old master paintings and drawings, especially Rubens, Michelangelo, and Tiepolo. The galleries are air-

conditioned, and some of the paintings are shown without glass. Hours are Monday to Saturday from 10 a.m. to 5 p.m., on Sunday from 2 to 5 p.m. Admission is £1.50 ($2.65) for adults, 50p (90¢) for students or children. The galleries are near the Euston Square, Goodge Street, and Russell Square Underground stations.

WALLACE COLLECTION: Manchester Square, W.1 (tel. 935-0687). Gathered in a palatial setting (the modestly described "town house" of the late Lady Wallace) are a contrasting array of artists and armaments. The former (mostly French) include Watteau, Boucher, Fragonard, and Greuze, as well as such classics as Frans Hals's *Laughing Cavalier* and Rembrandt's portrait of his son, *Titus*.

The arms, European and Oriental, are shown on the ground floor and are works of art in their own right. Superb inlaid suits of armor, some obviously more for parade than battle, are exhibited together with more businesslike swords, halberds, and magnificent Persian scimitars. The crescent sabres were reputedly tested by striking the blade against a stone, then examining it for even the minutest dent. If one was found, the sword was rejected.

The paintings of the Dutch, English, Spanish, and Italian schools are outstanding. The collection also contains one of the most important groups of French 18th-century works of art in the world, including furniture from a number of royal palaces, Sèvres porcelain, and gold boxes.

Take the tube to Bond Street or Baker Street or buses to Oxford Street (Selfridges). It is open Monday to Saturday from 10 a.m. to 5 p.m. and on Sunday from 2 to 5 p.m.; closed Christmas Eve, Christmas Day, Boxing Day, New Year's Day, Good Friday, and the first Monday in May. Admission is free.

HAYWARD GALLERY: Opened by Queen Elizabeth II in 1968, this gallery, South Bank, S.E.1 (tel. 928-3144), presents a changing program of major exhibitions. The gallery forms part of the **South Bank Centre,** which also includes the Royal Festival Hall, the Queen Elizabeth Hall, the Purcell Room, the National Film Theatre, and the National Theatre. Admission to the gallery varies according to exhibitions, from £1.50 ($2.65) to £3 ($5.25), with cheap entry all day Monday and from 6 to 8 p.m. on Tuesday and Wednesday. Hours are Monday through Wednesday from 10 a.m. to 8 p.m.; on Thursday, Friday, and Saturday from 10 a.m. to 6 p.m.; and on Sunday from noon to 6 p.m. The gallery is closed between exhibitions, so check the listings before crossing the Thames. For recorded information, phone 261-0127. Tube: Waterloo Station.

SCIENCE MUSEUM: Exhibition Road, S.W.7 (tel. 589-3456). This museum traces the development of both science and industry, particularly their application to everyday life.

Exhibits vary from models and facsimiles to the actual machines. You'll find Stephenson's original *Rocket,* the tiny locomotive that won a race against all competitors and thus became the world's prototype railroad engine. The earliest motor-propelled airplanes, a cavalcade of antique cars, steam engines from their crudest to their most refined form. Greatest fascinators are the working models of machinery (visitor-operable by pushbuttons). Recent additions are the Exploration of Space gallery, the Chemical Industries gallery, and the Plastics gallery, which tells the story of plastic from its invention to the present day. The museum also has a "launch pad," a hands-on gallery of experiments and demonstrations in technology and science. The museum is open Mondays to Saturdays from 10 a.m. to 6 p.m., on Sunday from 2:30 to 6 p.m. Admission is free. Take the tube to South Kensington or bus 14.

NATIONAL PORTRAIT GALLERY: Visitors have a chance to outstare the stiff-necked greats and not-so-greats of English history in this portrait gallery on St. Martin's Place, W.C.2 (tel. 930-1552); entrance around the corner from the National Gallery on Trafalgar Square. In a gallery of remarkable and unremarkable pictures, a few paintings tower over the rest, including Sir Joshua Reynolds's first portrait of Samuel Johnson ("a man of most dreadful appearance").

Among the best are Nicholas Hilliard's miniature of a handsome Sir Walter Raleigh and a full-length Elizabeth I (painted to commemorate her visit to Sir Henry Lee at Ditchley in 1592), along with the Holbein cartoon of Henry VIII (sketched for a family portrait that hung, before it was burned, in the Privy Chamber of Whitehall Palace). There is a portrait of William Shakespeare (with gold earring, no less) by an unknown artist but bearing the claim of being the "most authentic contemporary likeness" of its subject of any work known. The John Hayls portrait of Samuel Pepys is here, as is a portrait of Whistler, no mean painter in his own right.

One of the most unusual pictures in the gallery—a group portrait of the three Brontë sisters (Charlotte, Emily, and Anne)—was painted by their brother, Branwell. An idealized portrait of Lord Byron by Thomas Phillips is pleased with itself, and you can treat yourself to the likeness of the incomparable Aubrey Beardsley. For a finale, Princess Diana is on the Royal Landing.

The admission-free gallery is open from 10 a.m. to 5 p.m. Monday to Friday, to 6 p.m. on Saturday, and from 2 to 6 p.m. on Sunday. Tube: Charing Cross or Leicester Square.

APSLEY HOUSE WELLINGTON MUSEUM: At 149 Piccadilly, W.1, this was the mansion of the Duke of Wellington, one of Britain's greatest generals and one of her prime ministers. The "Iron Duke" defeated Napoleon at Waterloo, but later, for a short period, had to have iron shutters fitted to his windows as a protection from the mob. His temporary unpopularity soon passed, however.

The house is crammed with art treasures, military mementos, and a regal china and porcelain collection. You can admire the duke's medals, the array of field marshal's batons, the battlefield orders, plus three original Velázquez paintings among a score of other greats. One of the features of the museum is a colossal marble statue of Napoleon by Canova in the vestibule. It was a present from the grateful King George IV.

Take the tube to Hyde Park Corner. The museum is open Tuesday to Sunday from 11 a.m. to 6 p.m.; closed Monday. Admission is £2 ($3.50) for adults, £1 ($1.75) for children.

NATIONAL ARMY MUSEUM: Royal Hospital Road, Chelsea, S.W.3 (tel. 730-0717). We may abhor war in all its forms, but there's no doubt that it makes for fascinating viewing. The National Army Museum occupies a building adjoining the Chelsea Hospital (a thoughtful combination, this, but not intentional).

Whereas the Imperial War Museum is concerned only with wars in the 20th century, the National Army Museum tells the colorful story of British armies from 1485. Here you'll find the rainbow uniforms British soldiers wore in every corner of the world and many of the items they brought back. Included is the regional flag of a Connecticut unit captured in the War of 1812. The skeleton of Napoleon's favorite charger is here too. Displayed also is the actual battle order which—through its hazy wording—launched the lunatic and heroic Charge of the Light Brigade at Balaklava.

A permanent exhibition is called "From Flanders to the Falklands." The perspective here ranges from the trenches of the western front in the so-called Great War, from the "Tommy Atkins" of 1914 to the national service soldiers of the 1950s, and from the beaches of Dunkirk to the hills overlooking Port Stanley.

In all, here are weapons, the gear, the colors and medals Britain's soldiers wore, and some of the magnificent paintings that glorified them.

Take the tube to Sloane Square. The admission-free museum is open Monday to Saturday from 10 a.m. to 5:30 p.m. and on Sunday from 2 p.m. to 5:30 p.m. It's closed on New Year's Day, Good Friday, December 24 through 26, and the May bank holiday. The cafeteria is open from 10:30 a.m. to 4:15 p.m.

NATIONAL POSTAL MUSEUM: King Edward Building, King Edward St., E.C.1 (tel. 432-3851). This museum attracts philatelists and even vaguely kindred spirits. Actually part of the Post Office, it features permanent exhibitions of the stamps of Great Britain and the world and special displays of stamps and postal history, changing every few months according to certain themes.

For example, recent displays have included one on "Travelling Post Offices" and one on how stamps are produced.

The museum is open from 10 a.m. to 4:30 p.m. Monday through Thursday, to 4 p.m. on Friday. Admission is free. Tube: St. Paul's or Barbican.

LONDON TRANSPORT MUSEUM: A collection of historic vehicles is displayed in a splendid Victorian building which formerly housed the Flower Market at Covent Garden, W.C.2 (tel. 379-6344). The museum shows how London's transport system evolved, and exhibits include a representative collection of road vehicles, featuring a reconstruction of George Shillibeer's Omnibus of 1829.

Nearly two centuries of London's public transport are represented by these historic buses, trams, trolleybuses, locomotives, rolling stock, posters, models, working exhibits, and audio-visual displays. A steam locomotive which ran on the world's first underground railway, a knifeboard horse bus, the "B" type motor bus, London's first trolleybus, and the Feltham tram are of particular interest. One of the features of the exhibition is the number of participatory exhibits, which are unique and popular with visitors. These allow visitors to operate the controls of a tube train, a tram, a bus, and full-size signaling equipment.

The museum is open every day of the year except December 24, 25, and 26 from 10 a.m. to 6 p.m. (last entrance at 5:15 p.m.). Admission charges are £2.40 ($4.20) for adults, £1.10 ($2) for children. There is free admission to the museum shop which sells a range of unusual and attractive souvenirs. Tube: Covent Garden.

HAMPSTEAD: Standing on a ridge overlooking the City of London and the River Thames, **Hampstead Heath** encompasses 785 acres of wild royal parkland about 4 miles north from the cen-

ter of London, and the village of Hampstead, plus other small en-
claves on the rim of the heath, are an important part of London. Its
features vary from formal park to woodland to heath and
meadowland to ponds. There are a wide variety of recreational facilities ranging from athletics to a small zoo. The heath draws hundreds of visitors each year for the walks, views, and traditional
Bank Holiday fairs.

Hampstead Village, especially since the coming of the Underground (Northern Line) in 1907, has been a favorite residential area for literary figures (H. G. Wells, John le Carré, Kingsley
Amis) and other notables (Freud, actress Gracie Fields). Even before that time, however, it was transformed from a village which
grew up amid substantial mansions into a fashionable spa of the
18th century and counted among its residents the painter John
Constable, Shelley, Keats, and many other eminent persons.

History-rich pubs offer good stopping places after visits to the
two mansions, Kenwood House (the Iveagh Bequest, a 17th-
century house filled with period furniture and paintings by Turner, Rembrandt, Vermeer, and Gainsborough) and Fenton House,
which are fine architectural examples, as well as to the house once
lived in by Keats or Freud's last home. Tube: Hampstead Heath.

A stone's throw east from Hampstead Heath is Highgate Village, where **Highgate Cemetery** is the main drawing card, containing, among others, the grave of Karl Marx, architect of
Communism. Tube: Highgate.

CLERKENWELL: London's "hidden village," Clerkenwell,
just to the north of Clerkenwell Road and east of Farringdon
Road, has been carefully restored, so that a visit to its green and to
the Gatehouse of St. John and the museum, as well as to the fascinating little shops and workshops is worth the time. Tube:
Farringdon.

Close by is the **London Charterhouse,** of historic importance since its foundation in 1350, and Smithfield, London's great
meat market and scene of the burning of religious dissidents in the
time of the Tudors. Tube: Barbican.

ORGANIZED TOURS

Given unlimited time, the stamina of a veteran jogger, plus
permanent good weather, the ideal way to see the sights of London would, of course, be on foot. And there are sections—such as
Soho and the actual City—which can't be seen any other way. At
least not properly.

But if you have to budget your time and still want to get as
much London as possible for your money, there's an enormous

variety of touring arrangements at your fingertips, including by bus, by car, by boat.

I'll give you a quick run-down of a few sample tours. Each of them has several variations, expanding or telescoping the amount of sightseeing involved. If the particular tour I happen to mention doesn't quite suit your particular schedule, the organization involved will be glad to list alternatives.

ORIGINAL LONDON TRANSPORT SIGHTSEEING TOUR: For the first-timer, the quickest and most economical way to bring the big city into focus is to take a two-hour, 20-mile circular tour of the West End and the City of London on the guided Original London Transport Sightseeing Tour, which passes virtually all the major places of interest in central London. Operated by London Transport Tours, part of the city's official bus company, the journeys leave at frequent intervals daily from Victoria, Piccadilly Circus, Marble Arch, and Baker Street. Tickets cost £6 ($10.50) for adults and £4 ($7) for children and are available from the conductor. Tickets can also be purchased from London Regional Transport Travel Information Centres, where you can get a discount of £1 ($1.75) off each ticket. Locations of the travel centers are listed under "Transportation in Greater London," Chapter III.

LONDON'S WEST END AND THE CITY: If you want a detailed look at the city's sights, then **London Transport** offers two highly regarded conducted coach tours.

For a look at the West End, a three-hour tour is offered, passing Westminster Abbey (guided tour), Houses of Parliament, Horse Guards, Changing of the Guard at Buckingham Palace, Trafalgar Square, and Piccadilly Circus.

London Transport's other popular three-hour tour is of the City, and includes guided trips to the Tower of London and St. Paul's Cathedral. The fare for the Westminster and Changing of the Guard tour is £10 ($17.50) for adults and £8 ($14) for children under 14. For the City and Tower tour, the cost is £14.50 ($25.50) for adults, £12 ($21) for children under 14. The City tour leaves at 2 p.m. Monday through Saturday from March to October. For about three months during the summer the tour also runs on Sunday.

These two tours are also combined to form the London Day tour, which costs £28 ($49) for adults and £24 ($42) for children under 14, including lunch.

The tours begin at London Transport's own Wilton Road coach station, alongside Victoria train station. To reserve seats or for information, phone 227-3456, or go to a London Transport Travel Information Centre.

LONDON PRIDE SIGHTSEEING TOUR: A 90-minute panoramic **Grand Tour of London** aboard double-decker buses (open top in summer) is offered by London Pride, taking in all the sights and with a commentary. Buses run at least every 30 minutes beginning daily at 10 a.m., and run until late, so this is a good way to see London at night when many of the buildings are floodlit. Buses leave from near Piccadilly Circus, outside the Trocadero on Coventry Street. Just show up and jump on. Tickets cost £5 ($8.75) for adults, £2 ($3.50) for children. For information, call 0708/86-5656 day or night. London Pride tours are operated by Ensign Bus Services Ltd. in Essex.

HARRODS SIGHTSEEING BUS: A double-decker bus in the discreet green-and-gold livery of Harrods, the **Luxury Observation Coach,** takes sightseeing tours around London's attractions. The first departure from door 8 of Harrods in Brompton Road is at 10 a.m., and there are also tours at 1 and 4 p.m. Tea, coffee, and orange juice are served on board. The tour costs £12 ($21) for adults, £7.50 ($13.25) for children under 12. All-day excursion tours to Bath, Windsor, Stratford-upon-Avon, and around all of London are also available. You can purchase tickets at the desks either on the store's fourth floor or on the ground floor by door 8. You can obtain information by telephoning Harrods at 730-1234 or 581-3603.

THE THAMES BY NIGHT: An evening River Thames cruise by **Frames Rickards,** 11 Herbrand St., W.C.1 (tel. 837-3111), leaves Herbrand Street at 7 p.m. on Wednesday and Sunday from June to the end of September. Adult fare is £20 ($35), inclusive of a light supper.

A VIEW FROM ABOVE: Sightseeing trips over London by helicopter are available from **UK Air Taxis,** Westland Heliport, Lombard Road, S.W.11 (tel. 228-3232), with panoramic and unforgettable views over the city, past Greenwich, and to within sight of the Thames Barrier. Departures are only between April and October and leave every Thursday after 10 a.m. in as many 15-minute blocks as are scheduled and reserved for that day. The cost is £45 ($78.75) per person. Call for departure information and reservations.

CANAL CRUISES: The London canals were once major highways. Since the Festival of Britain in 1951, some of the traditional painted canal boats have been resurrected for Venetian-style trips through these waterways.

One of them is the *Jason,* which takes you on a 90-minute trip through the long Maida Hill tunnel under Edgware Road, through Regent's Park, the Mosque, the Zoo, Lord Snowdon's Aviary, past the Pirate's Castle to Camden Lock, and returns to Little Venice. The season begins Good Friday and lasts through September. During April and May, the boats run at 12:30 and 2:30 p.m. In June, July, August, and September, there is an additional trip during the afternoon, but always telephone first. A Boatman's Basket salad lunch can be enjoyed on the 12:30 and 2:30 p.m. trips, as well as a cream tea on the 4:30 p.m. voyage. Refreshments are served on all trips. The fare is £2.95 ($5.25) for adults, £1.75 ($3) for children.

To inquire about bookings, get in touch with **Jason's Trip,** opposite 60 Blomfield Rd., Little Venice, W.9 (tel. 286-3428). Advance booking is essential in season.

Also offered are one-way trips to Camden Lock on Saturday and Sunday to enable passengers to view the flea market and craft shops. Passengers may finish the trip there or return to Little Venice on a later boat.

ORGANIZED LONDON WALKS: John Wittich, who owns
J.W. Travel, 66 St. Michael's St., W.2 (tel. 262-9572), started walking tours of London in 1960. He is a Freeman of the City of London and a member of two of the ancient guilds of London, as well as having written several books on London walks. He is also director of the London History Fellowship. There is no better way to search out the unusual, the beautiful, and the historic than to take a walking tour. The company concentrates on personal walking tours for families and groups who have booked in advance. John Wittich conducts all tours. The cost for 1½-hour walks is £10 ($17.50) for a family of up to four adults, while groups are charged £30 ($52.50) for up to 20 adults.

Hunt for ghosts or walk in the steps of Jack the Ripper. Retrace the legal system through the Inns of Court. Visit peaceful Hampstead or elegant Mayfair. Investigate the London of Shakespeare, Dickens, and Sherlock Holmes, or taste the delights of an evening's drinking in four historic pubs. These and many other walks are included in the program of unusual and historical walks organized by **London Walks,** 10 Greenbrook Ave., Hadley Wood, Herts EN4 OLS (tel. 882-2763). Walks take place on weekends throughout the year and also during the week from April to October. The cost is £2.50 ($4.50) for adults, £2 ($3.50) for students with ID cards. Children under 16 go free. No reservations are required.

Another small and enthusiastic company, a husband-and-wife team offering a vast variety of London walks, is **Discovering London,** operated by a Scot, Alex Cobban, a historian of some note whose guides are professionals. Mainly on Saturday and Sunday, but sometimes during the week, scheduled walks are planned, starting at easily found Underground stations, to Dickens's London, Roman London, Ghosts of the City, the Inns of Court–Lawyers' London, and Jack the Ripper. No advance booking is necessary, and the walks cost £2.50 ($4.50). Children under 16 go free, and students with ID cards are charged £2.25 ($4). Each walk takes about 1½ to 2 hours, except for the pub tours, which are usually in the evening and allow time for drinking in interesting pubs. Write, enclosing an international reply coupon, for a detailed schedule of the walks available during your stay in London. The address is Discovering London, 11 Pennyfields, Warley, Brentwood, Essex CM14 5JP (tel. 0277/21-3704).

THE HOMES OF THE GREAT

There is, unfortunately, no conducted tour catering to one of the most popular pursuits for visitors: viewing the birthplaces or working abodes of great historical figures. The map of London is peppered with them, but only the home of Charles Dickens gets included in the regular sightseeing jaunts.

Over the years the Historical Society has marked most of these sites with the characteristic blue-and-white plaques that now adorn thousands of London buildings, telling you which celebrity lived there, when, and for how long. But you still have to track them down for yourself. I have therefore compiled a selective list of some of the most sought-after sites, with the idea of saving you some leg work. But please remember that the following is merely a sampling from a register that could be as big as a city telephone book. I'm bound to have left out somebody's particular hero, and for this I apologize and plead lack of space.

William Blake, artist and poet, 74 Broadwick St., Soho.

James Boswell, biographer of Samuel Johnson, 122 Great Portland St., W.1.

Elizabeth Barrett Browning, poet, 50 Wimpole St., W.1.

Robert Browning, poet, 19 Warwick Crescent, W.2.

Samuel Taylor Coleridge, poet, 71 Berners St., W.1.

Daniel Defoe, author of *Robinson Crusoe,* 95 Newington Church St., N.16.

Benjamin Disraeli, statesman, 19 Curzon St., W.1.

George Eliot (actually Mary Ann Cross), novelist, 4 Cheyne Walk, S.W.3.

Benjamin Franklin, statesman and scientist, 36 Craven St., W.C.2.

Thomas Gainsborough, painter, 82 Pall Mall, S.W.1.

John Galsworthy, novelist, Grove Lodge, Hampstead.

Mahatma Gandhi, statesman, Kingsley Hall, Powis Road, E.3.

George Frederick Handel, composer, 25 Brook St., W.1.

John Keats, poet, Keats House, Keats Grove, N.W.3.

Rudyard Kipling, poet and novelist, 43 Villiers St., W.C.2.

Horatio Nelson, naval hero, 103 New Bond St., W.1.

Isaac Newton, scientist, 87 Jermyn St., W.1.

Florence Nightingale, pioneer of modern nursing, 10 South St., N.W.1.

Dante Gabriel Rossetti, artist and poet, 16 Cheyne Walk, Chelsea.

Percy Bysshe Shelley, poet, 20 Nelson Square, S.E.1.

Arthur Sullivan, composer (Gilbert and Sullivan), 58 Victoria St., S.W.1.

William Makepeace Thackeray, novelist, 36 Onslow Square, S.W.7.

John Wesley, founder of Methodism, 47 City Rd., Finsbury.

Richard Whittington, London's most celebrated mayor and cat owner, 20 College Hill, E.C.4.

Finally I have the astonishingly famous address of a man who never was: 221b Baker Street, as most people know, was the place where Sherlock Holmes occupied "furnished lodgings." But a startling number of folks never accepted the fact that the pipe-puffing sleuth didn't exist outside the imagination of his creator, Arthur Conan Doyle. The company actually on the premises, the Abbey National Building Society, has a special switchboard operator to answer the 60 or more calls a week from people wanting to become clients of the illustrious detective. She tells most of them that Mr. Holmes is currently out of the country and therefore can't take their case. "And Dr. Watson?"

"Oh, he is with him, naturally."

ALONG THE THAMES

There is a row of fascinating attractions lying on, across, and alongside the River Thames. All of London's history and development is linked with this winding ribbon of water. The Thames connects the city with the sea, from which it drew its wealth and its power. For centuries the river was London's highway and main street.

Some of the bridges that span the Thames are household words. London Bridge, which—contrary to the nursery rhyme—has never "fallen down," but has been dismantled and shipped to the United States, ran from the Monument (a tall pillar commemorating the Great Fire of 1666) to Southwark Cathedral, parts of which date back to 1207.

Its neighbor to the east is the still-standing **Tower Bridge,** E.1 (tel. 407-0922), one of the city's most celebrated landmarks and possibly the most photographed and painted bridge on earth. Its outward appearance is familiar to Londoners and visitors alike, and it is that same bridge that a certain American thought he'd purchased instead of the one farther up the river.

Tower Bridge, in spite of its medieval appearance, was built during 1886–1894 with two towers 200 feet apart, joined by footbridges that provide grass-covered walkways for the public, who can enter the north tower, take the elevator to the walkway, cross the river to the south tower, and return to street level. It's a photographer's dream, with interesting views of St. Paul's, the Tower of London, and in the distance, a part of the Houses of Parliament. You can also visit the main engine room with its Victorian boilers and steam-pumping engines that used to raise and lower the roadway across the river.

There are models showing how the 1,000-ton arms of the bridge can be raised in 1½ minutes to allow ships passage upstream. These days the bridge is only opened four or five times a week, and you'll be lucky to catch the real thing. You'll know if it's going to open, however, as a bell sounds throughout the bridge and road traffic is stopped. Admission is £2 ($3.50) for adults, £1 ($1.75) for children. It's open daily in summer from 10 a.m. to 6:30 p.m. (to 4:45 p.m. in winter). For more information, call 407-0922.

The piece of river between the site of the old London Bridge and Tower Bridge marks the city end of the immense row of docks stretching 26 miles to the coast. Although most of them are no longer in use, collectively they have long been known as the Port of London.

But the Thames meant more to London than a port. It was also her chief commercial thoroughfare and a royal highway, the only regal one in the days of winding cobblestone streets. Every royal procession was undertaken by barge, gorgeously painted and gilded vessels, which you can still see at the National Maritime Museum in Greenwich. All important state prisoners were delivered to the Tower by water: it eliminated the chance of an ambush by their friends in one of those narrow, crooked alleys surrounding the fortress.

When Henry VIII had his country residence at Hampton Court, there was a constant stream of messenger boats shuttling between his other riverside palaces all the way to Greenwich. His illustrious daughter, Queen Elizabeth I, revved up the practice to such a degree that a contemporary chronicler complained he couldn't spit in the Thames for fear of hitting a royal craft.

The royal boats and much of the commercial traffic disappeared when the streets were widened enough for horse coaches to maintain a decent pace. But a trip up or down the river today will give you an entirely different view of London from the one you get from dry land. You'll see exactly how the city grew along and around the Thames and how many of her landmarks turn their faces toward the water. It's like Manhattan from a ferry.

There are pleasure launches sailing from Charing Cross and Westminster piers from April to September. You can take them upstream, past the Houses of Parliament, to Kew, Richmond, and Hampton Court. The downstream journey takes about 50 minutes and ends at Greenwich.

The multitude of small companies operating boat services from Westminster Pier have organized themselves into the **Westminster Passenger Service Association,** Westminster Pier, Victoria Embankment, S.W.1 (tel. 930-4097). Boats leave the pier for cruises of varying lengths throughout the day and evening.

Particular note should be taken of the striking removal of pollution from the Thames in the past few decades. The river, so polluted in the 1950s that no marine life could exist in it, can now lay claim to being "the cleanest metropolitan estuary in the world," with many varieties of fish, even salmon, back as happy denizens of the waters.

THE THAMES FLOOD BARRIER: Since its official opening in 1984, the engineering spectacle known as the Thames Flood Barrier has drawn increasing crowds to the site, at a point in the river known as Woolwich Reach in east London, where the Thames is a straight stretch about a third of a mile in width. For centuries the Thames estuary has from time to time brought tidal surges, which have on occasion caused disastrous flooding at Woolwich, Hammersmith, Whitehall, Westminster, and elsewhere within the river's flood reaches. The flooding peril has increased during this century from a number of natural causes. These include the unstoppable rise of tide levels in the Thames, surge tides from the Atlantic, and the down-tilt of the country of some 12 inches a century. Also, London is sinking at about that same rate into its clay foundations.

All this led to the construction, beginning in 1975, of a great barrier with huge piers linking mammoth steel gates, smaller rising sector gates, and falling radial gates, all of which when in use make a solid steel wall about the height of a five-story building, which completely dams the waters of the Thames, keeping the surge tides from passage up the estuary. The gates are operated every month or so to remove river silt and to be sure the operation is smooth.

London Launches offers trips to the barrier, operating from Westminster Pier. Four trips sail daily in summer at 10 and 11:15 a.m. and at 1:30 and 2:45 p.m. Except on the last trip, passengers can get off at the barrier pier, visit the Barrier Centre, and return by a later boat or by bus. An audio-visual show depicting the need for the barrier and its operation is presented at the center, where there are also a souvenir shop, a snackbar, and a cafeteria. Round-trip fare from Westminster Pier is £3.50 ($6.25) for adults, £2 ($3.50) for children. For further information, phone 740-8263.

LONDON DOCKLANDS:
What was a dilapidated wasteland in eight square miles of property surrounded by water—some 55 miles of waterfront acreage within a sailor's cry of London's major attractions—has been reclaimed, restored, rejuvenated, whatever, until now London Docklands is coming into its own as a leisure, residential, and commercial lure.

Included in this complex are Wapping, the Isle of Dogs, the Surrey and Royal Docks, and more, all with Limehouse at its heart. The former urban wasteland of deserted warehouses and derelict wharves and the many facilities already completed can be visited by taking the **Dockland Light Railway,** which links the Isle of Dogs and London Underground's Tower Hill station, via several new local stations. To see the whole complex, take the railway at the Tower Gateway near Tower Bridge for a short journey through Wapping and the Isle of Dogs. You can get off at Island Gardens and then cross through the 100-year-old Greenwich Tunnel under the Thames to see the attractions at Greenwich.

A regular water-bus service connects Greenwich with Charing Cross in a river voyage of about half an hour, and other tunnels are planned to link the Docklands with port points and motorways. An STOL airport in the old Royal Docks area should be in operation by the time of your visit, with service to major U.K. and European cities as well as the Channel Islands.

A visit to the **Exhibition Centre** on the Isle of Dogs gives an opportunity to see what the Docklands past, present, and future include. Already the area has given space for overflow from the City of London's square mile, and it looks as though the growth and development is more than promising.

A shopping Village at Tobacco Dock, a new home at Shadwell Basin for the Academy of St. Martin-in-the-Fields Orchestra, and the London Arena (largest man-made sport and leisure complex in the country) at the tip of the Isle of Dogs are being joined by luxury condominiums, offices, hotels, museums, theaters, and all the other amenities aimed at making the East End of London a shining star have been or soon will be completed.

A FLOATING MUSEUM: An 11,500-ton cruiser, H.M.S. *Belfast,* Morgan's Lane, Tooley Street (tel. 407-6434), is a World War II veteran now preserved as a floating naval museum. She is moored opposite the Tower of London, between Tower Bridge and London Bridge. During the Russian convoys and D-Day she saw distinguished service, and in the Korean War she was known as "that straight shootin' ship." Exhibitions both above and below deck show how sailors lived and fought over the past 50 years. H.M.S. *Belfast* can be explored from her bridge right down to her engine and boiler rooms seven decks below. The museum ship is open seven days a week from 11 a.m., with last boarding at 5:30 p.m. in summer, 4 p.m. in winter. Admission is £3 ($5.25) for adults, £1.50 ($2.65) for children. Refreshments are available. Nearest tube stops: Monument, Tower Hill, and London Bridge. A ferry runs from Tower Pier (weekends only in winter).

TWO SHIPS AT GREENWICH: Two other ships, both world famous, are at Greenwich, four miles east of London. You can make the trip faster by train from Charing Cross, but the leisurely journey downriver from Westminster Pier is definitely more enjoyable. The river launch chugs you past a full-length view of the imposing County Hall—London's equivalent of City Hall—the Royal Festival Hall, and the immense Shell Centre.

Rising from the Victoria Embankment is a tall white stone obelisk, popularly misnamed "Cleopatra's Needle." The pillar is, in fact, far older than Cleopatra and once stood in front of the temple of Heliopolis, erected sometime between 1600 and 1500 B.C. In 1878 it was presented to Britain by the khedive of Egypt and brought here in a ship specially fitted for the purpose. On its re-erection by the Thames, the Victorians couldn't resist adding some contemporary objects to the interior of the foundation stone. To wit: a Bible, a straight razor, several morning newspapers, a baby's feeding bottle, and a box of hairpins, presumably to impress whomever would excavate the site with the splendors of 19th-century civilization.

At Greenwich Pier, now in permanent drydock, lies the last and ultimate word on sailpower . . . the **Cutty Sark.** Named after the witch in Robert Burns's poem "Tam o'Shanter," she was the greatest of the breed of clipper ships that carried tea from China and wool from Australia in the most exciting ocean races ever sailed. Her record stood at a then unsurpassed 363 miles in 24 hours. Launched in Scotland in 1869, the sleek, black three-master represented the final fighting run of canvas against steam. Although the age of the clippers was brief, they did outpace the steamers as long as there was wind to fill their billowing mountain of sheets.

On board the *Cutty Sark* you'll find a museum devoted to clipper lore, plus all the fittings that made her the fastest thing at sea.

The admission is £1.20 ($2.10) for adults, 60p ($1.05) for children. The vessel may be boarded Monday to Saturday from 10:30 a.m. to 6 p.m. and on Sunday (and Good Friday) from noon to 6 p.m. It closes at 5 p.m. in winter.

Next to the clipper—and looking like a sardine beside a shark—lies the equally famous **Gipsy Moth IV.** This, in case you don't remember, was the ridiculously tiny sailing craft in which Sir Francis Chichester circumnavigated the globe . . . solo! You can go on board and marvel at the minuteness of the vessel in which the gray-haired old seadog made his incredible 119-day journey. His chief worry—or so he claimed—was running out of ale before he reached land. The admission to go aboard is 20p (35¢) for adults, 10p (18¢) for children under the age of 14. The *Gipsy* keeps the same hours as the *Cutty Sark,* and is usually closed on Friday.

THE SPORTING SCENE

London can be as exciting for sports enthusiasts as for theater fans. That is, if they happen to be *British* sports enthusiasts.

The trouble is that Britain's two main sporting obsessions—soccer and cricket—are respectively unknown and incomprehensible to the average American visitor.

Soccer is the national winter sport. The teams that set British pulses racing—Chelsea, Leyton Orient, Tottenham Hotspurs—sound like so many brands of cheese spread to a Statesider.

In summer there is cricket, played at Lord's or Oval Cricket Ground in London. During the international test matches between Britain and Australia, the West Indies, or India (equivalent in importance to the World Series), the country goes into a state of collective trance, hanging glassy-eyed on every ball as described over the radio or TV.

Cricket is a game of infinite skill and subtlety and—to the initiate—a source of unending delight and occasional bursts of high passion. (The closest England and Australia ever came to going to war against each other was during the so-called body-line cricket scandal of the 1930s.) But it's not what you might call a fast game. Decisions fall in a matter of hours (unless postponed by rain) and our average American may be slumbering peacefully by the time the last embattled wicket topples.

Luckily, there are a number of sports and events that can be shared by all transatlantic visitors.

At the **All England Lawn Tennis & Croquet Club** at Wimbledon, you can see some of the world's greatest tennis players in action. The annual championship Fortnight comprises the last week in June and the first in July, with matches lasting from about 2 p.m. till dark. Although the British founded the All England Lawn Tennis & Croquet Club back in 1877, they now rarely manage to win against the Australian and American latecomers to the game. Take the tube to Southfields Station, then a special bus from there. The gates open at 11:30 a.m.

Attracting all equestrians is the annual **Horse of the Year Show** in the Wembley Arena. This takes place in October and consists of six days of jumping, riding teams, men's and women's championships, and team competitions. Matinees are at 1:30 p.m., evening shows at 7 p.m. Take the tube to Wembley Park.

Within easy reach of central London, there are horse-racing tracks at **Kempton Park, Sandown Park,** and the most famous of them all, **Epsom,** where the Derby is the main feature of the summer meeting. Racing takes place both midweek and on weekends, but not continuously. Sometimes during the summer there are evening race meetings, so you should telephone **United Racecourses Ltd.,** Epsom, Surrey (tel. 03727/26311) for information of the next meeting at Epsom, Sandown Park, or Kempton Park. You can drive yourself or, if you want to travel by rail, phone 928-5100 in London for details of train services.

Finally, we come to a spectacle for which it is difficult to find a comprehensive tag. The **Royal Tournament,** which takes place in mid-July for a 2½-week run, is one of London's longest-running shows. For more than 110 years this military tattoo has been thrilling the public with its special blend of color, pageantry, and seat-edge excitement. It's a cross between a military and a sporting display put on by the three British services, plus foreign visiting displays.

The show includes the massed bands presenting stirring music, the Royal Navy field gun competition, the Royal Air Force with their dogs, the Royal Marines in action, the King's Troop Royal Horse Artillery, the Household Cavalry, and many other spectacular acts.

There are two performances daily, at 2:30 and 7:30 p.m., at Earl's Court Exhibition Centre, Warwick Road, S.W.5. There are no performances on Sunday and no matinees on Monday. Seats cost from about £5 ($8.75) upward. For tickets and other information, write to the Royal Tournament Exhibition Centre, Warwick Road, London S.W.5 (tel. 373-8141). For any other information, get in touch with the Royal Tournament, Horse Guards, Whitehall, London S.W.1. (tel. 930-4288).

CHAPTER VII

A LONDON SHOPPING SPREE

□ □ □

When Prussian Field Marshal Blücher, Wellington's stout ally at Waterloo, first laid eyes on London, he allegedly slapped his thigh and exclaimed, "Herr Gott, what a city to plunder!"

He was gazing at what, for the early 19th century, was a phenomenal mass of shops and stores, overwhelming to Herr Blücher's unsophisticated eyes. Since those days, other cities have drawn level with London as shopping centers, but none has ever surpassed her.

London's shopping world today is a superbly balanced mixture of luxury and utility, of small personalized boutiques and giant department stores, of junk-heaped market stalls and breathtakingly elegant specialty shops.

As for bargains—that magic word in every traveler's dictionary—they are everywhere, but likely to be limited by the U.S. Customs regulations.

According to the latest rules, you—and everyone traveling with you—are entitled to bring back $400 worth of foreign-made merchandise without paying U.S. duty. This applies only to goods actually accompanying you. You can quite legitimately stretch that amount by mailing gifts back from abroad. No gift, however, can be worth more than $50, and you are not permitted to send more than one present per day to the same address.

Many London shops will help you beat the whopping purchase tax levied on much of England's merchandise. By presenting your passport, you can frequently purchase goods tax-free, but only on condition that:

□ You either have your purchase sent directly to your home address or

□ You have it delivered to the plane you're taking back.

The huge purchase taxes imposed on so-called luxury goods are responsible for the extremely high cost of items such as wines, spirits, tobacco, cigarettes, and gasoline.

When bargain-hunting, zero in on those goods that are manufactured in England and liable to cost a lot more when exported to America. These are—above all—men's and women's suits, woolens, tweeds, overcoats, scarves, tartans, bone china, cutlery, and prints, plus specialties such as antiques, rare books, and those magnificent old world and city maps in most bookstores.

SHOPPING DISTRICTS

London stores keep fairly uniform hours, mostly shorter than their American equivalents. The norm is a 5:30 p.m. closing, with a late Wednesday or Thursday night, until 7 p.m. Most central shops close Saturday around 1 p.m. They don't, however, go in for the French-style lunch-hour closing.

Any minor hindrances are more than compensated for by the tact, courtesy, and patience you'll meet in English shops, coupled—in some of the smaller establishments—with an almost courtly sense of pride in craftsmanship.

London's retail stores tend to cluster in certain areas, a hangover from the times when each guild or craft had its own street. This is what gives a London shopping spree its special flavor: you head in a certain direction to find a certain style of merchandise.

Herewith, I present a very rough outline of the main shopping districts (not including the "Two Singular Shopping Districts," which I will detail below):

REGENT STREET: Curving down elegantly from Oxford Circus to Piccadilly Circus, this stylish thoroughfare is crammed with fashionable stores, selling everything from silks to silverware. It has both department stores and boutiques, but the accent is on the medium-size establishment in the upper-medium price range.

OXFORD STREET: *The* shopping drag of the metropolis, it runs from St. Giles Circus to Marble Arch, an endless, faceless, totally uninspiring but utility-crammed band of stores, stores, and yet more stores. It contains six of London's major department stores, apart from just about every kind of retailing establishment under the sun.

PICCADILLY: Unlike the circus, the street Piccadilly is distinctly in the upper bracket, specializing in mouthwatering automobile showrooms, travel offices, art galleries, plus London's poshest grocery store, Fortnum & Mason.

BOND STREET: Divided into New and Old, Bond Street connects Piccadilly with Oxford Street and is synonymous with the luxury trade. Here are found the very finest—and most expensive—of tailors, hatters, milliners, shoe stores, sporting goods, and antiques.

KNIGHTSBRIDGE: Together with Kensington and Brompton Roads, this forms an extremely svelte shopping district south of Hyde Park. It's patronized for furniture, antiques, jewelry, and Harrods department store.

THE STRAND: Stately, broad, and dignified, the Strand runs from Trafalgar Square into Fleet Street. It's lined with hotels and theaters, and a selection of specialty stores you could spend a whole day peeking into.

SHOPPING ARCADES

Running off the above streets are a dozen or so arcades, housing some of the most exclusive and intriguing shops and boutiques in London. The best-known arcade of all is the . . .

BURLINGTON ARCADE: This is a glass-roofed, Regency-style passage leading off Piccadilly, looking like a period exhibition. It has been celebrated in several music hall ditties (to wit: "I'm Burlington Bertie, I rise at ten-thirty, and I saunter along like a toff . . .").

Lit by wrought-iron lamps, decorated with clusters of ferns and flowers, it makes shopping feel like strolling through a classy hotel lobby. Goods here, naturally, aren't cheap. The small, smart stores specialize in lines such as high fashions, jewelry, Irish linen, camera equipment, stationery, pipes and smoking accessories, and model soldiers.

TOP DEPARTMENT STORES

London has some 25 department stores, nearly all of them in the centers listed above. Shopping emporiums tend to look alike the world over, but London boasts at least two for which you'll find no parallels anywhere. Some American counterparts may be larger, some Parisian ones may be older, and some German and Scandinavian ones more streamlined, but both of the following enterprises have a unique touch of their own that no one has so far succeeded in copying.

Harrods, Brompton Road, Knightsbridge, S.W.3 (tel. 730-1234), is London's—indeed Europe's—top store. Harrods is really an institution, and visitors to the city come to view it as a sightseeing attraction, like the Tower of London. Some of the goods displayed for sale are works of art, and so are the departments displaying them. The sheer range and variety of merchandise is dazzling, from silver and pewter ware to clothing, from food to furs, from pianos to delicatessen. Every department seems to have had a different architect, but each one unmistakably carries Harrods's distinctive stamp of the best quality, taste, and décor. The store has undergone refurbishment to restore it to the elegance and luxury of the '20 and '30s.

You have a choice of ten restaurants and bars at Harrods. The fourth floor is devoted to leisure. Here, there is a Toy Kingdom with everything a child could want, from the latest video games to a large collection of traditional teddy bears. Other departments include an American Ice Cream Parlor, the first in-store one in the country; a jewelry department; a fantastic sports department called "Olympic Way," a huge complex which has brought together sports equipment and fashionable sports clothing and accessories for dozens of different sports in one department; and the redesigned "Way In" Department for the younger customers. Tube: Knightsbridge.

Much more economical, however, is **Selfridges,** on Oxford Street, W.1 (tel. 629-1234), one of the biggest department stores in Europe, with more than 500 divisions selling everything from artificial flowers to groceries. The specialty shops are particularly enticing, with good buys in Irish linen, Wedgwood, leather goods, silver-plated goblets, cashmere and woolen scarves. There's also the Miss Selfridge Boutique, for the young or those who'd like to be. To help you travel light, the Export Bureau will air-freight your purchases to anywhere in the world, completely tax free. In the basement Services Arcade, the London Tourist Board will help you find your way around London's sights with plenty of maps, tips, and friendly advice. Tube: Bond Street.

Liberty & Company Limited, Regent Street, W.1 (tel. 734-1234), is renowned worldwide for selling high-quality, stylish merchandise in charming surroundings. Its flagship store on Regent Street houses six floors of fashion, fabrics, china, and home furnishings, plus the Oriental department in the basement. As well as the famous Liberty Print fashion fabrics, furnishing fabrics, scarves, ties, luggage, and gifts, the shop sells well-designed high-quality merchandise from all over the world. Liberty offers a personal "corner shop" service with helpful and informed assistants selling it's stylish and often unique merchandise. Tube: Oxford Street.

Simpson's, 203 Piccadilly, W.1 (tel. 734-2002), opened in 1936 as the home of DAKS clothing, and it's been going strong ever since. It is known not only for men's wear, but women's fashions, perfume, jewelry, and lingerie. Its basement-level men's shoe department, for example, is a model of the way quality shoes should be fitted. Many of the clothes are light-hearted, carefully made, and well suited to casual elegance. More formal clothing is also sold, always by staff who seem to be polite and thoughtful. A restaurant serves fine English food. Tube: Piccadilly Circus.

The world's most elegant grocery store, **Fortnum & Mason Ltd.,** 181 Piccadilly, W.1 (tel. 734-8040), down the street from the Ritz, draws the carriage trade, the well-heeled dowager from Mayfair or Belgravia who comes seeking such tinned treasures as pâté de foie gras or a boar's head. She would never set foot in a regular grocery store, but Fortnum & Mason, with its swallow-tailed attendants, is no mere grocery store: it's a British tradition dating back to 1707. In fact, the establishment likes to think that Mr. Fortnum and Mr. Mason "created a union surpassed in its importance to the human race by the meeting of Adam and Eve."

In the Mezzanine Restaurant, you can mingle at lunch with the caviar and champagne shoppers. The pastries are calorie-loaded but divine. The chocolate and confectionery department is on the ground floor. The Fountain Restaurant has both store and street entrances (Jermyn Street), and is open from 9:30 a.m. until 11:30 p.m. Monday to Saturday for the benefit of theater-goers. The St. James's Room Restaurant on the fourth floor is open during normal store hours. Tube: Piccadilly Circus.

TWO SINGULAR SHOPPING STREETS

If London has unique department stores, it also has a couple of equally unique streets. The first one achieved such legendary fame abroad that you owe yourself a visit. I'm talking, of course, about . . .

CARNABY STREET: Just off Regent, Carnaby is a legend, and legends take time to build. Often, by the time they are entrenched, fickle fashion has moved on elsewhere. Alas, Carnaby Street no longer dominates the world of pacesetting fashion as it did in the '60s. But it is still visited by the young, especially punkers, and some of its shops display lots of claptrap and quick-quid merchandise. For value, style, and imagination in design, the Chelsea

(King's Road) and Kensington boutiques have left Carnaby far behind.

KING'S ROAD: The formerly village-like main street of Chelsea, although still the cutting edge for fashion trends, has undergone yet another metamorphosis: the trendies of the '70s who replaced the hippies of the '60s have been pushed aside by the punk scene. Numerous stores sporting American clothes have sprung up along its length.

King's Road starts at Sloane Square (with Peter Jones's classy department store) and meanders on for a mile before losing its personality and dissolving into drabness at a sharp bend appropriately known as World's End.

Along the way, you'll see the tokens of Chelsea's former claims to fame: cozy pubs, smart nightclubs and discos, coffee bars, cosmopolitan restaurants, and possibly the most casually attractive of London's "Beautiful People."

The leap of King's Road to the mod throne in the late '60s came with the advent of designer Mary Quant, who scored bull's eyes on the English as well as the world's fashion target. Ms. Quant is no longer there, but what seems like myriad others have taken her place.

More and more, however, King's Road is becoming a lineup of markets and "multistores," large or small conglomerations of in- and outdoor stands, stalls, and booths fulfilling half a dozen different functions within one building or enclosure. They're springing up so fast that it's impossible to keep them tabulated.

STREET MARKETS

Markets are considerably more ancient than shops as a retailing medium. Most of the Old World's large cities began as market towns, and in London you still have a few thriving survivors of the open-air trading tradition. They're great fun to visit, even if you don't plan on buying anything. But I'm willing to bet that you'll go home with something . . . anything.

PETTICOAT LANE: The most popular of London markets, this functions only on Sunday morning. There's furious bargaining for every conceivable kind of object, from old clothing to brand-new "antiques," the air vibrating with voices, canned and human. It's no place for hangover victims, but a gas otherwise. Take the tube to Liverpool Street Station.

PORTOBELLO ROAD: A magnet for collectors of virtually everything, this Saturday event occasionally turns up real treasures at bargain prices. Only don't take the stallholder's word for it that the mildewed fiddle he's holding is a genuine Stradivarius left to him in the will of his Italian great-uncle. It might just as well have been "nicked" from an East End pawn shop. You can browse around jewelry, weapons modern and antique, toys, kitchenware, scientific instruments, china, books, old cigarette cards, movie posters, magazines long defunct, watches, pens, music boxes. . . .

Anyway, take the tube to Ladbroke Grove, then turn east, and the best of finder's luck to you.

BERWICK STREET MARKET: This may be the only street market in the world that is flanked by two rows of strip clubs, porno stores, and adult movie dens. Don't let that put you off, however. Humming six days a week in the scarlet heart of Soho, this array of stalls and booths sells probably the best and cheapest fruit and vegetables in town. It also sells ancient records that may turn out to be collectors' items, tapes, books, and old magazines. It's in action from 8 a.m. to 5 p.m. Monday through Saturday.

NEW CALEDONIAN MARKET: Commonly known as the **Bermondsey Market** because of its location on the corner of Long Lane and Bermondsey Street. At its extreme east end, it begins at Tower Bridge Road. This is one of Europe's outstanding street markets in size and quality of goods offered. The stalls are well known, and many dealers come into London from the country. The market gets under way on Friday at 5 a.m. (take a flashlight, as the light is poor at that early hour), before the Underground opens. Antiques and other items are generally lower in price here than at Portobello Road and the other street markets, but bargains are gone by 9 a.m. The market closes at noon. It's best reached by taking the Underground to London Bridge, then bus 78 or walk down Bermondsey Street.

LEATHER LANE: A daily market, reached by taking the tube to Chancery Lane, it's open Monday to Friday from 11 a.m. to 3 p.m. At this lively market, you'll find a good variety of items for sale: fruit from carts, vegetables, books, men's shirts and sweaters, and women's clothing. There are no try-ons at this outdoor market.

ANTIQUE MARKETS

GRAYS and **GRAYS IN THE MEWS ANTIQUE MARKETS:** These two, at 58 Davies St. and 1-7 Davies Mews, W.1 (tel. 629-7034), just south of Oxford Street and opposite Bond Street tube station, are in a triangle formed by Davies Street, South

Molton Lane, and Davies Mews. The two old buildings have been converted into walk-in stands with independent dealers. The term "antique" here covers items from oil paintings to, say, the 1894 edition of the *Encyclopaedia Britannica*. Also sold here are exquisite antique jewelry, silver, gold, antiquarian books, maps and prints, paintings and drawings, bronzes and ivories, arms and armor, Victorian and Edwardian toys, furniture, art nouveau and art deco, antique luggage, antique lace, scientific instruments, craftsmen's tools, and Oriental, Persian, and Islamic pottery, porcelain, miniatures, and antiquities. There is also a whole floor of repair workshops and a Bureau de Change.

ALFIES ANTIQUE MARKET: This is one of the cheapest covered markets in London, and it's where the dealers come to buy. It's at 13–25 Church St., N.W.8 (tel. 723-6066). Alfies is named after the father of Bennie Gray, the owner of Grays and Grays in the Mews and former owner of the Antique Hypermarket, Kensington, and Antiquarius. The market has increased in size until it is the largest covered antique market in Europe. Tube: Edgware Road.

ANTIQUARIUS: At 135–141 King's Rd. and 15 Flood St., S.W.3 (tel. 351-5353), Antiquarius echoes the artistic diversity of King's Road. More than 200 standholders offer specialized and general antiques of all periods from ancient times to the 1950s, including statuary and metalwork, early domestic and craftsmen's tools, timepieces, silver and silver plate, precious and costume jewelry, period clothes, lace, theatrical items, porcelain, glass, early writing and travel accessories, tiles, ethnic items, Delft and faïence, antiquarian books and prints, fine paintings, and small furniture. It's open Monday to Saturday from 10 a.m. to 6 p.m. Tube: Sloane Square. Bus 11, 19, or 22 will also take you there, or you can travel on bus 137, alighting at Sloane Square.

CHENIL GALLERIES: At 181–183 King's Rd., S.W.3 (tel. 351-5353), Chenil offers a blend of fine art and antiques set in spacious surroundings. A permanent exhibit of an Epstein statue reflects the long association with the arts which is also recorded on a rotunda mural. Here you can find 17th- and 18th-century paintings, long case clocks, scientific instruments, antiquarian books, prints and maps, fine porcelain, silverware, art nouveau and deco items, jewelry, boxes, chess sets, fine period furniture, and objets d'art. Here also you'll find Oriental carpets, collector's dolls, and teddy bears. The gallery also contains the Chenil Garden Restaurant which serves food throughout the day and the Chenil Art Gallery with changing exhibitions of contemporary art. It's open Monday to Saturday from 10 a.m. to 6 p.m. Tube: Sloane Square.

COVENT GARDEN

After four centuries the most famous market in all England—possibly all Europe—has gone suburban, Covent Garden, London's legendary fruit, vegetable, and flower market, has followed the lead of Les Halles in Paris and shifted to more contemporary but less colorful quarters south of the River Thames. The move relieves some of the wild congestion it generated, but a lot of memories are left behind.

In 1662 Samuel Pepys, a diarist, watched a Punch and Judy show there and was so impressed that he brought Mrs. Pepys along for the next performance. And, of course, Professor Higgins met Eliza Doolittle under the portico of St. Paul's Church in Covent Garden. George Bernard Shaw spent weeks eavesdropping around the market to catch the sound of Eliza's 'orrible Cockney, which he then immortalized in *Pygmalion,* alias *My Fair Lady.*

The new Covent Garden has developed into an impressive array of shops, pubs, and other attractions. The following are places that have caught my interest.

Contemporary Applied Arts, 43 Earlham St., W.C.2 (tel. 836-6993), is an association of craftspeople that is pioneering in its energetic encouragement of contemporary art work, both traditional and progressive. The galleries at the center are used to house a diverse retail display of members' work that includes glass, rugs, lights, ceramics for both use and decoration, fabric, clothing, paper, metalwork, and jewelry, all selected from the work of the most outstanding artisans currently producing in the country. There is also a program of special exhibitions that focuses on innovations in the crafts. These are lone or small group shows from the membership. Many of Britain's best-established makers are represented, as well as promising, lesser-known ones. The center is open Monday to Friday from 10 a.m. to 5:30 p.m., on Saturday from 11 a.m. to 5 p.m.

The **Covent Garden General Store,** 111 Long Acre, W.C.2 (tel. 240-0331), offers thousands of ideas for gifts and souvenirs at reasonable prices. It is ideally situated in Covent Garden, and because of the entertainment nature of the area, the store offers extended trading hours: from 10 a.m. to midnight Monday to Saturday, and 11 a.m. to 7 p.m. Sunday. The store also features The Green & Pleasant soup-and-salad restaurant.

At 21 Neal St., W.C.2 (tel. 836-5254), the **Natural Shoe Store** sells all manner of comfort and quality footwear from Birkenstock to the best of the British classics.

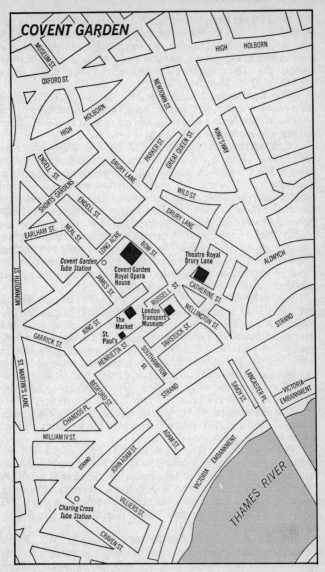

COVENT GARDEN

Neal Street East, 5 Neal St., W.C.2 (tel. 240-0135), is a vast shop devoted to Oriental or Orient-inspired merchandise. Here you can find artificial flowers, pottery, baskets, chinoiserie, and toys, as well as calligraphy, modern and antique clothing textiles, and jewelry. There is also an extensive cookware section and a bookshop. Open Monday to Saturday.

The **Tea House,** 15a Neal St., W.C.2 (tel. 240-7539), is a shop devoted to tea and "tea-phernalia," which includes anything associated with tea, tea drinking, and tea time. It boasts 45 different teas and more than 250 teapots.

Coppershop, 48 Neal St. W.C.2 (tel. 836-2984), offers the widest range of exclusively English-manufactured copper goods in Britain. For the kitchen, you'll find jelly molds depicting lions, unicorns, fruit, whatever . . . along with hard-wearing frying and omelet pans, plus more exotic sauté pans, pomme Anna pans, and zabaglione pans. In addition to fish kettles, jardinières, and traditional coal scuttles, ideal as flowerpot holders, Coppershop has copper clocks, lamps, ship's lanterns, ice buckets, trays, watering cans, and much else besides. The shop is run by Sally and Michael Crosfield, and they will airmail your goods home at a low cost, because on exports they can deduct the VAT and put this against postage. A mail-order catalog is available.

Naturally British, 13 New Row (by Covent Garden), W.C.2 (tel. 240-0551), specializes in items handmade in Britain and displayed on excellent antique furniture of oak, pine, yew, and fruitwood. Naturally British aims to present the best of contemporary craftworks from many fields: pottery, jewelry, glass, clothes from Ireland, Wales, and Scotland, cosmetics, rocking horses, games, puzzles, painted firescreens, and iron works, as well as soft toys. There is a wide range of prices. Open Monday to Saturday from 10:30 a.m. to 6:45 p.m. (and on Sunday in summer).

The Glasshouse, 65 Long Acre, W.C.2 (tel. 836-9785), sells beautiful glass and also invites visitors into the workshops to see the craftspeople producing their wares.

Penhaligon's, 41 Wellington St., W.C.2 (tel. 836-2150), is a Victorian perfumery established in 1870, holding a Royal Warrant to H.R.H. the Duke of Edinburgh. It offers a large selection of perfumes, after-shave, soap, and bath oils for men and women. Perfect gifts include antique silver perfume bottles. It is also at 20a Brook St., W.1.; 55 Burlington Arcade, W.1; 69 Moorgate, E.C.2; and 4 Knights Arcade, S.W.1.

The **Royal School of Needlework,** 5 King St., W.C.2 (tel. 240-3186), offers in kit form many of the classic tapestry designs bequeathed to them by such designers as Burne-Jones and William Morris. The kits also include the wools and instructions. A good stock of books on the subject of needlework as well as materials are for sale. The school's shop is open Monday to Friday from 10 a.m. to 5:30 p.m., on Saturday to 4 p.m.

Off Neal Street runs a narrow road leading to **Neal's Yard,** a mews of warehouses which seem to retain some of the old London atmosphere. The open warehouses display such goods as vegetables, health foods, fresh-baked breads, cakes, sandwiches, and, in an immaculate dairy, the largest variety of flavored cream cheeses you are likely to encounter.

At the top of Burleigh Street, off the Strand, beside the old Flower Market, is the **Covent Garden Flea Market,** in the old Jubilee Hall (a Victorian wholesale vegetable market). This is a real browser's paradise, with its good, bad, and indifferent clothing, fruit, and vegetables . . . you name it. The stalls are mainly under cover, and stall holders range from the aristocratic through punk. Specialty days are Monday for antiques and atticana, Saturday and Sunday for arts and crafts.

OTHER LEADING SHOPS

ARTS AND CRAFTS: A public body, the **Crafts Council,** 12 Waterloo Pl., S.W.1 (tel. 930-4811), exists to promote crafts in England and Wales. It has galleries which offer a broad program of changing crafts exhibitions from British domestic pottery to American traditional patchwork. Most exhibitions are free; otherwise, concessions are available. Other facilities include a lively information center which can direct you to crafts events throughout Britain, a slide library, and a bookstall. (*Note:* The Crafts Council runs a craft shop at the Victoria and Albert Museum, South Kensington.) The galleries and information center are open Tuesday to Saturday from 10 a.m. to 5 p.m., on Sunday from 2 to 5 p.m. Tube: Charing Cross or Piccadilly Circus.

BOOKS: Claiming to be the world's largest bookstore, **W. & G. Foyle, Ltd.,** 113–119 Charing Cross Rd., W.C.2 (tel. 439-8501), has an impressive array of hardcovers and paperbacks, including travel maps. The stock includes records, videotapes, and sheet music. Tube: Leicester Square.

BRASS RUBBING: Formerly at St. James's Church in Piccadilly, the **London Brass Rubbing Centre** is now at St. Martin-in-the-Fields Church, Trafalgar Square, W.C.2 (tel. 437-6023), in the big brick-vaulted 1730s crypt, alongside a brasserie restaurant, a bookshop, and a craft market, all additions to London's visitor attractions. The center has 70 exact copies of celebrated bronze portraits ready for use. Paper, rubbing materials, and instructions on how to begin are furnished. Classical music is played as visitors work at the task. The charges range from 50p (90¢) for a small copy to £12 ($21) for the largest, a life-size Crusader knight. The center is open all year except Christmas Day and Easter Thursday through Sunday from 10 a.m. to 6 p.m. Monday to Saturday, noon to 6 p.m. on Sunday. A gift area is open, selling brass-rubbing kits for children, budget-priced ready-made rubbings, plaques, a wide variety of books, souvenirs with a heritage theme, posters, and postcards. You can order a shield with your family coat-of-arms. For those who wish to make brass rubbings in the countryside churches, the center offers instructions and sells guidebooks and the necessary materials. Tube: Leicester Square.

BRITISH DESIGN: Regularly changing exhibitions on all aspects of British design are shown at **The Design Centre,** 28 Haymarket, S.W.1 (tel. 839-8000). In the refurbished Design Centre Shop, you can purchase items ranging from toys to household products to jewelry, bearing the black-and-white triangular label that says "Selected for The Design Centre, London." The café on the top floor sells a wide selection of refreshments and is ideal for morning coffee, a lunchtime snack, three-course meals, or pretheater drinks. The Design Centre is open from 10 a.m. to 6 p.m. on Monday and Tuesday, from 10 a.m. to 8 p.m. Wednesday to Saturday, and from 1 to 6 p.m. on Sunday. Tube: Piccadilly Circus.

CHINA: A wide range of English bone china, as well as crystal and giftware, is sold at **Lawleys,** 154 Regent St., W.1 (tel. 734-8184). The firm specializes in Royal Doulton, Minton, Royal Crown Derby, Wedgwood, Denby, and Aynsley porcelain; Webb Corbett, Stuart, Waterford, and Edinburgh crystal; and Lladrò figures. Tube: Piccadilly Circus or Oxford Street.

    Waterford-Wedgwood has a large shop at 249 Oxford St., W.1 (tel. 734-5656), at the corner of Regent Street. The staff there will explain their export plan to save you money on your souvenir buying. Besides selling tableware and glassware, the store offers inexpensive ashtrays in the traditional blue-and-white or sage-green-and-white. In any case, the store is like a miniature museum and well worth a visit. It also carries a collection of china, jewelry, pendants, earrings, and brooches. Tube: Oxford Circus. There are also Waterford-Wedgwood shops at 158 Regent St. and 173 Piccadilly.

    Goodes, 19 S. Audley St., Grosvenor Square, W.1 (tel. 499-2823), a fine glass and china shop with three Royal Warrants, has Minton majolica elephants gracing its front windows. The main entrance gives access through its famous mechanical doors.

The china, glass, and silverware are displayed in 14 showrooms. You can choose a small gift or purchase a unique dinner service with cresting and a monogram. A Goodes catalog is available. Tube: Hyde Park Corner.

CHOCOLATES:
What may be the finest chocolates in the world are made by **Charbonnel et Walker Ltd.,** 28 Old Bond St., W.1 (tel. 629-4396). They will send messages of thanks or love, spelled out on the chocolates themselves. The staff of this bow-fronted shop on the corner of the Royal Arcade off Old Bond Street will help you choose from the variety of centers. A box is priced according to what you decide to put in it. They have ready-made presentation boxes as well. Tube: Green Park.

CONTEMPORARY ART:
Originally established as a branch office of Christie's, specializing in modern art, **CCA Galleries,** 8 Dover St., W.1 (tel. 499-6701), in 1987 broke away from its illustrious mother. Today it offers etchings, lithographs, and screenprints by up-and-coming artists, priced from £35 ($61.25) to £200 ($350). It also offers major works by such world masters as Henry Moore. The gallery is considered innovative and creative even within the competitive world of London galleries. Tube: Green Park.

IRISH WARES:
Northern Ireland and the Republic of Ireland are united in the stock of a wide variety of stuff in a small area at the **Irish Shop,** 11 Duke St., W.1 (tel. 935-1366), and 80 Buckingham Gate, S.W.1 (tel. 222-7132). Directed by Charles Bruton and Anthony Tarrant, it sells only genuine articles. Prices are reportedly as close to those you'd pay in Ireland as possible. Merchandise ranges from china to woolens, from "tea-cosies" to Celtic-designed jewelry to Irish linen. Waterford crystal comes in all styles and types. Belleek china and Gaelic coffee glasses—single or in a set—are also featured. Women's suits and men's jackets in fine Donegal tweeds are offered. Duke Street is off Wigmore, a street running alongside Selfridges from Oxford Street. Tube: Bond Street or Oxford Circus.

Kilkenny, 150–151 New Bond St., W.1 (tel. 493-5455), established by the national design authority of Ireland, brings to London the finest fashions from young Irish designers for both men and women. Soft wools are blended with silks; knits are in jewel-like colors or the muted neutrals of nature, such as heathers, peats, and mosses. Traditional sportswear includes rugged Donegal jackets and knits for men and country wear for women. Irish linen is brought up-to-date in fashions or timelessly used for tables and beds. There are beautiful baby clothes in lace, crochet, and linen, as well as a fine selection of handmade pieces in sterling silver, wood, glass, and leather from the studios and workshops of artists and craftworkers in Ireland. Tube: Bond Street.

JEWELRY: A family firm, **Sanford Brothers Ltd.,** the jewelers at 3 Holborn Bars, Old Elizabethan Houses, E.C.3, (tel. 405-2352), has been in business since 1923. They sell anything in jewelry, both modern and Victorian, silver of all kinds, and a fine selection of clocks and watches. The Old Elizabethan buildings are one of the sights of Old London. Tube: Chancery Lane.

MEN'S CLOTHING: Long a name for quality men's wear, **Austin Reed,** 113 Regent St., W.1 (tel. 734-6789), offers both British and international designers. For example, the suits of Chester Barrie are said to fit like bespoke models. The battalions of polite employees are usually honest about telling you what looks good on you. The store always stocks top-notch but expensive cashmere jackets along with well-made, conventional clothes. Men can outfit themselves from dressing gowns to gloves to overcoats, but women will find a more limited selection of items. The Cue Shop is aimed at a young, fashion-conscious man-about-town. An entire floor, the third, is devoted to the clothing needs of women, with carefully selected suits, separates, coats, shoes, shirts, knitwear, and accessories. Tube: Piccadilly Circus.

At the **Man's Shops** at the London Hilton on Park Lane, W.1 (tel. 493-3740), a man can equip himself sartorially from neck to feet. The masculine boutique in the international arcade features subtly superb ties, cashmere and mink jackets, original shirts, alpaca slipovers with antelope-suede fronts, cufflinks of crafted silver, and the latest in belt designs. The shop has lounge suits and silk suits by famous makers like Chester Barrie and Brioni of Italy. You'll find Aquascutum raincoats, cashmere and vicuna cardigans, magnificent silk dressing gowns from India, brocaded braces, and a range of allied items, all with that custom-built look that somehow blends with Park Lane.

NOTIONS: A variety of toilet articles and fragrances is found at **Floris,** 89 Jermyn St., S.W.1 (tel. 930-2885). The floor-to-ceiling mahogany cabinets that line its walls are considered architectural curiosities in their own right. They were installed relatively late in the establishment's history (that is, 1851), long after the shop had received its Royal Warrants as suppliers of toilet articles to the king and queen. The business was established in 1730 by a Minorcan entrepreneur, Juan Floris, who brought from his Mediterranean home a technique for extracting fragrances from local flowers. Fashionable residents of St. James's flocked to his shop, purchasing his soaps, perfumes, and grooming aids. Today you can buy essences of flowers grown in English gardens, including stephanotis, rose geranium, lily of the valley, violet, Madagascar white jasmine, and carnation. Other items include cologne for gentlemen, badger-hair shaving brushes, ivory comb-and-brush sets, Chinese cloisonné, and combs made of horn. Tube: Piccadilly Circus.

OLD SILVER AND PLATE: A very special place is **Stanley Leslie,** 15 Beauchamp Pl., S.W.3 (tel. 589-2333). Behind a cramped and black-painted, big-windowed storefront lies a staggering array of Georgian, Victorian, and early 20th-century silver. It's just the place to spend hours ferreting around for a special present. The quality is high—and it's amazing that Mr. Leslie knows just what he's got there and how much is a fair price. He's a lovely London character, hovering ready to help in his glasses and jeweler's apron. Tube: Knightsbridge.

PHILATELY: Interested in stamps? The **National Postal Museum,** King Edward Building, King Edward Street, E.C.1 (tel. 432-3851), is open Monday to Thursday from 10 a.m. to 4:30 p.m., to 4 p.m. on Friday, and houses a magnificent collection of postage stamps and allied material. It also sells postcards illustrating the collection and has a distinctive Maltese Cross postmark first used on the Penny Black. Tube: St. Paul's.

PIPES AND TOBACCO: A pipe-smoker's paradise, **Astleys,** 109 Jermyn St., S.W.1 (tel. 930-1687), is masculine to the core. Apart from selling superb pipes (some of them special freehand models) and virtually every conceivable blend of their own tobaccos, Astleys features a kind of pipe museum, consisting of antique smoking utensils which tell the history of the ancient and noble art of "tobacco drinking." Briar pipes start at £18 ($31.50) and go upward. Tube: Piccadilly Circus.

POSTERS: A fine selection of posters is offered at the **London Transport Museum Shop,** Covent Garden, W.C.2 (tel. 379-6344), open daily from 10 a.m. to 5:45 p.m. except the Christmas holidays. This unique shop carries a wide range of posters, costing £2 ($3.50) to £6 ($10.50). The London Underground maps in their original size, as seen on every tube station, can be purchased here for £6 ($10.50). The shop also carries books, cards, T-shirts, and other souvenir items. Tube: Covent Garden.

RAINCOATS: Where else but **Burberry,** 18 Haymarket, S.W.1 (tel. 930-3343), near the London offices of American Express? The word Burberry has been synonymous with raincoats ever since King Edward VII publicly ordered his valet to "bring my Burberry" when the skies threatened rain. Its circa 1912 Haymarket store connects three lavishly stocked floors to an oak-lined staircase upon which have trod some of the biggest names in politics, the stage, and screen. An impeccably trained staff sells the famous raincoat, along with a collection of excellent men's shirts, sportswear, knitwear, and accessories. Raincoats are available in women's sizes and styles as well as men's. Don't think you'll get anything cheap from such a world-famous retailer. You'll get quality and prestige. Tube: Piccadilly Circus.

SOUVENIRS: Closely linked to Charles Dickens, **The Old Curiosity Shop,** 13–14 Portsmouth St., off Lincoln's Inn Fields, W.C.2 (tel. 405-9891), was used by the writer as the abode of Little Nell. One of the old Tudor buildings remaining in London, dating from 1567, the shop crams every nook and cranny with general knickknackery, whatnots, china, silver, pewter, prints, and souvenirs, even Dickens first editions. A popular item is an unframed silhouette of one of Dickens's characters. Horse brasses are also sold, as are Old Curiosity Shop bookmarks and ashtrays with Dickensian engravings. The shop is open every day of the week, including Sunday and holidays. Tube: Holborn.

SPORTS GOODS: Britain's biggest sports store, **Lillywhites Ltd.,** Piccadilly Circus, S.W.1 (tel. 930-3181), has floor after floor of sports clothing, equipment, and footwear. Established in 1863 and Europe's most famous sports store, Lillywhites offers everything connected with sport, together with new and exciting ranges of stylish and fashionable leisurewear for both men and women. For overseas customers, the Lillywhites Special Orders and International Departments offer a worldwide service. Tube: Piccadilly Circus.

WOOLENS: For top-quality woolen fabric and garments, go to **The Scotch House,** 84 Regent St., S.W.1 (tel. 734-0203), renowned worldwide for its comprehensive selection of cashmere and wool knitwear for both men and women. Also available is a wide range of tartan garments and accessories, as well as Scottish tweed classics. The children's collection covers ages 2 to 13 and also offers excellent value and quality. Tube: Piccadilly Circus. The Scotch House also has stores at 191 Regent St., W.1; 2 Brompton Rd., S.W.1; and 187 Oxford St., W.1.

Westaway & Westaway, opposite the British Museum at 62–65 Great Russell St., W.C.1 (tel. 405-4479), is a substitute for a shopping trip to Scotland. They stock an enormous range of kilts, scarves, waistcoats, capes, dressing gowns, and rugs in authentic clan tartans. What's more, they're knowledgeable on the subject of these minutely intricate clan symbols. They also sell superb—and untartaned—cashmere, camel-hair, and Shetland knitwear, along with Harris tweed jackets, Burberry raincoats, and cashmere overcoats for men. Tube: Tottenham Court Road. Another branch is at 92–93 Great Russell St., W.C.1.

Berk, at 46 Burlington Arcade, Piccadilly, W.1 (tel. 493-0028), is one of those irresistible "fancy shops" for which London is famous. The store is believed to have one of the largest collections of cashmere sweaters in London, at least of the top brands. And all this is displayed in the 150-year-old Burlington Arcade, an attraction in its own right. Tube: Piccadilly Circus.

CHAPTER VIII

THE THEATERS OF LONDON

□ □ □

London today is the theatrical capital of the world by any criterion you want to apply. It shows both more and better plays than any other city, enjoys a standard of acting unequaled anywhere, and holds a wide lead in both the traditional and the experimental forms of stagecraft.

This is partly, but only partly, because of a theatrical tradition going back well over 400 years. The city's first theater, in the Fields at Shoreditch, opened in 1576 under the patronage of Queen Elizabeth I. The following year saw the debut of the Curtain, and 1598 the most famous of all—the Globe. This was Shakespeare's and Marlowe's stage, and as long as the shrewd, tough, and efficient Queen Bess ruled England, the legitimate theater held its own against such rival attractions as bullbaiting, cockfighting, and public executions.

But from then on, the nation's dramatic glory suffered periodic declines which almost extinguished it, the first under Cromwell's official puritanism, which banned *all* stage performances (along with the celebration of Christmas) as "heathenish and un-Godly."

In more recent times, the causes lay in the social and moral rigidity Britain had acquired along with her Empire. At the turn of the century France became the country with the best theater. In the 1920s Germany took the lead. During the '30s the focus shifted to the United States, while England floundered in the most dismal theatrical shallows of her history, and turned out her worst movies to boot.

This doesn't mean that the country at any time lacked great playwrights, actors, or directors. But her stage and film craft had become largely removed from real life. It tended to reflect little beyond the stilted formalism of a thin upper-middle crust who went to the theater to admire their own petrified reflection in a kind of polite distortion mirror.

Attempts in earthier directions were rigorously sat upon by an official called the Lord Chamberlain, who had unlimited powers of censorship and used them like the proverbial "Little Old Lady from Dubuque." This Mandarin figure was responsible for the creation of London's theater clubs, which—being private rather than public stages—were outside his jurisdiction. One such club was specially founded to present Arthur Miller's *A View from the Bridge* to English audiences, who would have been deprived of this masterpiece otherwise.

The Great Thaw occurred some time during the mid-1950s, although it was more like a volcanic eruption. The pressures of talent, creativeness, and expressive urges had been building up ever since the war. Now they broke loose in a veritable lava stream of stage and film productions, which flooded the globe, swept away most of London's dusty theatrical mores, and swung open the gates of a second Elizabethan dramatic era.

Britain hasn't looked back since. The tide is still running, originality still rampant. No one can say for how long. So my advice is to use your stay in London for a theater orgy: you may never get opportunities like this again.

London's live stage presents a unique combination of variety, accessibility, and economy. No other city anywhere can currently boast a similar trio of advantages.

Variety is assured by the sheer number of productions on view. London currently has more than 35 active theaters, and this figure does not include opera, ballet, amateur stages, or the semi-private theater clubs mentioned earlier.

Accessibility, of course, is linked to the enormously wide choice available to patrons. With the exception of one or two smash hits, for which advance booking is advisable, you can literally walk up to any box office five minutes before the opening curtain and buy whatever seat you fancy. Compare this to the woes of Broadway, which features only two types of plays: those that flop and those you can't get into. Strangely enough, things are much tighter in the movie realm. You frequently have to book ahead or "queue up" for major film releases.

Finally, there's economy. London theater prices are—by U.S. standards—very reasonable. The **Leicester Square Half-Price Ticket Booth,** Leicester Square, W.C.2, sells theater tickets on the day of a performance for half price (cash only), plus a £1 ($1.75) service charge. It's open from noon to 2 p.m. for matinee performances and from 2:30 to 6:30 p.m. for evening performances. The staff there has a wide range of seats available. Obviously, tickets for "hits" are not available often. There is a long queue, but it moves quickly, and it's well worth the effort if you want to take in a lot of theater when you're in London. Saving money is important, naturally. The shows for which tickets are available are displayed at the booth, so you can make up your mind on what to see as you wait in the queue.

Apart from this, many London theaters offer additional trimmings in the shape of licensed bars on the premises and hot coffee during intermissions.

London theaters generally start and finish earlier than their American cousins. Evening performances are between 7:30 and 8:30, midweek matinees at 2:30 and 3 p.m., Saturday at 5:45 p.m.

For full details on West End productions, pick up a free biweekly *London Theatre Guide* at the Booth or at any West End theater, tourist or travel information center, hotel, or library on your arrival in London. Alternatively, if you want to receive details regularly, subscription is £20 ($35) per year. Write to the **Society of West End Theatre**, Bedford Chambers, The Piazza, Covent Garden, London WC2E 8HQ, U.K.

There are two weekly publications giving full entertainment listings, *Time Out* and *What's On in London,* available at newsstands and containing information on restaurants, theaters, and nightclubs.

THE THEATERS

Since it is quite impossible to describe all of London's live theaters in this space, I'll just pick out a few for your benefit. Don't forget, these are merely gleanings from a treasure trove:

ADELPHI: The Strand, W.C.2 (tel. 836-7611). This theater offers light comedies and musicals, mainly, but not exclusively. Performances are at 7:30 p.m. on weeknights. Matinees are on Wednesday at 2:30 p.m. and Saturday at 4:30 p.m. Tube: Charing Cross.

DRURY LANE, THEATRE ROYAL: Covent Garden, W.C.2 (tel. 836-8108). This is one of the oldest and most prestigious establishments in town, crammed with traditions, not all of them venerable. Nell Gwynne, the rough-tongued, well-stacked Cockney wench who became King Charles's mistress, used to have her orange pitch under the long colonnade in front. Nearly every star of the London stage heaven played here at some time. It has a wide-open repertoire, but leans toward musicals. Shows are at 8 p.m. Monday to Saturday, with matinees at 3 p.m. on Wednesday and Saturday. Take the tube to Covent Garden. Guided tours of this historic theater may be arranged through George Hoare, the theater historian for Stoll Moss theaters.

FORTUNE: Russell Street, W.C.2 (tel. 836-2238). Like the Drury Lane, this is part of the ancient and odd theater concentration around Covent Garden, an intimate theater of 440 seats. Shows are presented daily at 8 p.m., except on Saturday when two presentations are given, at 6 and 8:30 p.m. Tube: Covent Garden.

GLOBE: Shaftesbury Avenue, W.1 (tel. 437-1592). Only a name connection with Shakespeare's playhouse (which was down by the Thames), this is one of a row of theaters in the same street, leading off Piccadilly Circus. Dramas and comedies are presented. Check the daily press for shows and times of performances. Tube: Piccadilly Circus.

HER MAJESTY'S: Haymarket, W.1 (tel. 930-6606). Big, plush, and ornate, this is one of London's traditional homes for top musicals, standing in what used to be *the* street for mustached "toffs" and scarlet women. Shows daily are at 7:45 p.m., and matinees are presented on Wednesday and Saturday at 3 p.m. Tube: Piccadilly Circus.

MERMAID: Puddle Dock, E.C.4 (tel. 236-5568). Although this is one of London's newest theaters (reopened 1981), it stands on hallowed stage ground. Shakespeare's Globe rose on the opposite Bankside, and he bought a house in an adjoining alley for £140. The Mermaid is an entire complex: two riverside restaurants, a coffee bar in the foyer, and two other bars adjacent. Shows range from classics to comedies and musicals. After you take the tube to Blackfriars station, it's one minute's walk to the right.

NATIONAL THEATRE: South Bank, S.E.1 (tel. 928-2252 for the box office). This is the home of Britain's National Theatre, one of the greatest stage companies on earth. Not one, but three theaters, each radically different in design, all under the same roof, offer a wide mixture of plays: new works, revivals of ancient and modern classics, contemporary foreign plays, experimental drama. The theaters are the Olivier, the Lyttelton, and the Cottesloe. The building, with its bars, restaurants, buffets, foyers, river walks, and terraces, is a full-time theater center offering—alongside its main work—short, early-evening performances, poetry, live foyer music, bookshops, tours of the building, and exhibitions.

Tickets range from £6 ($10.50) to £13 ($22.75), but midweek matinees are cheaper. Some tickets are available on the day of the performance, at £6 ($10.50) and £8 ($14). You can have a meal in the National Theatre Restaurant for around £12 ($21), or at one of the coffee bars, a snack will cost around £3.50 ($6.25). Tube: Waterloo Station.

THE OLD VIC: This 170-year-old theater is on Waterloo Road, S.E.1 (tel. 928-2651, or the box office at 928-7616). The façade and much of the interior have been restored to their original early 19th-century style, and most of the modernization is behind the scenes. The proscenium arch has been moved back, the stage trebled in size, and more seats and stage boxes added. It is air-conditioned and contains five bars. It presents short seasons of varied plays, and several subscription offers have been introduced with reductions of up to £3 ($5.25) a seat if you purchase six tickets for different shows at once. Otherwise, top prices vary, with the best stalls or dress circle going for about £13.50 ($23.75) a ticket. Tube: Waterloo.

THE YOUNG VIC: At 66 The Cut, Waterloo, S.E.1 (tel. 928-6363), the Young Vic aims primarily at the 15 to 25 age group, but many older and younger people use the theater as well. The repertoire here includes such authors as Shakespeare, Ben Jonson, Arthur Miller, and Harold Pinter, plus specially written new plays. Performances normally begin at 7:30 p.m. Seats cost £7.50 ($13.25), reduced to £3.75 ($6.50) for students and children. Tube: Waterloo Station.

OPEN AIR: Regent's Park, N.W.1 (tel. 486-2431). As the name indicates, this is an outdoor theater, right in the center of Regent's Park. The setting is idyllic, and the longest theater bar in London provides both drink and food. Performances are given in June, July, August, and the first half of September, evenings at 7:45 p.m., with matinees on Wednesday, Thursday, and Saturday at 2:30 p.m. Presentations are mainly Shakespeare, usually in period costume. Both seating and acoustics are excellent. If it rains, you're given tickets for another performance. Prices are £4 ($7) to £10 ($17.50). Tube: Baker Street.

BARBICAN CENTRE: The **Royal Shakespeare Company** has

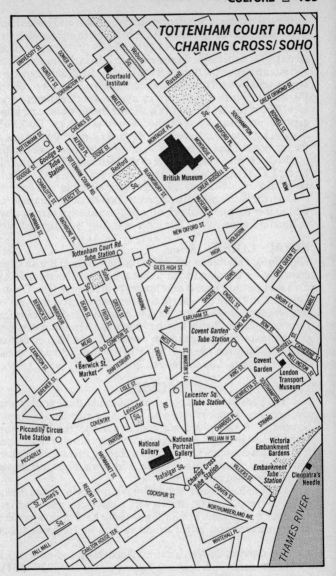

TOTTENHAM COURT ROAD/
CHARING CROSS/ SOHO

its famous theater in Stratford-upon-Avon but is also housed here in the Barbican Centre, E.C.2 (tube to Barbican or Moorgate; tel. 628-8795 in London or 0789/295-623 in Stratford-upon-Avon). This is the single theater group in Britain that most seriously concentrates on the theatrical works of the Bard, although it presents works by such relatively modern playwrights as Jean Genet. Plays run in repertoire and are presented two or three times a week each. The company also has two smaller theaters where new and experimental plays are performed as well as classics: The Other Place (a.k.a. the Swan) as well as the famous main theater (a.k.a. the Memorial Theatre), both in Stratford-upon-Avon. The company also occasionally leases space at the Mermaid Theatre, Puddle Dock, E.C.4 (tel. 236-5568; Tube: Blackfriars or St. Paul's). Dedicated theater addicts on a limited time schedule can arrange, through the Barbican Centre, a theater-hotel-restaurant-transportation junket for one fixed price for performances of certain plays at Stratford-upon-Avon. Transport is usually by chartered bus.

ROYAL COURT: Sloane Square, Chelsea, S.W.1 (tel. 730-1745). This theater ushered in the New Wave of British stagecraft when it presented John Osborne's (then) sensational *Look Back in Anger* in 1956. It now houses twin theaters. The Theatre Upstairs—60 steps up—is a theater concentrating on the work of new writers, open to the public. The main theater downstairs features new plays by better-known writers and new interpretations of the classics. Shows are at 8 p.m. weekdays, 4 and 8 p.m. on Saturday; 7:30 p.m. on weekdays and 3:30 p.m. and 7:30 p.m. for the Theatre Upstairs. Take the tube to Sloane Square.

MOVIES

The films shown in London are much like those you'd see in any large American city, but with a stronger international flavor. Screenings, however, are not continuous and the last performances start around 8 p.m., so you'd better consult a newspaper for the exact showtimes. Prices vary according to seats, all of them considerably cheaper than at home. And don't forget that movie theaters are called cinemas.

London has a dozen or so real movie palaces in the old meaning of the term, gigantic citadels with plush loges, grand buffets, and triple curtains. But her prime piece is the kind of ultra-modern movie mansion you might expect to find in Hollywood, but won't.

The **Cannon Cinema** is a streamlined, black-and-white block on Panton Street, off Leicester Square, S.W.1 (tel. 930-0631), housing four superb theaters under one roof. They share one sleekly plush lobby, but each runs a separate program, always including at least one European film. Tube: Leicester Square.

OPERA AND BALLET

You might be getting a little tired of superlatives, but in this particular chapter it's unavoidable. For in the operatic and ballet field as well as in legitimate theater, the British currently lead the world.

In a way this is rather strange, because historically neither singing nor dancing has been a particularly English talent. But over the past couple of decades (and with a strong influx of foreigners), both have developed in an almost breathtaking fashion.

The central shrine is the **Royal Opera House,** a classical building on Bow Street, W.C.2, actually the northeast corner of Covent Garden. Covent Garden was London's first square, originally laid out by Inigo Jones as a residential piazza. Until a few years ago the whole area was a thriving fruit and vegetable market, originally started by the nuns selling surplus stocks from their convent garden. In the 16th century the area became fashionable to live in and was soon to become one of the centers of London nightlife. The first theater was built on the present site in 1732. The existing opera house, one of the most beautiful theaters in Europe, was built in 1858 and is now the home of the Royal Opera and Royal Ballet, the leading international opera and ballet companies. Newspapers give full details of performances.

The Opera House advance box office, at 48 Floral St., W.C.2 (tel. 240-1066), is open from 10 a.m. to 8 p.m. Monday to Saturday. Seat prices range from £1 ($1.75) to £27.50 ($48.25) for ballet, £2 ($3.50) to £70 ($122.50) for opera.

The **Barbican Centre,** The Barbican, in the City, E.C.2, is considered to be Western Europe's largest art and exhibition center. It was created to make a perfect setting in which to enjoy good music and theater from comfortable and roomy seating. In addition to the theater, which, as stated, is the London home of the Royal Shakespeare Company, the concert hall is the permanent home of the London Symphony Orchestra and host to visiting players.

There are often lunchtime concerts, when the admission is £3 ($5.25) for the 45 minutes or so. Otherwise, seats are priced from £5 ($8.75) to £17.50 ($30.75) for the evening performances. Matinees in the theater cost £5.50 ($9.75) to £13.50 ($23.75). You can call the box office for seats for concerts and theaters (tel. 638-8891 or 628-8795). There are a number of bars, a self-service café, and a restaurant (see my restaurant recommendations, Chapter V). Tube: Barbican or Moorgate.

English National Opera (formerly Sadler's Wells), London Coliseum, St. Martin's Lane, W.C.2 (tel. 836-3161), features a wide range of opera—from Wagner and Verdi to Berlioz and Richard Strauss—usually in English. Ticket prices start as low as £4.50 ($8). Upper Circle seats, which are preferable, begin at £9.50 ($16.75). Tube: Charing Cross or Leicester Square.

Sadler's Wells Theatre, Rosebery Avenue, E.C.1 (tel. 278-8916 for the box office), is on a site where a theater has stood since 1683, a short walk from Camden Passage. Resident companies—Sadler's Wells Royal Ballet and the New Sadler's Wells Opera (producing light opera, operetta, and fresh productions of that most English of theatrical institutions, the work of Gilbert and Sullivan)—are complemented by a program of British and foreign dance, opera, and ballet. Seats are offered at prices ranging from £3.50 ($6.25) to £16.50 ($29). Performances generally begin at 7:30 p.m. Reach the theater by the Angel tube or bus 19 or 38 from Piccadilly, Charing Cross, or Holborn. A theater buffet (hot and cold) is open from 6:30 p.m. on performance days, from 1:30 p.m. on matinee days.

CONCERTS

In recent years the musical focal point has shifted to a superbly specialized complex of buildings on the South Bank side of Waterloo Bridge, called the **South Bank Centre,** at South Bank, S.E.1. It includes the Hayward Gallery and houses three of the most stylish, comfortable, and acoustically perfect concert structures in the world: the **Royal Festival Hall,** the **Queen Elizabeth Hall,** and the **Purcell Room.** Here, more than 1,200 performances a year are presented, and it's not all classical music: included are ballet, jazz, popular classics, pop, and folk. The Royal Festival Hall is open from 10 a.m. every day and offers an extensive range of things to see and do. There are free exhibitions in the foyers and free lunchtime music from 12:30 to 2 p.m., plus guided tours of the building, and book, record, and gift shops. The Festival Buffet has a wide selection of food at reasonable prices, and there are a number of bars throughout the foyers.

Tickets are available from the Royal Festival Hall box office (tel. 928-3191; for credit-card bookings, 928-6544), or booking agents. They usually range in price from £3.50 ($6.25) to £10 ($17.50).

London's oldest established concert auditorium is the **Royal Albert Hall,** Kensington Gore, S.W.7 (tel. 589-8212). Dating back to 1871, the building is a fine example of Victorian architecture on a grand scale. The design of the auditorium makes it equally suitable for meetings, conferences, tennis and badminton tournaments, boxing, wrestling, and a multitude of other activities apart from its renowned musical events. During the eight-week season of BBC Promenade concerts held each summer, up to 7,000 people gather together under this great dome and yet there is still an intimate atmosphere that has to be experienced to be appreciated. Ticket prices vary with the programs. Tube: South Kensington, High Street Kensington, or Knightsbridge.

Wigmore Hall, 36 Wigmore St., W.1 (tel. 935-2141). At this intimate auditorium, you'll hear excellent recitals and concerts. There are regular series, master concerts by chamber music groups and instrumentalists, song recital series, and concerts featuring special composers or themes throughout the year. There are nightly performances, plus Sunday Morning Coffee Concerts and also concerts on Sunday at 4 and 7 p.m. Many good seats are in the £4 ($7) range. A free list of the month's programs is available from the hall. Tube: Bond Street or Oxford Circus.

GILBERT AND SULLIVAN EVENINGS

The English Heritage Singers present Gilbert and Sullivan programs at the **Mansion House at Grim's Dyke,** Old Redding, Harrow Weald, Middlesex HA3 6SH (tel. 01/954-4227), every other Sunday in winter and every Sunday the rest of the year. This is a dinner event, costing £22.50 ($39.50) per person. You arrive for cocktails in the Library Bar of the house where Gilbert once lived and where he and Sullivan worked on their charming operettas—when they were at peace with each other. A full Edwardian-style dinner is served at 8 p.m., with costumed performances of the most beloved of Gilbert and Sullivan songs both during and after the meal. You can request your favorite melodies from the Gilbert and Sullivan works—the singers know them all.

CHAPTER IX

LONDON AFTER DARK

□ □ □

Midnight runs through the length and width of London's nightlife like an invisible Iron Curtain. The entire world of bright lights, in fact, can be divided into Pre and Post Midnight.

The division is achieved partly by the pub closing hour (11 p.m.) and the cessation of public transport (around midnight). But it is subtly reinforced by a tangled coil of bylaws, unwritten rules, precedents, and traditions laid down for one express purpose: to get the lower (i.e., working) orders into bed at what local magistrates still term "a respectable hour," so they would be bright and lively at work the next morning. The original purpose went the way of bloomers and spats, but the regulations remained, others were added, half of them were ignored, until the whole thing came to resemble a jigsaw puzzle of paragraphs assembled with the singular aim of driving travel writers to distraction.

Take the matter of clubs. In every other metropolis, from Buenos Aires to Tokyo, a club means the same thing and requires no further explanation. Not so in London. Here a club can mean virtually anything, depending on where it is, what it does, and how long it does it. A club can be a rigidly exclusive institution, vetoing prospective members like candidates for the diplomatic service. Or it can be as wide-open as a Reno gambling parlor, blithely disregarding its own rules as well as those laid down by the law . . . and getting away with it.

You cannot formulate an overall picture with the word "club"; each has to be dealt with individually. Some "nightclubs," for example, are clubs in name only, like their American counterparts. Others take their tag dead serious and rigorously exclude strangers, no matter how affluent. Some clubs stick to precise opening and closing hours; others regard them as a practical joke. Some clubs . . .

Anyway, this will give you an idea of the general situation. Which amounts to the fact that there is no *general* situation, only an encyclopedic mass of half-remembered, rarely enforced, occasionally applied ordinances with which you learn to live like you can learn to live with hay fever.

But don't let the above mislead you into thinking that London is in any way short of nightlife. It's there in vast quantities, except that some of it takes a little finding.

Geographically, about 90% of the bright lights burn in the area roughly defined as the West End. There are no great outer patches like Paris's Montmartre, San Francisco's North Beach, or Chicago's Old Town. The core of this region is Piccadilly Circus which, with Coventry Street running down to Leicester Square, resembles Broadway. To the north lies Soho, chockablock with entertainment in various hues of scarlet. To the east the theaterland of Covent Garden, to the south Trafalgar Square, and to the west the fashionable and expensive night world of Mayfair.

With a few widely scattered exceptions, this area encompasses all the nightlife of interest to visitors, most of the attractions within easy walking distance of each other. But there are a few peculiarities you should be warned about.

The midnight curtain mentioned earlier operates against *simple* nighttime pleasures. It prevents you, for instance, from just dropping into a place for a drink (you must have something to eat with a drink served after 11 p.m.). It doesn't prevent you, after hours, from paying a cover charge (frequently disguised as a membership fee) and enjoying a stage show, taking a spin on a dance floor, trying your luck at a gambling table, eating a five-course meal, and drinking yourself into oblivion.

If this sounds slightly wacky to you, be assured that it sounds precisely the same to some 20 million-odd English people.

Most of the places I'll take you to have some kind of front-door mumbo-jumbo that passes as membership enrollment. What it amounts to is a so-called temporary membership, which satisfies the letter (if not the spirit) of the law and enables you to get in without delay. In many cases the temporary membership fee is deducted from the cost of dinner. There is, however, no hard and fast rule.

At this point, however, I'll add a word for the benefit of male travelers. London's club world is full of "hostesses." Their purpose is to make you buy things—from drinks to dolls and cigarettes—and they can shoot up your tab to much more than you intended to spend.

London's recognized meeting spots, particularly for the younger set, are the ballrooms and discos, neither of which employ hostesses.

Now, moving from generalities to particulars, let's start swinging with . . .

SOME TOP CLUBS

Eve, 189 Regent St., W.1 (tel. 734-0557), is London's longest-established late-night club. Doyen of London's nightlife, owner Jimmy O'Brien launched it in 1953. Strip cabaret and erotic entertainment (at 1 a.m.) have replaced the floor shows previously presented. Dancing is to disco, alternating with live music of a high standard. Eve is open Monday to Friday from 10 p.m. to 3:30 a.m. Admittance is by membership only. There is an annual subscription of £5 ($8.75), but a special temporary membership for overseas visitors, valid for one night only, is available for £1 ($1.75). Only one person in a party need be a member, and overseas visitors may be admitted on application without waiting the customary 48 hours. There is an entrance fee or cover charge of £7 ($12.25) for a member and each guest. An à la carte menu is offered throughout the night. Charming and attractive young women, many of whom speak more than one language, are available as dining or dancing partners for unaccompanied men. Tube: Oxford Circus.

The **Royal Roof Restaurant,** Royal Garden Hotel, Kensington High Street, W.8 (tel. 937-8000), on the top floor of the hotel, is elegant and refined, and overlooks Kensington Gardens and Hyde Park. From your table you will see the lights of Kensington and Knightsbridge, with a view of London's West End skyline. In a romantic candlelit aura, you can dance to the resident band and enjoy a three-course dinner costing from £25 ($43.75). The restaurant is open from 7 p.m. to 1 a.m. Monday to Saturday (last orders taken at 11:30 p.m.). A live band plays for dancing. Reservations are necessary. Tube: High Street Kensington.

l'Hirondelle, Swallow Street, off Regent Street, W.1 (tel. 734-6666). Rather misnamed, for it doesn't in the least resemble the streamlined, functional swallow, the Hirondelle puts on some of the most lavishly gorgeous floor shows in town. What's more, it lets you dine, drink, and dance from 7:30 in the evening till 3:45 a.m. without the ceremonial "temporary memberships." Neither does it charge an entrance fee. The shows are really full-scale revues and come on at 11 p.m. and 1:30 a.m. It is closed on Sunday. Dancing is from 8 p.m. to two live bands. Dancing-dining partners are available. There is a minimum charge of £7.50 ($13.25) for nondiners, but the club offers a good meal for about £40

($70), and a bottle of wine costs from £21 ($36.75). Tube: Piccadilly Circus.

The Talk of London

A unique theater restaurant in a unique setting, that's the Talk of London, in the New London Centre, an entertainment complex at Parker Street, off Drury Lane, W.C.2, the heart and soul of the city's theaterland. The restaurant is ingeniously designed so that every guest gets "the best seat in the house." By using a circular layout and varying floor levels, everyone has an uninterrupted view of the show.

The Talk of London offers a complete evening's entertainment from 8 p.m. to 1 a.m.: a four-course dinner of your choice, dancing to the Johnny Howard orchestra, Europe's top show band, Afrodisiac, and an international cabaret at 10:30 p.m. All this and coffee, service, and VAT are included in the price of £22 ($38.50) Monday to Friday and on Sunday, and £24 ($42) on Saturday. Drinks are extra. For reservations, which are essential, phone 408-1001). Tube: Covent Garden/Holborn.

The **Rheingold Club** thrives in a century-old wine cellar at Sedley Place, just off 361 Oxford St., W.1 (tel. 629-5343), and has a restaurant, two bars, and a good-sized dance floor. The main attraction is a top-class band playing daily except Sunday and bank holidays from 9:30 p.m. to about 2 a.m. There is also an occasional cabaret, usually with big-time guest stars, but most of the entertainment is created by the patrons themselves. The Rheingold, founded in 1959, is the oldest and most successful "singles club" in London, existing long before the term had been coined. It is a safe place for men to take their wives or girlfriends, and respectable single women are welcome and safe here. The temporary membership you purchase at the club's reception desk includes admission for the first visit and costs £5 ($8.75) per person. There is also a one-night membership for £3 ($5.25). The club offers a tasty German dish called champignon-schnitzel, a tender escallop of Dutch veal served with rice and peas in a cream-and-mushroom sauce, costing £4.20 ($7.25). It has a strong German draft beer at 90p ($1.60) for a half pint and excellent French and German wines from £6 ($10.50) for an *appellation controlée* or *qualitaetswein* to £10 ($17.50) for château-bottled bordeaux or a Moselle Auslese. The club is open from 8 p.m. to 1:30 a.m. on Monday and Tuesday, to 2 a.m. on Wednesday, Thursday, and cabaret nights, and to 2:30 a.m. on Friday and Saturday. Take the tube to Bond Street station, use the main exit to Oxford Street, turn right and turn right again to Sedley Place. It's only 40 yards from the station.

CABARETS AND MUSIC HALLS

Cockney Cabaret and Music Hall, 18 Charing Cross Rd., W.C.2 (tel. 408-1001), recaptures the atmosphere of a Victorian music hall. At the whisky-and-gin reception, you'll have the cockles of your heart warmed and learn about "Mother's ruin" (large gins). The lively waiters and waitresses join the guests to sing along to the sounds of a honky-tonk piano. An East End meal, four courses of Cockney nosh, is served. Music to sing and dance by mark the evening. The show is divided into two parts, featuring cabaret with both production numbers and solo performances. The club charges £25 ($43.75) per person Wednesday to Friday, rising to £27 ($47.25) on Saturday. The club is open from 8 p.m. to midnight. Phone for reservations. Tube: Charing Cross.

The **Players Theatre** is located at the Duchess Theatre, Catherine Street, W.C.2 (tel. 839-1134; Tube: Aldwych), during preparation of their new theater on Villiers Street (probably to be occupied by 1989 or 1990). The Players is a Victorian music hall variety club. The acts are not takeoffs or imitations, but the real thing, authentic from the costumes to the backdrops. The effect on modern, allegedly blasé, audiences is overwhelming. This might just possibly be your best night in London.

The entire setting is delightful. You can start by having a sumptuously old-fashioned dinner in the adjoining restaurant, which forms part of the club. Or get snacks (liquid or biteable) served at your table during the show. The stage is a piece of pure Victoriana, but the emcee—here called the "chairman"—is in a class quite his own. He introduces each act, tells anecdotes, keeps up a running patter of remarks and asides to and about the audience, trades insults with the patrons (and he takes as good as he gives), and ceremonially welcomes "Visitors from the Colonies," meaning Americans, Canadians, Australians, and such-like.

The acts are the immortal music hall melodies and lyrics . . . and you'll be surprised at their immortality. You'll know at least half of them, except that you probably didn't suspect them of being 90 or so years old.

You can join the Players by filling out a form and paying a temporary membership fee of £8 ($14) for one week, £15 ($26.25) quarterly. Then you have to wait 48 hours for the membership to become effective. Incidentally, memberships must be paid in sterling. After that *you* go in free, but you have to pay extra for each guest you bring. Dinner, from £11 ($19.25), is served in the restaurant from 6 p.m. (book a table ahead). The show starts nightly at 8 p.m. There's a new program every two weeks.

The Water Rats, 328 Grays Inn Rd., W.C.1 (tel. 837-7269 for reservations), formerly The Pindar of Wakefield and Aba Daba, perpetuates the world of the Victorian music hall contained in a famous London pub since 1655. It is now the headquarters of the Grand Order of Water Rats, a charitable organization of Britain's top variety performers. The admission charge is £6 ($10.50) to the theater, where you can dine on traditional fare for an additional £8 ($14). Shows are presented on Thursday, Friday, and Saturday at 9:15 p.m. However, most visitors arrive for the pre-theater dinner beginning at 7:30 p.m. The consumption of dinner seems to guarantee a good table for the show. Tube: King's Cross Station.

The **Romance of London** is a cabaret river cruise complete with a commentary through the heart of London, cruising down to the Thames Barrier. A superior three-course meal is served with wine shortly after boarding, while musicians stroll among the tables. A barbershop quartet, cabaret, and dancing are also featured. The Romance of London cruises are available on Sunday from May to September and also on Tuesday from June to September. They depart from Westminster Pier at 7 p.m., returning at 9:30 p.m. The price is £27.50 ($48.25) per person. For information and reservations, call 620-0474.

DISCOS

The discos originated in Paris just after the war, but were taken up enthusiastically by the rest of Europe and by North America. London, strangely enough, was one of the last cities to catch the bug, but has since more than made up for lost time.

For the past few years discos have been springing up and closing down in London with such bewildering rapidity—besides changing their names, their image, character, and patrons—that a list compiled now is liable to be hopelessly out of date by the time this book appears. Yet the "discs" play such a vital part in London's nightlife that to ignore them would mean to eliminate nearly half the fun spots in town.

So, with the perils of instant obsolescence in mind, here's a fractional survey of the disco field *at this moment.* I offer no guarantee that the picture will be the same, say, a week from next Wednesday.

One of the dilemmas in trying to classify these ephemeral establishments is that many of them have totally forgotten their original concept. A disco was meant to be a place where you danced or listened to recorded music, hence the name. But a solid proportion now offer live bands, floor shows, movies, gaming tables, and what-have-you, while still insisting on their original title.

Whatever we choose to tag them, London now has more of their breed than Paris and New York combined, and the ranks are still swelling.

The following, therefore, is merely a sample patchwork of the field.

Stringfellows, 16 Upper St. Martins Lane, W.C.2 (tel. 240-5534), is one of London's most elegant nighttime rendezvous spots, the creation of its owner and manager, Peter Stringfellow of the Hippodrome fame. It is said to have £1 million worth of velvet and hi-tech gloss and glitter. In theory it's a members-only club, but—and only at the discretion of management—nonmembers may be admitted. It offers two lively bars, a first-class restaurant, and a hi-tech theater. Its disco has a stunning glass dance floor and a dazzling sound-and-light system. It's been called "an exquisite oasis of elegance," and its nightclub food "the best in London," (for a nightclub, that is). Dancing starts at 11 p.m., dinner at 8, and the fun continues until 3 a.m. daily except Sunday. Prices start at £3 ($5.25) Monday to Wednesday, £6 ($10.50) on Thursday, and £8 ($14) on Friday and Saturday; closed Sunday. Tube: Leicester Square.

The Hippodrome, corner of Charing Cross Road and Leicester Square, W.C.2 (tel. 437-4311). Peter Stringfellow has created one of London's greatest discos, an enormous place where light and sound beam in on you from all directions. Revolving speakers even descend from the roof to deafen you in patches, and you can watch yourself on closed-circuit video. There are six bars, together with a balcony restaurant, where well-prepared food is served. Lasers and a hydraulically controlled stage for visiting international performers are only part of the attraction of this place. Admission Monday to Thursday is £4 ($7). On Friday and Saturday the charge is £7.50 ($13.25) before 11 p.m., £10 ($17.50) after. The Hippodrome is open Monday (which is gay night) to Saturday from 9 p.m. to 3:30 a.m. Tube: Leicester Square.

Camden Palace, la Camden High St., N.1 (tel. 387-0428), is a gigantic funtime disco, one of the most fashionable in London, the creation of impresario of the nighttime circuit Steve Strange (don't you love that name?). Avant-garde and spectacular, it is preening proud of its lavish lights and sound system. Live music and cabaret, in addition to recorded music, are featured. Guests enjoy the finest of drinks in the cocktail bars or can patronize a first-class restaurant. It's been called "strictly for the outré and adventurous," and whether you fall into that category may be determined by the management at the door. It is open Tuesday to Saturday from 9:30 p.m. to 3 a.m., charging an admission of £3 ($5.25) on Tuesday and Wednesday, £4 ($7) on Thursday and Friday, and £5 ($8.75) on Saturday. Tube: Camden Town, Mornington Crescent.

Samantha's, 3 New Burlington St., W.1 (tel. 734-6249), just off Regent Street, has been one of London's most popular discos and nightspots since it opened more than two decades ago. There are two discos side by side, and the disco is, of course, the central feature of the club. The sound-and-light system is controlled by a disc jockey. Flashing colored lights and curved mirrors create a surrealistic setting for the endless parade of youthful, energetic dancers. Depending on the night, the entrance fee ranges from £4 ($7) to £6 ($10.50), a pint of lager costing from 50p (90¢) to £1.20 ($2.10). The place is open every night but Sunday from 9 p.m. to 3:30 a.m. Tube: Oxford Circus.

Le Beat Route, 17 Greek St., W.1 (tel. 734-6308), is a luxurious club with both live and disco music, open every day. Top recording artists make personal appearances here. There's a superb sprung dance floor. Admission ranges from £5 ($8.75) to £7 ($12.25). It opens at 9 p.m., closing at 3:30 a.m. Closed Sunday. Tube: Tottenham Court Road.

THE BIG BALLROOMS

Although the straight dance hall is by now almost defunct in America, it continues to draw crowds in London. There are several reasons for this survival, all of them having to do with the boy-meets-girl syndrome. As places for casual encounters, the ballrooms are unbeatable. The music is not so loud that you can't hear each others' names, the illumination is bright enough to see whom you're meeting, and the floor is sufficiently large for actual dancing, as distinct from the postage stamp that passes for it in the discos. The hunters of both sexes usually prowl in pairs, but will split up as readily as amoebas when opportunity beckons.

The **Café de Paris,** on Coventry Street, off Piccadilly Circus, W.1 (tel. 437-2036), is the grandest of institutions, and still basks in a rosy glow of nostalgia. Opened in 1924, it was once the chicest nitery in the Empire, patronized by the Prince of Wales (the late Duke of Windsor) and on one occasion counted four reigning kings in its audience. Merle Oberon worked there as a dance hostess, Marlene Dietrich and Noël Coward topped the floor shows, and Robert Graves wrote a book about it.

Today the Café is still plush, chandelier-blazing, and large enough to land a plane on the dance floor. But instead of the aristocratic smart set, patrons today consist largely of regular folks who like to dance rather than to "be seen." They get to do so on a truly superb maple floor, to continuous music. The floor is bathed in changing "mood lights" and surrounded by gilded balustrades. One band alternates with disco for dancing seven nights a week. They are open Monday to Thursday from 8:30 p.m. to 1 a.m., on Friday and Saturday to 2 a.m., and Sunday to midnight. Afternoon tea dances are held from 3 to 5:45 p.m. Admission in the afternoon is £2 ($3.50); in the evening, from £3.60 ($6.25) to £3.90 ($6.75). Tube: Leicester Square.

The **Empire Discothèque,** Leicester Square, W.C.2 (tel. 437-1446), Europe's largest disco ballroom, is in the heart of London's entertainment area. Top DJs and spectacular light shows are presented, along with live bands Tuesday to Saturday. The place is open seven days a week from 8 p.m. to 3 a.m. (to 1:30 a.m. on Sunday). Admission is £3 ($5.25) to £7 ($12.25), the higher price charged on weekends. Tube: Leicester Square or Piccadilly.

JAZZ

Mention the word "jazz" in London and people immediately think of **Ronnie Scott's.** This citadel of Europe's aficionados is a svelte three-story establishment at 47 Frith St., Soho, W.1 (tel. 439-0747), crowded on weeknights, bursting at the seams on weekends. But don't let the throng discourage you. This is one of the—perhaps *the*—greatest jazz dispensary outside America and worth braving any size mob for. Featured on almost every bill is an American band, often with a top-notch singer. The best English and American groups are booked. It's in the heart of Soho, a ten-minute walk from Piccadilly Circus via Shaftesbury Avenue, and worth an entire evening. You can not only saturate yourself in the best of jazz, but you get reasonably priced drinks and dinners as well.

There are three separate areas: the Main Room, the Upstairs Room, and the Downstairs Bar. You don't have to be a member, although you can join if you wish. Admission begins at £8 ($14), going up to £10 ($17.50) if an international jazz band is playing. If you have a student ID you are granted considerable reductions on entrance fees. Drinks cost around £1.30 ($2.25) for whisky.

The Main Room is open Monday to Saturday from 8:30 p.m. to 3 a.m. You can either stand at the bar to watch the show or sit at tables, where you can order a three-course dinner from around £12 ($21).

The Downstairs Bar is more intimate, a quiet rendezvous where you can meet and talk with the regulars, usually some of the world's most talented musicians.

The Upstairs Room is a part of the club where you can either dance or drink. On most nights a live band is featured. Tube: Tottenham Court Road or Leicester Square.

Although considerably less plush and cheaper, the **100 Club** is considered a serious rival of the above among many dedicated jazz gourmets. At 100 Oxford St., W.1 (tel. 636-0933), the 100 Club sprinkles disco-dance nights among its cavalcade of bands which include the best British jazz musicians, as well as many touring Americans.

Sessions go from 7:30 p.m. till midnight weeknights, till 1 a.m. on Friday and Saturday. Admission prices vary according to who's playing, and hover between £2.50 ($4.50) and £3.50 ($6.25). Without membership, you pay an additional £1 ($1.75). Tube: Tottenham Court Road or Oxford Circus.

ROCK

The place where new bands are launched, **Rock Garden Restaurant & Rock Music Venue,** 6-7 The Piazza, Covent Garden, W.C.2 (tel. 240-3961), is where such renowned groups as Dire Straits, The Police, U2, and The Stanglers all played before becoming famous. The restaurant is open from noon to midnight Sunday to Thursday, to 1 a.m. on Friday and Saturday. In summer there is outside seating in the heart of Covent Garden. The cover charge in the Venue ranges from £3 ($5.25) to £6 ($10.50), depending on the performance. A wide range of meals is offered, costing from £8 ($14). The Venue is open from 7:30 p.m. to 3 a.m. six days a week, to midnight on Sunday. Both the restaurant and the Venue have licensed bars. Tube: Covent Garden; night buses from neighboring Trafalgar Square.

The Marquee, 90 Wardour St., W.1 (tel. 437-6603), is considered one of the best-known centers for rock in Europe. Its reputation goes back to the '50s, but it remains forever young, in touch with the sounds of the future. Famous groups such as the Stones played at the Marquee long before their names spread beyond the shores of England. Fortunately, you don't have to be a member—you just pay at the door. If you have a Student I.D. card from any country, it will cost you less to enter. The entrance fees vary, but usually fall in the £3.50 ($6.25) to £5 ($8.75) range, depending on who is appearing. There's a coffee and a Coke bar for light snacks; those 18 or older can order hard drinks. Many well-known musicians frequent the place regularly on their nights off. The quite small and very crowded club is one of the few that feature live music. Hours are 8 p.m. to 1 a.m. seven nights a week. Tube: Piccadilly Circus.

VAUDEVILLE

Virtually extinct in America, the variety stage not only lives but flourishes in London. Streamlined and updated, it has dropped most of the corn and preserved all of the excitement of the old vaudeville fare.

Top house in the field (not merely in London but in the world) is the **London Palladium,** Argyle Street, W.1 (tel. 437-7373), although it presents more than just vaudeville. It's hard to encapsulate the prestige of this establishment in a paragraph. Performers from Britain, Europe, and America consider that they have "arrived" when they've appeared here. Highlight of the season is the "Royal Command Performance" held before the Queen, which includes an introduction of the artists to Her Majesty. It's amazing to watch hardboiled showbiz champions moved close to tears after receiving the royal handshake.

In days of yore the Palladium has starred aces such as Frank Sinatra, Shirley MacLaine, Andy Williams, Perry Como, Julie Andrews, Tom Jones, Sammy Davis, Jr., and so on, like the Milky Way of stardom. Second-line program attractions are likely to include, say, "Los Paraguayos" and the Ukrainian Cossack Ensemble. Ticket prices, usually in the £8 ($14) to £17 ($29.75) range, and showtimes vary. Tube: Oxford Circus.

BOUZOUKI AND MIDDLE EASTERN

Omar Khayyam, 177 Regent St., W.1 (tel. 437-3693), is the best address for Middle Eastern cabaret. A long-established and well-known West End address, it is open Monday to Saturday from 10 p.m. to 6 a.m., charging £30 ($52.50) per person for a three-course dinner. There's no action on Sunday, however. Arab musicians, singers, and dancers entertain you, and every night members of the audience are invited to join the show. The main show is from midnight to 2 a.m. Tube: Oxford Circus or Piccadilly Circus.

The **Elysée,** 13 Percy St., W.1 (tel. 636-4804), boasts the biggest roof-garden restaurant in London and is bursting with Greek atmosphere. Run by the three Karageorgis brothers, who also participate in the cabaret, the place is alive with the strains of Hellenic strings and redolent with the aroma of Balkan cooking.

The twice-nightly shows feature Greek dancing and singing, mixed with some astonishing feats of wine-glass balancing while swaying to the rhythmic clapping of the musicians. If you dug

Zorba, this place will send you. The full and fragrant meal costs around £25 ($43.75) per person, including a bottle of wine, but there's a £3 ($5.25) cover charge. The club is open nightly from 6:30 p.m. until 3:30 a.m. (on Sunday to 2 a.m.). Dinner is served from 7 p.m. to 2:45 a.m. Dancing to music by a quartet is from 9 p.m. The Greek cabaret shows are staged at 11 p.m. and again at 1 a.m. (on Sunday at 10:30 p.m. and again at 12:15 a.m.). Tube: Goodge Street or Tottenham Court Road.

MEDIEVAL "FEESTES"

1520 A.D. Medieval Tavern, 17 Swallow St., W.1 (tel. 240-3978), is the place to be if you want to eat, drink, and be merry, beginning at 7:30 p.m. You get a sumptuous banquet and continuous medieval pageantry, with actors impersonating King Henry VIII, Anne Boleyn, Jane Seymour, the court jester, minstrels, and a dancing bear, while guests are served by so-called wenches. The feast is made up of game soup, pâté, a glass of Olde English mead, Henry's fish delight, puff pastry with a seafood filling, roast baby chicken with fresh vegetables, and to finish, Master Edwarde's treat, made with fresh fruit, cream, and Grand Marnier. After the show, return to the 20th century with disco dancing until 12:30 a.m. The cost is £19 ($33.25) Sunday to Thursday, £21 ($36.75) Friday and Saturday. Wine or ale is included with your meal. Tube: Piccadilly Circus.

Shakespeare's Feast, Blackfriars Lane, E.C.4 (tel. 408-1001), plays tribute to the Bard. Here many of the most famous characters from Shakespeare's plays are re-created for a riotous night of fun, aided in no small part by jugglers, jesters, and magicians. There are even duellists. At the reception the costumed staff serves traditional honeyed wines, and later at a six-course feast, diners can enjoy unlimited amounts of ale and wine. It's open from 8 p.m. to midnight, and after dinner there's dancing. The all-inclusive price is £22.50 ($39.50) Sunday to Friday and £24.50 ($43) on Saturday. Tube: Blackfriars.

A FAMOUS BAR ·

For those who like bars instead of pubs, **Jules,** 85 Jermyn St., S.W.1 (tel. 930-4700), is the best-known watering hole in St. James's. It was constructed originally as the Waterloo Hotel in 1830. After Jules Ribstein bought it in 1903, he turned it into a ground-floor restaurant, and in time it became a rendezvous for the "bucks and blades." Today it serves many purposes. It will even serve you lunch from 11 a.m. to 3 p.m. But it's known mainly for its cocktails, some 50 in all, ranging from those made with champagne to Hawaiian dream. "Godfather" is scotch and amaretto; "Godmother," vodka and amaretto. Cocktails cost from £2.90 ($5). At the restaurant in back you can order such treats as smoked salmon pâté, salmon and sole "as you like it," or perhaps one of a variety of steaks, with meals costing from £18 ($31.50). Evening hours are 5:30 to 11 p.m. Monday to Saturday. Tube: Piccadilly Circus.

STRIP SHOWS

Once upon a time, Britain's film censors were kept busy snipping the bare patches out of those "daring" French movies, and London's stage regulations permitted braless belles only on condition that they didn't move a limb while thus exposed.

All this might just as well have happened in the last century for all the relevance it has today, for the sheer acreage of undress currently on view in London outshows anything in Paris, New York, San Francisco, or Hamburg. Only Tokyo might be on the same par.

Some of this clothes-shedding mania is undoubtedly a reaction to the years of Mrs. Grundy's dictatorship, when even a semitransparent nightgown had to be struck out of a play as "bordering on the indecent." But by now it has gone past the saturation point. London's entertainment world, in fact, is in danger of being smothered by a pink tidal wave of nudity, lapping into every nook and cranny of the West End and sweeping before it every other brand of amusement.

Entire blocks of Soho now consist of little else but strip shows, sometimes two in one building. Along Frith Street, Greek Street, Old Compton Street, Brewer Street, Windmill Street, Dean and Wardour Streets, and the little courts and alleys in between, the disrobing establishments jostle cheek by jowl. Big ones and small ones, fancy and dingy, elaborate and primitive, they all sport outsize photos of the inside attractions, gloriously exotic names, and bellowing speakers to draw your attention.

The basic commodity is the same, but the packaging varies considerably. Some of the large—and fairly expensive—places are regular theaters, putting on lavish productions, complete with musical scores, choreography, trained dancers, and intricate, if insufficient, costuming.

At the other extreme are dozens of cellar dens, holding a few rows of creaking chairs, a torn curtain, and a few boards knocked together as a stage. The women appearing there can neither dance nor strip gracefully, but they can take their clothes off.

Regarding their acts, you'd better forget what you know about American burlesque. There's no trace of humor, no slapstick gags with girdles, no wisecracking with the boys in the front row, and no fans and fluttering pigeons. Here, the stripping is total, minus modesty gimmicks such as flickering strobe lights or climactic blackouts. The women go through a series of vaguely undulating movements and strip right down to their skins. And that's that.

The big, plush establishments, of course, have regular and highly paid casts, and among the most spectacular is the **Raymond Revuebar,** Walker's Court, Brewer St., W.1 (tel. 734-1593). Proprietor Paul Raymond is considered the doyen of strip society and his young, beautiful, hand-picked women are among the best in Europe. The stage show, Festival of Erotica, is presented Monday to Saturday from 8 to 10 p.m. There are licensed bars, and patrons may take their drinks into the theater. The price of admission is £12.50 ($22), and there is no membership fee. Whisky is around £1.50 ($2.65) per large measure. Tube: Piccadilly Circus.

GAMBLING

London was a gambling metropolis long before anyone had ever heard of Monte Carlo and when Las Vegas was an anonymous sandpile in the desert. From the Regency period until halfway into the 19th century, Britain was more or less governed by gamblers. Lord Sandwich invented the snack named after him so he wouldn't have to leave the card table for a meal. Prime Minister Fox was so addicted that he frequently went to a cabinet meeting straight from the green baize table.

Queen Victoria's reign changed all that, as usual, by jumping to the other extreme. For more than a century, games of chance were so rigorously outlawed that no barmaid dared to keep a dice cup on her counter.

The pendulum swung again in 1960, when the present Queen gave her Royal Assent to the new "Betting and Gaming Act." According to this legislation, gambling was again permitted in "bona fide clubs" by members and their guests.

There are at least 25 of them in the West End alone, with many more scattered through the suburbs. And the contrasts between them are much sharper than you find in the Nevada casinos.

However, I can no longer make specific recommendations. Under a new law, casinos aren't allowed to advertise, which in this context would mean appearing in a guidebook. It isn't illegal to gamble, only to advertise that you do. Most hall porters can tell you where you can gamble in London.

You will be required to become a member of your chosen club, and in addition you must wait 24 hours before you can play at the tables . . . then strictly for cash. Most common games are roulette, blackjack, punto banco, and baccarat.

CHAPTER X

CHILDREN'S LONDON

□ □ □

It's hard to draw a clear distinguishing line between junior and senior brands of entertainment. In London it's almost impossible.

The British Museum, for instance, is definitely rated as an adult attraction. Yet I've watched group after group of kids stand absolutely spellbound in front of the Egyptian mummies, still completely absorbed long after their parents were champing at the bit to trot along.

Conversely, the Zoo is supposed to be primarily for the younger set. But I've seen dignified daddies become so hypnotized by the ant colony and the nest-stitching Indian tailor bird that they had to be literally dragged away by their brood.

One variation or another of the same scene is constantly enacted at the Tower, Madame Tussaud's, the *Discovery*, Billingsgate Market, Battersea Park, and a dozen other places.

I've seen small girls react with frozen unamusement to royal dollhouses that had their mothers cooing with delight. And I've observed those same little ladies aglow with enthusiasm before the oil painting of a particularly gruesome 17th-century massacre. Their spiritual brothers meanwhile disdained even to glance at a model car racetrack and preferred to give their total attention to the activities of a window cleaner.

All of which merely goes to prove that children are at least as individualistic in their tastes as adults. It also goes to make my classification job difficult.

SIGHTS AND ATTRACTIONS

The attractions to follow are *not* meant specifically for children. They are general and universal fun places to which you can take youngsters without having to worry about either their physical or moral safety. There's nothing to stop you from going to any of them minus a juvenile escort. It is even possible that you'll enjoy them more thoroughly than any kid around.

THE LONDON DUNGEON: The premises at 34 Tooley St., S.E.1 (tel. 403-0606), simulate a ghoulish atmosphere designed deliberately to chill the blood while reproducing the conditions that existed in the Middle Ages. Set under the arches of London Bridge Station, the dungeon is a series of tableaux, more grisly than Madame Tussaud's, depicting life in medieval London. The rumble of trains overhead adds to the spine-chilling horror of the place. Bells toll and there is constant melancholy chanting in the background. Dripping water and live rats (caged!) make for even more atmosphere.

The heads of executed criminals were stuck on spikes for onlookers to observe through glasses hired for the occasion. The murder of Thomas à Becket in Canterbury Cathedral is also depicted. Naturally, there's a burning at the stake, as well as a torture chamber with racking, branding, and fingernail extraction.

If you survive, there is a souvenir shop selling certificates which testify that you have been through the works.

The dungeon charges £3.50 ($6.25) for adults, £2 ($3.50) for children under 14. From April to September it's open daily from 10 a.m. to 5:30 p.m., and from October to March hours are 10 a.m. to 4:30 p.m. Tube: London Bridge.

BATTERSEA PARK: The park is a vast patch of woodland, lakes, and lawns on the south bank of the Thames, opposite Chelsea Embankment. It boasts just about everything that makes for happiness on a dry day: a tree-lined boulevard, fountains, and a children's zoo with baby animals.

LONDON ZOO: One of the greatest zoos in the world, the London Zoo is more than a century and a half old. Run by the Zoological Society of London, Regent's Park, N.W.1 (tel. 722-3333), with an equal measure of showmanship and scholarly know-how, this 36-acre garden houses some 8,000 animals, including some of the rarest species on earth. The most famous is the giant panda, Chia-Chia, a gift to Britain from the People's Republic of China. One of the most fascinating exhibits is the Snowdon Aviary. Separate houses are reserved for some species: the insect house (incredible bird-eating spiders, a cross-sectioned ant colony), the reptile house (huge dragon-like monitor lizards and a fantastic 15-foot python), and other additions, such as the Sobell Pavilion for Apes and Monkeys and the Lion Terraces.

Designed for the largest collection of small mammals in the world, the Clore Pavilion has a basement called the Moonlight World, where special lighting effects simulate night for the nocturnal beasties, while rendering them clearly visible to onlookers. You can see all the night rovers in action: leaping bush babies, rare kiwis, a fierce Tasmanian devil, and giant Indian fruit bats with heads like prehistoric dogs.

Many families budget almost an entire day to spend with the animals, watching the sea lions being fed, enjoying an animal ride in summer, and meeting the baby elephant on its walks around the zoo. The zoo is open daily from 9 a.m. in summer and from 10 a.m. in winter, until 6 p.m. or dusk, whichever is earlier. Last admission is a half hour before closing. Admission is £3.60 ($6.25) for adults, £1.80 ($3.25) for children 5 to 16 (under 5, free). On the grounds are two fully licensed restaurants, one self-service, the other with waitresses. Take the tube to Baker Street or Camden Town, then take bus 74 (Camden Town is nearer and an easy ten-minute walk).

WHIPSNADE PARK ZOO: This is the country breeding park of the Zoological Society of London (which also operates the London Zoo), where the animals roam free in large paddocks and certain species even wander among visitors. Situated on the edge of the Chiltern escarpment in Bedfordshire, Whipsnade lays claim to being the world's first open-air zoo. Many endangered species are here, including the cheetah, Père David deer, oryx, and Indian and white rhinos. There are also 12 species of crane, including the rare and beautiful red-naped, or Manchurian, crane. There is a lot of walking here to see everything in a single day, but the opportunities for photography are second to none. Exhibits include dolphins, a steam railway, a birds-of-prey show, a Discovery Centre, and a family center. Animals are in geographical groupings. Cars are admitted for £3.75 ($6.50) in July and August and for £2.75 ($4.75) at other times of year, except from November 1 to February 28 when they are admitted free. In addition, you must pay £3.25 ($5.75) for adults and £1.75 ($3) for children. Children under the age of 5 are admitted free. The zoo is open daily from 10 a.m. to 6 p.m. or sunset, whichever is earlier. Take the train from St. Pancras to Luton, then a no. 43 bus to Whipsnade Park.

NATURAL HISTORY MUSEUM: This museum, on Cromwell Road, S.W.7 (tel. 589-6323), is the home of the national collections of living and fossil plants and animals, minerals, rocks, and meteorites, with lots of magnificent specimens on display. Exciting exhibitions designed to encourage people of all ages to enjoy learning about modern natural history include "Human Biology—An Exhibition of Ourselves," "Dinosaurs and Their Living Relatives," "Man's Place in Evolution," "Introducing Ecology," "Origin of the Species," "British Natural History," and "Discovering Mammals."

Admission is £2 ($3.50) for adults, £1 ($1.75) for children. The museum is open Monday to Saturday from 10 a.m. to 6 p.m. and on Sunday from 1 to 6 p.m. Take the tube to South Kensington.

BETHNAL GREEN MUSEUM OF CHILDHOOD: Cambridge Heath Road, E.2. (tel. 980-2415). This establishment displays toys from over past centuries. The variety of dolls alone is staggering, some of them dressed in period costumes of such elaborateness that you don't even want to think of the price tags they must have carried.

With the dolls go dollhouses, from simple cottages to miniature mansions, complete with fireplaces and grand pianos, plus carriages, furniture, kitchen utensils, and household pets. It might be wise to explain to your children beforehand, that no, none of them is for sale.

In addition, the museum displays optical toys, toy theaters, marionettes, puppets, and a considerable exhibit of soldiers and warlike toys of both World Wars, plus trains and aircraft. There is also a display of children's clothing and furniture related to childhood. Often special activities for children are presented; telephone for information.

The museum is open Monday to Thursday from 10 a.m. to 6 p.m. and on Sunday from 2:30 p.m.; closed Friday. Admission is free. Take the tube to Bethnal Green.

THE LONDON TOY AND MODEL MUSEUM: A restored Victorian house at 23 Craven Hill, W.2 (tel. 262-7905), holds one of the finest collections of commercially made toys and models on public display in Europe, with items by all the major toy and model manufacturers. It also contains one of the most comprehensive die-cast model transport collections in existence, a fine doll collection, and amazing working dioramas.

In the large garden you'll see operating model railway tracks, an antique children's roundabout, and a vintage bus which is available for exploration. There is a café and shop. The museum is open Tuesday to Saturday from 10 a.m. to 5:30 p.m., on Sunday from

11 a.m. Admission is £2.20 ($3.75) for adults, 80p ($1.40) for children (free to children under 5 years of age). Tube: Paddington or Lancaster Gate.

POLLOCK'S TOY MUSEUM:
1 Scala St., W.1 (tel. 636-3452), is probably the most curious museum in London. A wee white corner house, it's like something out of Hans Christian Andersen, crammed to the bursting point with antique playthings.

Each of the three stories has its specialties. On the ground level, the museum is a shop displaying old-fashioned toys and dolls you can buy. One steep flight up is the world of toy theaters: Victorian wood and cardboard stages, colorful and ornate like wedding cakes, Balinese shadow screens, 19th-century French "living pictures." Another flight up are the dolls, from wooden Dutch to china English, not forgetting original American teddy bears.

In between is a vast array of miniature kitchen stoves, tin soldiers, ships, horses, and "flying machines," plus playtime rarities like magic lanterns dating from 1866, clockwork cars from 1902, and a working British bathtub submarine from 1904.

Admission is 60p ($1.05) for adults, 30p (55¢) for children. It's open from 10 a.m. to 5 p.m. Monday through Saturday; closed Sunday. Take the tube to Goodge Street Station, then it's a minute's walk to the corner of Whitfield and Scala Streets.

NATIONAL MARITIME MUSEUM:
Romney Road, Greenwich (tel. 858-4422, ext. 221). Down the Thames at Greenwich, about six miles from the city, the Maritime Museum stands in a beautiful royal park and has a special claim to fame, aside from its contents (see below).

A great many astronomical instruments still mingle with the navigation gadgets: it's easy to see the connection. Otherwise, the building harbors the glory that was Britain at sea. The wooden ships, the brass cannon, the iron men; the relics, models, and paintings tell the story of a thousand naval battles and a thousand victories. Also the price of those battles . . . among the exhibits is the uniform that Lord Nelson wore when he was struck by a French musket ball at the very moment of his triumph at the Battle of Trafalgar.

The museum is open from 10 a.m. to 6 p.m. Monday to Saturday and from 2 to 6 p.m. on Sunday in summer, closing at 5 p.m. in winter. It is closed January 1, Good Friday, May bank holiday, and the Christmas holidays. A combined ticket to the main buildings and the Old Royal Observatory (see below; open same hours) costs £2.20 ($3.75) for adults, £1.10 ($2) for children aged 7 to 16. For either the museum or the observatory only, admission is £1.50 ($2.65) for adults, 75p ($1.25) for children. A £6 ($10.50) family ticket admits two adults and up to five children. There is a licensed restaurant in the west wing.

The **Old Royal Observatory,** designed by Sir Christopher Wren, is where you can stand at 0° longitude, as the Greenwich Meridian line, or prime meridian, marks the first of the globe's vertical divisions. You can also see the big red time-ball used in olden days by ships sailing down the river from London to set their timepieces by.

You can take a Thames launch downstream from Westminster Pier or the train from Charing Cross Station to Maze Hill.

THE UNICORN THEATER FOR CHILDREN: Arts Theatre, Great Newport Street, W.C.2. The Unicorn commissions several new plays each year as well as presenting dramatizations of *Beowulf, Gulliver's Travels,* and *The Green-Eyed Monster of Ecrovid.* Professional adult actors play the parts. It's a good idea to go to the 2:30 p.m. matinee performances on weekends, because during the week the troupe usually plays at school auditoriums throughout Britain. Admission is £2.50 ($4.50) to £4.50 ($8). Each play is presented for a specific age range within the 4-to-12 age group, which is indicated on all publicity. Visiting children's theater companies perform at the Unicorn during the spring, and in the summer months the Unicorn Summer Tour goes to parks and playgrounds in the London area.

Anyone can see a Unicorn play by becoming a temporary member. For additional information, such as how to secure temporary memberships for foreigners, telephone 379-3280. To book tickets, call the box office (tel. 836-3334). Tube: Leicester Square.

THE LITTLE ANGEL MARIONETTE THEATRE: 14 Dagmar Passage, N.1. This is especially constructed for and devoted to the presentation of puppetry in all its forms. It is open to the general public, and between 200 and 300 performances are given here every year. The theater is the focal point of a loosely formed group of about 20 professional puppeteers who work there as occasion demands, sometimes presenting their own shows and often helping with the performances of the resident company.

In the current repertory, there are 25 programs. These vary in style and content from *The Soldier's Tale,* using eight-foot-high figures, to *Wonder Island* and *Lancelot the Lion,* written especially for the humble glove puppet. Many of the plays, such as Hans Christian Andersen's *The Little Mermaid,* are performed with marionettes (string puppets), but whatever is being presented you'll be enthralled with the exquisite lighting and the skill with which the puppets are handled.

The theater is beautifully decorated and well equipped. There is a coffee bar in the foyer and a workshop adjacent where the settings and costumes, as well as the puppets, are made. To find out what's playing and for what age group a performance is suitable, and to book your seats, call 226-1787. Performances are at 11 a.m. on Saturday, when the seats are £1.50 ($2.75) for children, £2.50 ($4.50) for adults; and at 3 p.m. on Saturday and Sunday, when the cost is £2 ($3.50) for children, £3 ($5.25) for adults.

Take the tube to Angel Station, then walk up Upper Street to St. Mary's Church and down the footpath to the left of the church. You can go by car or taxi to Essex Road and then up Dagmar Terrace.

HAMPSTEAD HEATH: This is the traditional playground of the Londoner, the 'Appy' Ampstead of Cockney legendry, the place dedicated "to the use of the public forever" by special Act of Parliament in 1872. Londoners might just possibly tolerate the conversion of, say, Hyde Park into housing estates or supermarkets, but they would certainly mount the barricades if Hampstead Heath were imperiled.

This 800-acre expanse of high heath entirely surrounded by London is a chain of continuous park, wood, and grassland, bearing different names in different portions. It contains just about every known form of outdoor amusement, with the exception of big-game hunting.

There are natural lakes for swimmers (who don't mind goosebumps), bridle paths for horseriders, athletic tracks, hills for kite flying, and a special pond for model yachting. You can catch bream and pike in several lakes, paddle your own boat on others, feed the squirrels or admire the interiors of two 17th-century mansions converted into museums.

At the shore of Kenwood Lake, in the northern section, is a concert platform devoted to symphony performances on summer evenings. Waterlow Park, the northeast corner, has the Grass Theatre, where ballets, operas, and comedies are staged in June and July.

At Easter, Whitsun, and August bank holidays, the heath becomes riotous with the noise and tunes of two fun fairs going full-blast, and even sophisticated Londoners make it a point of dropping in on them. It's all part of a tradition, as deeply rooted as orderly queuing and Christmas decorations.

If you're history minded, you can stand for a moment on top

of Parliament Hill on the south side. It was from that vantage point that the ancient British Queen Boadicea and her daughters watched the burning of the Roman camp of Londinium, which her tribesmen had put to the torch in A.D. 61.

Take the tube to Hampstead or Belsize Park.

SHOPPING FOR CHILDREN

The best place to go for both children's books and toys is **Young World,** 229 Kensington High St., W.8 (tel. 937-6314). It is thought to be the largest children's bookshop in the world and has thousands of titles. A feature of the bookshop is that fiction, both hardback and paperback, is arranged according to age, including the young adult reader in the 14 to 16 age group. The large toy department, which has been called the most imaginative in London, offers a wide selection of toys, games, and stationery for all ages. In the gift section are items suitable for children to give their parents and other relatives. The store is open from 9:30 a.m. to 6 p.m. Monday to Saturday and from noon to 6 p.m. on Sunday. Tube: High Street Kensington.

At 237 Kensington High St., W.8 (tel. 937-7497), the Young World people have a shop called **The Tree House** which is a gift shop for children, carrying a range of merchandise suitable for youngsters to give as presents to parents, friends, and relations. It's open Monday through Saturday from 9:30 a.m. to 6 p.m. and on Sunday from noon to 6 p.m. Tube: High Street Kensington.

Another Young World shop is in the Trocadero Centre, Piccadilly. Tube: Piccadilly Circus.

Hamleys of Regent Street, 188–196 Regent St., W.1 (tel. 734-3161), is an Ali Baba's cave of toys and games, ranging from electronic games and *Star Wars* robots on the ground floor to different toys on each of the other floors: table and card games, teddy bears, nursery animals, dolls, and outdoor games. The Hamleys train races around the walls. Tube: Oxford Circus.

CHAPTER XI

ONE-DAY EXCURSIONS FROM LONDON

□ □ □

You could spend the best part of a year—or a lifetime—exploring London, without risking either boredom or repetition. But since your stay is probably limited, I advise you to tear yourself away from Big Ben for at least a day or two.

For the Thames metropolis is surrounded by some of the most memorable spots on earth, entire clusters of scenic resorts, historic sites, cultural and religious shrines, and just-plain-fun places, all within comfortable commuting range.

The only trouble is that there are too many of them.

There's Shakespeare's town of Stratford-upon-Avon, the pilgrimage city of Canterbury, Churchill's country home at Chartwell, the Tudor turrets of Hampton Court, dozens of "stately mansions"—and resident dukes—awaiting your inspection, Windsor Castle of Queen Victoria's memory, the flowers of Syon Park, the great universities of Oxford and Cambridge, the roaming wild animals of Woburn Abbey, Runnymede of Magna Carta fame—the roll call goes on and on.

The small county of Hampshire alone contains the medieval cathedral city of Winchester, the great seaport of Southampton, and the New Forest nature preserve with deer and shaggy wild ponies.

STRATFORD-UPON-AVON

Starting with the farthest and most famous, this small town in Warwickshire lies 91 miles from London. The train from Paddington Station takes you there in 2½ hours.

As you probably know, Shakespeare was born there in 1564, and returned to live and die there after his successful and creative years in London had earned him enough money to settle down as the solid bourgeois he was at heart.

You can trace his life story in Stratford, from his birthplace on Henley Street to his tomb in the Holy Trinity Church. There's still an aura of old Elizabethan England among Stratford's timbered inns and 16th-century houses with their oddly protruding upper story. And the Avon is still the same gentle river in which young Will, the tanner's son, admired the reflection of his sprouting beard.

The Bard was first honored at a "birthday celebration" in Stratford in 1769. Ever since, Will has drawn a steady stream of tourists to his hometown. By the way, in Stratford—especially to the prospering innkeepers and shop owners—don't put forth the theory that Francis Bacon really wrote those plays.

All the Shakespearean properties are open from 9 a.m. till 6 p.m. Monday to Saturday (on Sunday from 2 to 6 p.m.; Shakespeare's Birthplace and Anne Hathaway's Cottage from 10 a.m.) from April to October. In the winter season they remain open from 9 a.m. to 4 p.m. On off-season Sundays, only the two most visited attractions, Shakespeare's Birthplace and the Cottage of Anne Hathaway, remain open (the hours are 1:30 to 4:30 p.m.).

It's recommended that you go first to **Shakespeare's Birthplace,** on Henley Street. The Elizabethan dramatist was born there on April 23, 1564, the son of a "whittawer," or glove maker. Since 1847, when fans of the Bard raised the pounds and purchased the property, the house has been operated as a national shrine. A museum on the premises reveals his "life and times." Built to honor the 400th anniversary of the writer's birth, the Shakespeare Centre next door was dedicated as a library and study center in 1964. An extension to the original building, opened in 1981, provides a reception center for visitors to the Birthplace. It contains some notable artistic features.

You can purchase a comprehensive ticket admitting you to all five trust properties. The cost is £4.50 ($8) for adults, £2 ($3.50) for children.

For many, the chief magnet here is **Anne Hathaway's Cottage,** in the small hamlet of Shottery, outside of Stratford. Poor

Anne had to remain behind when her roving husband wandered off to London in 1587 to pursue his career as a playwright and actor at the Blackfriars and Globe Theatres. At the cottage made of what the English call "wattle and daub," Miss Hathaway, the daughter of a yeoman farmer, lived before her marriage to Shakespeare. Of the furnishings remaining, the "courting settle" evokes the most interest.

If the weather is good, the best way to reach Shottery is from Evesham Place in town (the strolling path is marked), traversing a meadow. Otherwise, a bus leaves from Bridge Street in Stratford.

At the so-called **New Place** on Chapel Street, Shakespeare retired in comfort in 1610. His reputation was already secured, his purse full, although, I suspect, he could hardly imagine the fame that would one day come to him. He was to live there in peace for six years, enjoying the esteem and respect of the townspeople, in spite of his "scandalous" career in the theater. He died in 1616 at the age of 52.

The house that he purchased for his retirement was destroyed, but you can walk through the gardens (entered through the home of Thomas Nash, a man who married Shakespeare's granddaughter, Elizabeth Hall). Of chief interest in the garden is a mulberry tree, said to have been rooted from a cutting of a tree that Shakespeare planted.

Although often ignored by the casual visitor, **Mary Arden's House** is a delight, built in the charming Tudor style. Shakespeare's mother, who like his wife was the daughter of a yeoman farmer, lived here in Wilmcote, a village about three miles outside Stratford. A farming museum is accommodated in the barns.

In the "Old Town" is the **Hall's Croft,** not far from the parish church. It was here that Shakespeare's daughter, Susanna, lived with her husband, Dr. John Hall. It is a Tudor house with a beautiful walled garden. Exhibits illustrating the theory and practice of medicine in Dr. Hall's time are on view in the house. Visitors are welcome to use the adjoining Hall's Croft Club, which serves morning coffee, lunch, and afternoon tea. The house is only a short walk from the Royal Shakespeare Theatre, about a block from the river.

Although not administered by the trust association, the **Holy Trinity Church,** one of England's most beautiful parish churches, on the banks of the Avon, is also much visited. Shakespeare was buried here, leaving behind the threat engraved on his tombstone: "and curst be he who moves my bones." A contribution is requested from adults wishing to view Shakespeare's tomb.

Nearly every visitor to Stratford wants to attend at least one performance at the **Royal Shakespeare Theatre** (tel. 0789/295623), designed in 1932 to stand right on the Avon by Miss Elizabeth Scott (the building was the subject of much controversy). The old Memorial Theatre caught fire and burned down in the 1920s. The long season of the Bard's plays begins in April and lasts until January. Five or six of Shakespeare's dramas and comedies usually operate in repertory. Reservations, of course, should be made in advance, as the theater is popular. Chances are you won't get a good seat (or even a seat) if you should just arrive at the box office.

WINDSOR

Windsor means two things to an English person: a castle and a college. Windsor Castle, the largest inhabited castle in the world, has been the home of English sovereigns for more than 800 years. And nearby Eton College has been educating future sovereigns along with lesser fry for more than 500.

Windsor Castle stands 21 miles outside London. The train from either Waterloo or Paddington Station does the trip in 50 minutes. Green Line coaches 704 and 705 from Hyde Park Corner take about 1½ hours.

The castle was built by William the Conqueror and completed before his death in 1087. An immense, looming structure, it has distinctly mixed memories for Britain's royalty. King John waited here in seething rage before being forced to sign the Magna Carta by his obstreperous barons in 1215. Here, Queen Victoria's beloved consort Albert died in 1861, turning her into the eternally grieving "Widow of Windsor." The State Apartments are still used at certain times by the present Queen Elizabeth.

When the Royal Standard is up, you know the State Apartments are closed for "official residence," or else the Queen is in "private" residence at weekends. At other times they can be viewed by the public, the only glimpse of inhabited royal suites you're likely to get. Admission is £1.80 ($3.25) for adults, 80p ($1.50) for children. The rest of the castle—and it's a mighty big rest—is open free from 10 a.m. to 5:15 p.m. in April, September, and October; to 7:15 p.m. May to August; and to 4:15 p.m. November to March. To learn what will be open when you visit, phone 0753/868286.

Eton College, founded in 1440 by King Henry VI, is still the most illustrious "public" (meaning private) school in Britain, and its pupils still wear strange Edwardian garb, top hat and collar, that makes them look like period fashion plates, but carries a helluva load of snob appeal. You can visit the schoolyard and Cloisters free from 2 to 5 p.m.

Two miles beyond Windsor lies the meadow of **Runnymede,** where King John, chewing his beard in fury, signed the Magna Carta. But Runnymede is also the site of the John F. Kennedy Memorial, one acre of hallowed ground presented to the United States by the people of Great Britain.

CANTERBURY

The ancient pilgrimage center in Kent, 56 miles from London, is the site of the cathedral that is the Mother Church of the worldwide Episcopalian movement. By train from Victoria, Charing Cross, Waterloo, or London Bridge Stations, the journey takes 1½ hours. The bus from Victoria Coach Station does it in two to three hours.

Chaucer and his fellow pilgrims went there more than six centuries ago, and the gray West Gate through which they entered still forms the city's main gateway. The goal of their pilgrimage—and that of millions of others—was the Gothic cathedral, shrine of Archbishop Thomas à Becket, who was murdered there by four knights after their king had asked why no one would rid him of "that turbulent priest."

When the swords hacked into Becket in 1170, **Canterbury Cathedral** (tel. 0227/762862) was already a century old. Then, as now, it dominates the town, governs its spirit, somehow makes you aware of its presence even when hidden by other buildings.

The cathedral is neither as overpowering as Cologne Cathedral nor as awe-inspiring as Notre-Dame in Paris. It has a mellow, almost gentle, beauty and a touching simplicity, despite the splendor of the art treasures it houses: the stained-glass windows and the opulent tomb of Edward the Black Prince, hero of the "Longbow Battle" of Crécy.

The original church on the site now occupied by the cathedral was erected by St. Augustine in A.D. 597 and became the cradle of English Christianity among the pagan folk of Kent.

WOBURN ABBEY

The great 18th-century mansion of **Woburn Abbey** (tel. 0525/290666) is the traditional seat of the Dukes of Bedford and the most publicized of all of England's Stately Homes. A wondrous collection of art gems, it contains works of Rembrandt, Holbein, Van-Dyck, and Gainsborough—some $14-million worth of paintings, plus antique furniture, silver, and tapestries.

This ancestral seat, 44 miles from London, a Georgian mansion, has slept Queen Victoria as well as Marilyn Monroe. The Stately Antique Market consists of three streets of period shops selling objects d'art. Surrounding it is a 3,000-acre park, containing the Wild Animal Kingdom with herds of rare deer, European bison, a light railway, and a pets corner, as well as amusement rides, lake fishing, and gardening centers.

OXFORD

The university town of Oxford, 57 miles from London, can be reached in 1¼ hours by train from Paddington Station. The city is well over a thousand years old, and the earliest of the colleges—St. Edmund Hall, Merton, and Balliol—date from the 13th century.

It's difficult to decide where the university ends and the town begins; the scattered colleges, quads, and chapels blend in with the workaday buildings in a harmonious whole, giving every street scene dreaming spires and domes. The two main streets, oddly known as "The High" and "The Broad," are perhaps the most beautiful period thoroughfares in England, set off by the Sheldonian Theatre, the University Church of St. Mary, and the Bodleian Library, one of the most important book collections in the world.

On Broad Street, you'll see a cross marking the spot where England's martyr bishops, Latimer, Ridley, and Cranmer, were burned at the stake during the reign of "Bloody Queen Mary" in 1557.

BRIGHTON

London's favorite seaside resort lies on the Sussex coast, 51 miles from the capital. Fast trains from Victoria or London Bridge Station make the trip in 55 minutes. Buses from Victoria Coach Station take around two hours.

Brighton has lost the aura of fashionable wickedness it possessed when the prince regent built his incredible pseudo-Oriental Royal Pavilion there in 1787. Now it's very much a family resort, boasting the warmest sunshine and the best beaches on the British Isles.

Don't bank on actually swimming, however (the English are a hardy lot when it comes to water temperatures), but the seafront promenade and two amusement piers make it a fun town, as well as a beautiful one. Brighton has everything from wax-works and aquariums to three live theaters, every conceivable form of sports, cafés, plush restaurants, five miles of beaches, and the annual London–Brighton Veteran Car Run.

The town is still a picture of terraced Regency elegance, tranquil after the turmoil along the seafront. At night, the floodlights play on the Royal Pavilion and the floral boulevard.

HAMPTON COURT

On the north side of the Thames, 13 miles west of London in East Molesey, Surrey, Hampton Court, amid rolling green country by the River Thames, is the grandest of all the great palaces built in England during the Tudor period. It was originally intended as the homestead of Cardinal Wolsey, chancellor (meaning prime minister) to King Henry VIII. On second thought, however, the wily cardinal presented it as a gift to his royal master, who then added a few luxurious touches of his own. The Great Kitchens were restored as they were in the 1530s. Walk in and see the fantastic Astronomical Clock, made by Nicholas Oursian in 1540. It tells the time, the date, and number of days since the New Year, the phases of the moon, and the times of high water at London Bridge, and was regarded as one of the mechanical miracles of its period. Wander through the royal kitchens, where an ox could be roasted whole, and lounge on the original lawn where King Henry once serenaded his Anne Boleyn—whom he eventually married—and then beheaded.

Attached to the original palace is a later one, designed by Sir Christopher Wren for William of Orange and Queen Mary. Wren built the formal Fountain Court and the great East Front facing the gardens. Still standing there is the Great Vine (mentioned in Ripley's "Believe It or Not") which was planted in 1769 and has a main branch now more than 100 feet long. You can also lose yourself in the Maze.

The gardens—including the Great Vine, King's Privy Garden, Great Fountain Gardens, Tudor and Elizabethan Knot Gardens, Board Walk, Tiltyard, and Wilderness—are open daily year round from 7 a.m. until dusk, but not later than 9 p.m., and can be visited free. Cloisters, courtyards, and State Apartments are open from 9:30 a.m. to 5 p.m. from Monday to Saturday, from 2 to 7 p.m. on Sunday, from January 2 to March 31 and October 1 to December 31, closing at 6 p.m. from April 1 to September 30. The Great Kitchen and cellars, Tudor tennis court, king's private apartments, Hampton Court exhibition, and Mantegna Paintings gallery are open the same hours as the above, but only from April to September. Admission to all these attractions is £2.20 ($3.75) for adults, £1 ($1.75) for children 5 to 16 (under 5, free). To visit only the courtyards and cloisters, including the kitchens and cellars, costs 50p (90¢) for adults, 25p (45¢) for children 5 to 16.

The Maze is open daily from 10 a.m. to 5 p.m. March 1 to October 31, costing 30p (55¢) for adults, 25p (45¢) for children 5 to 16 (under 5, free). For inquiries regarding the palace and its appurtenances, get in touch with the Superintendent, Hampton Court Palace, East Molesey, Surrey KT8 9AU (tel. 01/977-8441).

You can go to Hampton Court by bus, train, boat, or car. London Regional Transport buses for routes 111, 131, 216, 267, and 461 make the trip, as do Green Line buses (ask at the nearest London Country Bus office) for routes 713, 715, 716, 718, 726, and 728. Frequent trains from Waterloo Station (Southern Region) go to Hampton Court Station. Boat service is offered to and from Kingston and Richmond.

CAMBRIDGE

It's one of the world's greatest university towns, its oldest college, **Peterhouse,** having been founded in 1284. The contrast between Cambridge and Oxford is pronounced. Oxford is not only a university town, but an industrial city as well; Cambridge adheres more to the traditional image of an English "town and gown" city.

To begin with, it lies in that part of England known as East Anglia, a bucolic land that embraces Essex and Suffolk, often called "Constable country." Cambridge is 80 miles from Oxford, but only 55 miles northeast of London.

The town boasts 29 colleges for both men and women. A good starting point for your exploration is the corner of Market Hill and King's Parade, the heart of Cambridge. Nearby is Great St. Mary's, the university church. Here, too, is the most brilliant jewel in the Cambridge crown: the 15th-century **King's College Chapel,** considered to be one of the most perfect buildings in the world (stained-glass windows, fan vaulting, lofty spires—all vividly explained in the exhibition in the lovely side chapels).

From here, you can walk to most of the colleges along the paths that scholars have followed for seven centuries of academic life. "The Backs," where the grounds of the colleges sweep down to the River Cam, are exciting to see.

Fifteen miles from Cambridge is one of the most magnificent cathedrals of England in **Ely,** that old lady of the "fen country."

CHARTWELL

Roger Lockyer once wrote, "Chartwell is a dull house, even from some aspects an ugly one, and it contains no collections of fine furniture or paintings, no magnificent ceilings or vaulted roofs. Its one claim to distinction is the quality of its owner . . . but, then, as Churchill himself said after a narrow vote in the House of Commons, 'One is enough.'"

For many years the former prime minister of Great Britain, its wartime leader, lived at this fairly modest home 1½ miles south of Westerham in Kent. However, as a descendant of the first Duke of Marlborough, he had been born in grander style at Blenheim Palace on November 30, 1874.

Administered by the National Trust, the house is open to the public April to October from noon to 5 p.m. on Tuesday, Wednesday, and Thursday, and from 11 a.m. to 5 p.m. on Saturday and Sunday. In March and November, it's open from 11 a.m. to 4 p.m. on Wednesday, Saturday, and Sunday. The gardens and Churchill's studio are not open in March and November. Admission to the house only in March and November is £1.60 ($2.75); to the house and garden April to October, £2.70 ($4.75); to the garden only, £1.10 ($2); and to Churchill's studio only, 40p (70¢). Children enter for half price.

AND AFTER LONDON

The scope of this book was London, along with some interesting day trips. However, for the intrepid traveler who would like to explore England and Scotland (or at least sections of it, including the Cotswolds, Cornwall, Devon, or the Highlands), we publish three different guides.

One, *England on $40 a Day,* describes hundreds of budget hotels, bed-and-breakfast places, restaurants, and pubs, and gives information on low-cost transportation, sightseeing, shopping bargains, and inexpensive nightlife.

Its companion guide, *Scotland and Wales on $40 a Day,* provides the same comprehensive treatment for the other two countries that share the island with England, ranging from Edinburgh and the Highlands to the major attractions of Wales, including a side trip to the Isle of Man.

A final volume, *Dollarwise Guide to England & Scotland,* tells you where to seek and find the best value for your dollar throughout these two countries. This guide contains hotels and restaurants that range from the ritzy establishments to the more modest inns, along with pubs, wine bars, and bistros. All price levels are included—from budget to deluxe—but the emphasis is on the medium-priced.

Index

NOW, SAVE MONEY ON ALL YOUR TRAVELS!
Join Frommer's™ Dollarwise® Travel Club

Saving money while traveling is never a simple matter, which is why, over 28 years ago, the **Dollarwise Travel Club** was formed. Actually, the idea came from readers of the Frommer publications who felt that such an organization could bring financial benefits, continuing travel information, and a sense of community to economy-minded travelers all over the world.

In keeping with the money-saving concept, the annual membership fee is low—$18 (U.S. residents) or $20 U.S. (Canadian, Mexican, and foreign residents)—and is immediately exceeded by the value of your benefits which include:

1. The latest edition of any TWO of the books listed on the following pages.
2. A copy of any Frommer City Guide.
3. An annual subscription to an 8-page quarterly newspaper *The Dollarwise Traveler* which keeps you up-to-date on fastbreaking developments in good-value travel in all parts of the world—bringing you the kind of information you'd have to pay over $35 a year to obtain elsewhere. This consumer-conscious publication also includes the following columns:
   Hospitality Exchange—members all over the world who are willing to provide hospitality to other members as they pass through their home cities.
   Share-a-Trip—requests from members for travel companions who can share costs and help avoid the burdensome single supplement.
   Readers Ask . . . Readers Reply—travel questions from members to which other members reply with authentic firsthand information.
4. Your personal membership card which entitles you to purchase through the club all Frommer publications for a third to a half off their regular retail prices during the term of your membership.

So why not join this hardy band of international Dollarwise travelers now and participate in its exchange of information and hospitality? Simply send $18 (U.S. residents) or $20 U.S. (Canadian, Mexican, and other foreign residents) along with your name and address to: Frommer's Dollarwise Travel Club, Inc., 15 Columbus Circle, New York, NY 10023. Remember to specify which *two* of the books in section (1) and which *one* in section (2) above you wish to receive in your initial package of member's benefits. Or tear out the next page, check off your choices, and send the page to us with your membership fee.

FROMMER BOOKS
PRENTICE HALL TRAVEL
15 COLUMBUS CIRCLE
NEW YORK, NY 10023

Date_____

Friends:
Please send me the books checked below:

FROMMER™ GUIDES
(Guides to sightseeing and tourist accommodations and facilities from budget to deluxe, with emphasis on the medium-priced.)

☐ Alaska	$13.95	☐ Japan & Hong Kong	$13.95
☐ Australia	$14.95	☐ Mid-Atlantic States	$13.95
☐ Austria & Hungary	$14.95	☐ New England	$14.95
☐ Belgium, Holland & Luxembourg	$13.95	☐ New York State	$13.95
☐ Bermuda & The Bahamas	$14.95	☐ Northwest	$14.95
☐ Brazil	$14.95	☐ Portugal, Madeira & the Azores	$13.95
☐ Canada	$14.95	☐ Skiing Europe	$14.95
☐ Caribbean	$14.95	☐ Skiing USA—East	$13.95
☐ Cruises (incl. Alask, Carib, Mex, Hawaii,		☐ Skiing USA—West	$13.95
Panama, Canada & US)	$14.95	☐ South Pacific	$13.95
☐ California & Las Vegas	$14.95	☐ Southeast & New Orleans	$13.95
☐ England & Scotland	$14.95	☐ Southeast Asia	$14.95
☐ Egypt	$13.95	☐ Southwest	$14.95
☐ Florida	$14.95	☐ Switzerland & Liechtenstein	$13.95
☐ France	$14.95	☐ Texas	$13.95
☐ Germany	$14.95	☐ USA	$15.95
☐ Italy	$14.95		

FROMMER $-A-DAY® GUIDES
(In-depth guides to sightseeing and low-cost tourist accommodations and facilities.)

☐ Europe on $40 a Day	$15.95	☐ New Zealand on $40 a Day	$12.95
☐ Australia on $30 a Day	$12.95	☐ New York on $50 a Day	$13.95
☐ Eastern Europe on $25 a Day	$13.95	☐ Scandinavia on $60 a Day	$13.95
☐ England on $50 a Day	$13.95	☐ Scotland & Wales on $40 a Day	$12.95
☐ Greece on $35 a Day	$12.95	☐ South America on $35 a Day	$13.95
☐ Hawaii on $60 a Day	$13.95	☐ Spain & Morocco on $40 a Day	$13.95
☐ India on $25 a Day	$12.95	☐ Turkey on $30 a Day	$12.95
☐ Ireland on $35 a Day	$13.95	☐ Washington, D.C., & Historic Va. on	
☐ Israel on $35 a Day	$13.95	$40 a Day	$13.95
☐ Mexico on $25 a Day	$13.95		

FROMMER TOURING GUIDES
(Color illustrated guides that include walking tours, cultural & historic sites, and other vital travel information.)

☐ Australia	$9.95	☐ Paris	$8.95
☐ Egypt	$8.95	☐ Scotland	$9.95
☐ Florence	$8.95	☐ Thailand	$9.95
☐ London	$8.95	☐ Venice	$8.95

TURN PAGE FOR ADDITIONAL BOOKS AND ORDER FORM.

FROMMER CITY GUIDES
(Pocket-size guides to sightseeing and tourist accommodations and facilities in all price ranges.)

☐ Amsterdam/Holland $5.95	☐ Minneapolis/St. Paul $5.95
☐ Athens. $5.95	☐ Montréal/Québec City. $5.95
☐ Atlantic City/Cape May $5.95	☐ New Orleans. $5.95
☐ Belgium. $5.95	☐ New York $5.95
☐ Boston. $5.95	☐ Orlando/Disney World/EPCOT $5.95
☐ Cancún/Cozumel/Yucatán. $5.95	☐ Paris $5.95
☐ Chicago. $5.95	☐ Philadelphia $5.95
☐ Dublin/Ireland $5.95	☐ Rio $5.95
☐ Hawaii. $5.95	☐ Rome. $5.95
☐ Las Vegas $5.95	☐ San Francisco $5.95
☐ Lisbon/Madrid/Costa del Sol $5.95	☐ Santa Fe/Taos/Albuquerque. $5.95
☐ London $5.95	☐ Sydney. $5.95
☐ Los Angeles $5.95	☐ Washington, D.C. $5.95
☐ Mexico City/Acapulco $5.95	

SPECIAL EDITIONS

☐ A Shopper's Guide to the Caribbean. .$12.95	☐ Motorist's Phrase Book (Fr/Ger/Sp) . . .$4.95
☐ Beat the High Cost of Travel $6.95	☐ Paris Rendez-Vous $10.95
☐ Bed & Breakfast—N. America $11.95	☐ Swap and Go (Home Exchanging). . . .$10.95
☐ California with Kids $14.95	☐ The Candy Apple (NY for Kids). $11.95
☐ Guide to Honeymoon Destinations	☐ Travel Diary and Record Book $5.95
(US, Canada, Mexico & Carib) $12.95	☐ Where to Stay USA (Lodging from $3
☐ Manhattan's Outdoor Sculpture $15.95	to $30 a night) $10.95

☐ Marilyn Wood's Wonderful Weekends (NY, Conn, Mass, RI, Vt, NH, NJ, Del, Pa) $11.95
☐ The New World of Travel (Annual sourcebook by Arthur Frommer previewing: new travel trends,
   new modes of travel, and the latest cost-cutting strategies for savvy travelers). $14.95

SERIOUS SHOPPER'S GUIDES
(Illustrated guides listing hundreds of stores, conveniently organized alphabetically by category)

☐ Italy. $15.95	☐ Los Angeles $14.95
☐ London $15.95	☐ Paris $15.95

GAULT MILLAU
(The only guides that distinguish the truly superlative from the merely overrated.)

☐ The Best of Chicago $15.95	☐ The Best of New England $15.95
☐ The Best of France $16.95	☐ The Best of New York. $14.95
☐ The Best of Italy $16.95	☐ The Best of San Francisco $14.95
☐ The Best of Los Angeles $14.95	☐ The Best of Washington, D.C. $14.95

ORDER NOW!

In U.S. include $2 shipping UPS for 1st book; $1 ea. add'l book. Outside U.S. $3 and $1, respectively.
Allow four to six weeks for delivery in U.S., longer outside U.S.

Enclosed is my check or money order for $_____

NAME _____

ADDRESS _____

CITY _____ STATE _____ ZIP _____